Prophet without Honor

F. Ross Peterson

Prophet without Honor

Glen H. Taylor & the Fight
for American Liberalism

The University Press of Kentucky

ISBN: 0-8131-1286-9

Library of Congress Catalog Card Number: 72-91668

Copyright © 1974 by The University Press of Kentucky

A statewide cooperative scholarly publishing agency
serving Berea College, Centre College of Kentucky,
Eastern Kentucky University, Georgetown College,
Kentucky Historical Society, Kentucky State University,
Morehead State University, Murray State University,
Northern Kentucky State College, Transylvania University,
University of Kentucky, University of Louisville, and
Western Kentucky University.

Editorial and Sales Offices: Lexington, Kentucky 40506

To Kay

Contents

Preface

No study of third-party movements, the origins of the Cold War, Harry S. Truman's Fair Deal, or contemporary American radicalism is complete without reference to the career of Glen H. Taylor. Taylor's colorful political career, which ran its course in a few short years, from 1944 to 1956, saw him rise from a barnstorming musician to candidate for the vice-presidency of the United States on the 1948 Progressive party ticket.

All political figures are products of their time and locale, but Glen Taylor was perhaps more so than most. In considering his political life, it is first necessary to understand the state of Idaho, which he represented as a United States Senator. Idaho has a rural agrarian tradition, which helps explain why its citizens harbor a basic distrust of eastern bigness, monopoly, and outside interference. In addition, Idaho voters are noted for their provincialism. The state's first presidential electoral vote, cast in 1892, went to the Populist candidate, James B. Weaver. William E. Borah, Idaho's most famous political figure, who served the state for thirty-four years in the Senate, skillfully used the Populist appeal as part of his arsenal. Throughout his long eventful career, Borah assailed bigness, whether in business or government. At the same time he advocated reforms which he believed would aid the "common man."

Taylor, a former entertainer, used an approach similar to Borah's and directed it toward obtaining reforms for the "common man" in post–World War II America. Both senators, one a Republican, the other a Democrat, had a great appeal with the Idaho voters. However, while Borah viewed both big government and big business as potential destroyers of individual rights, Taylor, who railed against big business, saw the federal government as the initiator of reforms and the guarantor of individual rights.

Naturally, Glen Taylor's career was shaped by the time in which he lived. Having come to political awareness during the depression days of the New Deal, he served in the Senate during a transitional period of world history. The decade following the Second World War saw significant social, economic, political, and scientific changes. To many Americans it was a time of bewilderment. It was difficult to understand why there was unemployment, inadequate housing, and spiraling inflation. Minority groups who had fought in the Second World War against racist Nazi Germany returned home to a segregated America. Farmers who had prospered while they fed the Allied nations were again suffering the problems of overproduction. Society seemed to lag behind the rapid rate of technological development. To Taylor, the situation seemed to demand a rapid renewal of the New Deal.

Taylor also believed that foreign policy had an effect on domestic reform. Like all those who had looked forward to a lasting world peace after the defeat of Hitler and the Japanese, he was frustrated by the events that resulted in the Cold War. An ideological struggle between the free world and international communism seemed to be leading the world toward atomic destruction. The loss of Eastern Europe and China to the Communists added to these anxieties. Taylor opposed the Truman administration's foreign policy, criticizing the Truman Doctrine, the Marshall Plan, and NATO as contributing to the Cold War. It was Taylor's opinion that the United States and the Soviet Union not only should share the responsibility for troubled world conditions but should work together for a peaceful solution. Taylor dedicated his Senate tenure to the search for peace.

Many of Taylor's contemporaries dismissed him as either a clown or a Communist dupe, but his record reveals that he was neither. Glen Taylor was more than a colorful ham actor, a hillbilly musician, and an egotistical opportunist. It is true that he was more than a little of each, but above all Taylor was a dedicated liberal and humanitarian. Devoted to ideological causes, Taylor, in part, sacrificed his political future for those causes and refused to abandon them.

It has been over a decade since he decided to leave political life, and his public career has never been fully submitted to scholarly analysis. The fact that there exists no single collection of Taylor's political papers is a major research handicap; however, I did examine a large amount of original source material relevant to his career. The task was made easier by the generous assistance of the staffs at the following libraries or archival depositories: Harry S. Truman Library, Independence, Missouri; Franklin

Delano Roosevelt Library, Hyde Park, New York; Dwight D.
Eisenhower Library, Abilene, Kansas; New York Public Library,
New York City; Library of Congress, Washington, D.C.; AFL-CIO
Committee on Political Education, Washington, D.C.; Idaho State
Historical Society, Boise; University of Idaho, Moscow; Idaho
State University, Pocatello; Washington State University, Pullman;
University of Iowa, Iowa City; and Utah State University, Logan.
The Harry S. Truman Collection at the Truman Library and the
Henry A. Wallace Collection at the University of Iowa were of
special value. Taylor gave helpful information and his assistance
is appreciated. Many of Taylor's political associates and opponents
from Idaho also provided useful insights in personal interviews
and through correspondence. A special thanks is given to Glyndean
LaPlante and Sarah Robertsen, the manuscript typists.

Since his defeat in 1956, Taylor has lived in California, where
he owns and manages Taylor Topper, Inc., which manufactures
toupees. Whether as an actor, musician, sheet-metal worker, politician, carpenter, or toupee manufacturer, Glen Taylor has economically survived the trauma of the depression, World War II,
and beyond. His political career is a vindication of the ancient
maxim that ideals have virtue and can be sacrificed only at a
loss of honor.

Prophet without Honor

I. *The Road to Politics*

Few scenes are more striking than the snowcapped Grand Tetons located near the Idaho-Wyoming border. Between Jackson, Wyoming, and Driggs, Idaho, lie sixty miles of the most picturesque scenery in the United States. But Glen Taylor was not overwhelmed by the beauty of Jackson Hole and the Grand Tetons on a cool clear morning in the fall of 1936. Taylor, the advance man for his theatrical and musical group, the Glendora Ranch Gang, was in a hurry to get to Driggs, locate an auditorium for a scheduled performance, and return to Jackson for an evening show.[1]

When he arrived in Driggs, Taylor found that the only theater was being used by a politician conducting a rally. Unable to locate the theater manager, Taylor decided to "waste" the morning listening to Idaho's three-term governor, "Cowboy" C. Ben Ross. Governor Ross was involved in a heated campaign against the famed "Lion of Idaho," Senator William E. Borah, for Borah's seat in the United States Senate.[2] Ross, an accomplished showman himself, put on a performance that morning in Driggs that greatly impressed Taylor. "Cowboy Ben" liked to walk down the aisles and rub shoulders with the audience while he spoke personally to them. Taylor never forgot Ross's technique.

"Why, Joe, how are you doing?"

"Fine, Governor, just fine."

"I haven't seen you since we pulled you out of that mud hole over on the road to Victor. You know we've got a nice new gravel road over there now. Old C. Ben, he got it for you. Yes, sir. The big boys, they tried to stop us, but we got it for you, and we saved the state and you a pile of money on the idea. Your Governor never forgot you, Joe. No, sir. He dosen't forget anyone."[3]

Taylor recalls that Ross's delivery was excellent, his comedy beautifully timed, and he was close to the people. The actor, who for years had been working on delivery, comedy, and the problems of communicating with people, began to compare himself to the governor. As Taylor watched Ross, the inspiration came to him—"If this is politics, why not? Ben Ross is an amateur [actor] and I'm a professional."⁴

Taylor continued to ponder the idea on the return trip around the Tetons to Jackson. Although in the past he had studied politics and economics in a limited way, the idea of actually attempting to serve as an elected official apparently had never before occurred to him. By the time he arrived in the Wyoming community, Taylor had definitely determined his future course of action. He proudly announced his decision to his wife, Dora, who was also his business partner. She immediately exclaimed, "Why, Glen, you can't run for office! We don't even have a permanent address or a home."⁵ But Taylor's mind was made up. He had decided to jump into politics, and he reassured his wife that he would take care of the minor detail of settling down in one community. Dora Taylor knew that when her husband reached a decision, he would be stubbornly devoted and dedicated to it; it could not be altered.

Taylor's life until he was thirty-two had been a tale of instability, continual setbacks, and a constant battle for economic survival. Born in a Portland, Oregon, boardinghouse on April 12, 1904, Glen Hearst Taylor was the twelfth of thirteen children of Pleasant John and Olive Higgins Taylor.⁶ Years later, on the Senate floor, Taylor would have reason to explain to his colleague, Senator Wayne Morse of Oregon, the circumstances surrounding his Portland birth.

It may interest the Senator from Oregon to know that I was born in Portland, Oregon. . . . My father was a minister of the gospel at the time. He and his family lived in Idaho; our home was there. He went to Portland to hold a protracted meeting, and in those days they were very protracted. He went to Portland to try to save the souls of some of the sinners there. . . . While he was there—and he took his family with him—and while he was holding this meeting, I was born in Portland. It has been a source of embarrassment to me, when I have run for office in Idaho and have been asked where I was born.

¹ Interview with Glen H. Taylor, June 14, 1967.

² Michael P. Malone, *C. Ben Ross and the New Deal in Idaho* (Seattle: University of Washington Press, 1970), p. 140.

³ Interview with Glen H. Taylor, June 14, 1967. The above quotation comes from a Taylor impersonation of Ross and is not a verbatim citation. During the interview, Taylor impersonated any public figure discussed and did so with ease. Although it has been nearly thirty years since Taylor acted professionally, he still enjoys an opportunity to exhibit his talents.

⁴ Ibid.

⁵ Ibid.

⁶ *Portland Oregonian*, January 11, 1948.

I should like to be able to say that I am native son of Idaho. But I have had to explain that, through an act of God, I was born in Portland.[7]

Pleasant John Taylor, according to his son, was a "hellfire and brimstone minister in the Christian Church [Disciples of Christ]."[8] The elder Taylor preached in mining camps and other outposts of civilization all across Idaho, Oregon, Montana, Colorado, and Utah. Westerners were quite unwilling to pay for pure religion, so the Taylor family also prepared musicals and melodramas to finance the trips.[9] The entire family of thirteen children had a measure of musical ability and all of them, at one time or another, went into some form of show business.[10]

Pleasant John was more than a nomadic preacher, however. Flexible and opportunistic, he was, at various times in his life, a Texas Ranger, a farmer, and an actor, as well as a minister. He also dabbled in Democratic politics. When Glen was sixteen years old, the elder Taylor served as an Idaho delegate to the 1920 Democratic National Convention. Pleasant John's politics were of the type that stressed the Golden Rule, brotherly love, and a modified Christian socialism. Long afterward, as a senator, Glen Taylor would crusade for civil equality, world peace, and equal opportunity. The father apparently had a permanent influence on his children; the lessons he taught were well learned.

Shortly before Glen's birth, Pleasant John, who moved often, had taken his family to a homestead on the banks of the Clearwater River three miles above Kooskia in northern Idaho.[11] He found it extremely difficult to support thirteen children on a 160-acre homestead, only about ten acres of which could be plowed. Poverty and hunger were more than possibilities, so each child was expected to help earn his keep. Taylor and his brothers snagged driftwood from the Clearwater River and traded it for flour at Kooskia. For what education they received, the Taylor children "rode horseback, or more often walked, six miles each day."[12] Because of economic necessity, Glen left school in 1916 at the age of twelve with perhaps the equivalent of a sixth-grade education. He took a job at ten

[7] U.S., Congress, Senate, *Congressional Record*, 79th Cong., 1st sess., 1945, 91, pt. 3:3069. Hereafter cited as *Cong. Rec.*
[8] Glen H. Taylor to the writer, July 24, 1967.
[9] Richard L. Neuberger, "Singing Cowboy to United States Senator," *Progressive* (May 7, 1945), p. 14.
[10] Glen H. Taylor to the writer, July 24, 1967.
[11] Ibid.
[12] *Cong. Rec.*, 79th Cong., 1st sess., 1945, 91, pt. 8:10498.

dollars a week helping herd a flock of sheep on their way to summer pasture. He went barefoot "for the simple reason that I had no shoes."[13] For Pleasant John Taylor's family, economic survival was of the essence; his offspring never forgot their struggles in the rural wilderness of Idaho.

Olive Higgins Taylor was a tolerant, kind frontier woman. Her life was not easy, and to see each of her children leave the homestead in search of survival deepened her sadness. Although she tried to encourage education and the professions, economic necessity deprived her children of the opportunity of reaching her goals.

Within a year after Glen left home to herd sheep, he moved back to Kooskia to work for his brother E. K. Taylor, who managed two moving picture theaters. One theater was located at Kooskia and the other at Stites, a hamlet four miles away. Glen's duties consisted of keeping the wooden benches in repair and splicing the film. Reminiscing, Taylor recalled that in this latter task he often "had a kiss looking like a collision."[14]

During the influenza epidemic of 1918–1919, Taylor's father became very ill, so Taylor contributed to the family budget by working for a short time as an apprentice sheet-metal worker.[15] But when another brother, Ferris, wrote home from California in 1921 asking the budding young craftsman to join him in a traveling vaudeville act, Glen jumped at the chance. He was not to stop traveling for fifteen years.

Now seventeen, Taylor had attained full physical growth. Of average height, he had broad shoulders and a trim physique. He had dark brown hair and a firm square chin. Perhaps his most striking feature was his crystal clear blue eyes.

As a member of the Taylor Players, Glen Taylor attempted legitimate theater for the first time. In the beginning, he played the villain and his brother assumed the role of the hero, but young Glen lacked the ability to scowl and act vicious, so the brothers switched roles and their productions became much more successful. Glen coveted the lead roles and once he obtained them, his acting came alive and his characterizations had more authenticity. By 1922 he was a full partner in the theatrical company.[16] The group traveled and played to audiences throughout the West.

13 Glen H. Taylor to the writer, July 24, 1967.
14 Frank Gervasi, "Low Man on the Wallace Poll," *Collier's* (May 8, 1948), p. 73.
15 *Cong. Rec.*, 79th Cong., 1st sess., 1945, 91, pt. 8:10498.
16 Gervasi, "Low Man on the Wallace Poll," p. 73.

Along the way, Taylor rushed into and out of a teen-age marriage in New Mexico as if it were another one-night stand. Little is known of Taylor's first wife or the daughter that was born to the brief union. Taylor did name his daughter Olive in memory of his mother. Taylor's life style at age eighteen was not conducive to a family setting and they soon parted company.[17]

Disaster struck the Taylor Players late in 1922 when a fire in Canyon City, Colorado, burned down their tent and destroyed their wardrobe collection.[18] The group disbanded and everyone went on his own.

Glen Taylor floated from job to job until he acquired a permanent place with the Slade Musical Comedy Company, which specialized in *Rose Marie*. While playing in Great Falls, Montana, in 1928, when Taylor was twenty-four, he met an attractive chief usherette, Dora Pike. He quickly convinced her, first, that she should join the company as a singer, and second, that she should become his wife.[19]

When Dora agreed to marry Glen Taylor, little did the pretty, dark-eyed girl realize that she was destined to act, play the trombone, and become the wife of a United States Senator. Throughout his career Dora Taylor was to have a tremendous influence on her husband. The striking brunette worked with Taylor in everything that he tried. Whether in show business or politics, she supported her husband and did it in such a manner that he knew he would succeed. They always survived as a family unit and developed a relationship based not only on love but on complete respect.

Soon after they were married—and after borrowing money for scenery, wardrobe, and a truck—Glen and Dora Taylor formed their own company, the Glendora Players. The venture was doomed to failure because of two external factors—the depression and "talkie" movies. If people had money, they preferred the new sensation, the talkies. Glen and Dora were continually forced to cut down their group and to play only the very small towns. They could no longer afford to rent theaters, so they had to use free Grange halls and Mormon recreation halls.

At the ticket window, the Taylors accepted anything as the price

---

[17] *New York Times*, October 4, 1945, p. 25. It is probable that Taylor got married only to give a child, presumably his, a name. Apparently he did not stay around very long nor did his bride accompany him on his perpetual tour. This marital venture would turn up again to plague him politically (see page 40).

[18] Kyle Crichton, "Idaho's Hot Potato," *Collier's* (June 30, 1945), p. 64.

[19] Gervasi, "Low Man on the Wallace Poll," p. 73.

of admission, including farm produce. "Many times," said Taylor, "we have taken farm produce, chickens—sometimes live chickens—and vegetables, in exchange for tickets to our show." When he saw children stand outside and beg to be admitted, he would admit them. About the third night afterward, instead of twenty children, there would be about 150 standing outside, and then he would have to draw the line.[20] Once a farmer brought his five youngsters, three fryers, and a sack of potatoes to the show. The farmer asked Taylor which he would take to let the kids see the play—chickens or potatoes. Taylor looked longingly at the fryers, then said, "I'll take the potatoes—they're more filling."[21] A choice between chickens and potatoes was not always available to the Taylors. Taylor recalled that they "ate jackrabbits more than once and sometimes we didn't eat at all."[22]

Finally, the Glendora Players consisted of only Glen and Dora, Glen's brother Paul, and Paul's wife. They constructed living quarters on the back of a truck and traveled from town to town, hoping to make enough at each performance to get them to the next community.

The depression had an unforgettable impact on Taylor. "The want and misery I saw during those years . . . made me do some serious thinking."[23] Although he saw people hungry, out of work, and poorly clothed, he believed the situation was not hopeless. Farmers could still grow crops and factories could still produce if some way could be found to provide people with money to buy the products. In 1932, practically penniless, Taylor read King C. Gillette's *The People's Corporation*. This book was a major influence in his career because it started him on a study of economics and politics.[24]

Gillette, a safety-razor king, wanted every citizen to be a stockholder in the United States of America. According to Gillette, a huge corporate state should be formed which would produce goods and then guarantee that customers had enough money to buy them. He advocated a guaranteed minimum annual wage, national health insurance, and price ceilings. Viewing the labor-capital conflict as a potential destroyer of the world, Gillette contended that

20 *Cong. Rec.*, 79th Cong., 1st sess., 1945, 91, pt. 7:9127.
21 Gervasi, "Low Man on the Wallace Poll," p. 73.
22 Glen H. Taylor to writer, December 11, 1967.
23 Neuberger, "Singing Cowboy to United States Senator," p. 16.
24 Interview with Glen H. Taylor, June 14, 1967.

his proposed corporate state would bring order, security, peace, and universal prosperity. He concluded with a grim warning that if a planned economy was not adopted, the struggle between labor and capital would bring violence, war, anarchy, and finally political and economic collapse.[25]

Taylor next read Stuart Chase's *A New Deal*, which also had a great influence on him. Among other things, Chase, like Gillette, called for the evolutionary change of the capitalistic system before it destroyed the United States. He saw public works, direct relief, and a planned economy as the only means of emerging from the depression and avoiding future economic disasters. Chase's book, clearly a product of the depression, closed with a question which impressed Glen Taylor: "Why should Russians have all the fun of remaking a world?"[26]

After further study of the works of Gillette and Chase, Taylor consulted other books that were more favorable to the established economic system.[27] But it was the economic theories of Gillette and Chase which influenced him most, and he was to rely heavily on them for his platform throughout his career.

Taylor felt that the purpose of all knowledge was action; he was determined that "never again should the people of America go hungry in the midst of plenty."[28] But he was not sure where to begin. During his travels he had participated in efforts to organize local Farmer-Labor parties in Montana and Nevada and realized the futility of these efforts. This experience convinced him that the Democratic party under Franklin D. Roosevelt offered the only real avenue to economic and social reform.[29] Although he talked

[25] King C. Gillette, *The People's Corporation* (New York: Boni and Liveright, 1924), pp. 129, 234-35.

[26] Stuart Chase, *A New Deal* (New York: Macmillan, 1932), p. 252.

[27] King C. Gillette, *World Corporation* (Boston: New England News, 1910). Other books by Stuart Chase that Taylor read were *The Tragedy of Waste* (New York: Grossett and Dunlap, 1925), *Your Money's Worth* (New York: Macmillan, 1927), *Rich Land, Poor Land* (New York: McGraw-Hill, 1936), *The Nemesis of American Business* (New York: Macmillan, 1931), and *The Economy of Abundance* (New York: Macmillan, 1934). Among the books favorable to orthodox capitalism were Carl Snyder, *Capitalism the Creator* (New York: Macmillan, 1940); and James H. R. Cromwell and Hugo E. Czerwonky, *In Defense of Capitalism* (New York: Charles Scribner's Sons, 1937). Jerome Davis, *Capitalism and Its Culture* (New York: Farrar and Rinehart, 1935), which Taylor also read, is very critical of the capitalist culture.

[28] *Cong. Rec.*, 79th Cong., 1st sess., 1945, 91, pt. 7:9128.

[29] Richard L. Neuberger, "Cowboy on Our Side," *Nation* (August 24, 1946), p. 210.

with Socialists and Communists, "splendid men who earnestly believed in what they fought for," he refused to ally himself with either group. Taylor was inclined to be a Democrat because of his father, but he also maintained that "even if my father had not been a Democrat I think I would have had enough sense to be a Democrat anyway."[30]

By the time he was in his thirties, a political Glen Taylor had begun to emerge, but he was only beginning to realize that an evolution had taken place. For over fifteen years, he had traveled the western United States. Nearly half of that time, the nation had been immersed in a disastrous depression. He had witnessed mass human suffering and had suffered himself, but he did not despair completely. His travels, studies, and upbringing had left an imprint on the man, and had given him food for thought.

Politics always had been an enigma to Taylor, as he was later to be to politics, but he realized that a people's government had to be established that would relieve deprivation. He believed that Roosevelt might be on the right track, but that it was necessary to go beyond the president. Huey Long, Father Charles Coughlin, and others did not provide a complete program so Taylor was willing to support Roosevelt. Taylor was a political and economic liberal, but was too radical to become involved personally and to be effective in influencing party policies and programs.

Taylor's economic views were radical even for those strenuous times. He felt that the profit system should be junked and that the economy should be altered to plan for plenty. His interest in the Montana Farmer-Labor movement during 1935 makes it evident that Taylor had given some consideration to translating his ideas into politics while he was reading the works of Gillette and Chase. In Taylor's mind, political issues were formulated in terms of "how," not "why." He never questioned why he should support civil rights for blacks, Indians, or Basques, or the public financing of dams and roads, or the preservation of natural resources. He knew where he stood on political and economic issues, but the difficulty lay in implementation. If accomplishing these aims meant personally going into politics, Taylor decided, that is what he would do. Glen Taylor was at this point in his intellectual and political development when he heard C. Ben Ross at the theater in Driggs, Idaho.

[30] *Cong. Rec.*, 79th Cong., 1st sess., 1945, 91, pt. 7:9128.

At about the same time the Glendora Players, or what was left of them, made a significant change which helped shape Taylor's initial political strategy. Through correspondence courses and long practice sessions, Glen mastered the guitar and banjo while Dora learned to play the piano and the trombone. The Paul Taylors also attempted to master some instruments. Glen hired a couple of experienced musical entertainers, and the Glendora Players became the Glendora Ranch Gang, with Glen as the lead vocalist.[31] The group was to become an integral part of Taylor's political force, but first Taylor had to find a potential home from which he could operate the Ranch Gang as well as plan for a political future.

Glen Taylor chose Pocatello, Idaho, as home for several carefully thought-out reasons. Pocatello was then a small city, with very strong unions, especially the railroad brotherhoods. As a native of northern Idaho, Taylor, by living in southern Idaho, hoped to create a greater voter appeal in the geographically divided state.[32] He realized early that if his liberal economics was going to get a hearing it would be with the common man. Knowing the state well, he was convinced that a liberal from traditionally conservative southern Idaho could carry the mining and lumbering north, and perhaps pick up enough votes in his home area to win. It seems evident at this early date that Taylor's ultimate goal was a seat in the Senate.

Finally, Taylor chose Pocatello because the Ranch Gang was able to procure time for a daily half-hour radio show on KSEI in Pocatello. The Taylors talked Henry Fletcher, the station's owner, into a two-week trial period for their live program. Fletcher later described the Taylors' music as "not perfect, or well done, but very homey. We weren't sure after one week, but the public response was amazing. They lasted nearly four years."[33] Their show opened with the group singing, "Oh, we like mountain music, good old mountain music, played by the old Glendora Band."[34]

[31] Interview with Henry Fletcher, owner of KSEI Radio (Pocatello, Idaho), August 25, 1967.

[32] Interview with Glen H. Taylor, June 14, 1967. Northern Idaho has traditionally felt isolated and discriminated against by the southern part of the state. Economically and socially, the Idaho panhandle is dominated by Spokane, Washington.

[33] Interview with Henry Fletcher, August 24, 1967.

[34] Interview with A. M. Rich, a former Bear Lake County Democratic chairman, August 20, 1967. Mr. Rich and his wife, teen-agers at the time the radio program ran, easily recalled the Taylor theme song.

The Taylors not only performed on these daytime broadcasts but used them to announce where they would be playing each evening. KSEI, one of the few radio stations in southern Idaho during the 1930s, had a range of approximately 100 miles from Pocatello in all directions.

During the winter of 1937–1938, the Glendora Ranch Gang traveled extensively throughout southeastern Idaho. Each week they paid for their own radio program in advance. The afternoon show attracted large crowds at the station, especially after Glen and Dora encouraged their three-year-old son Arod (Dora spelled backwards) to sing on the program. Arod, whom Mrs. Fletcher remembers as "an extremely beautiful boy," captured the hearts of many listeners. After the radio show, the group would put their instruments into a small rowboat, which was tied on top of the Taylor car as a luggage carrier, and leave for a dance in some small Idaho community. After playing for the dance and performing a short play, they would return to Pocatello, usually the same night. This was not an easy life, especially the long rides home in a cold car on winter nights. According to the Fletchers, the Taylors always had colds and appeared to subsist on cough drops.[35]

Glen Taylor continued to read and to formulate a political plan of action. The realities of the depression, combined with the economic theories of Gillette and Chase, gave him an ideology. Added to these were his father's Christian teachings which were an integral part of Glen Taylor's basic philosophy. Finally he was ready to put his ideas to the test. He decided to enter the Idaho Second District congressional race of 1938. If C. Ben Ross was politically successful as an amateur thespian, Taylor was interested in knowing how an experienced entertainer such as himself would do in politics. The election of 1938 would give him an answer.

[35] Interview with Henry Fletcher, August 25, 1967. Arod Taylor is now a dentist in Millbrae, California.

II. *Election to the Senate*

Six months after Glen and Dora Taylor moved into a small frame home in Pocatello, Taylor announced that he would run for Congress as a Democrat. Most political observers considered his candidacy a mere publicity stunt.[1] But Taylor was very serious, as he demonstrated by running for office four times, until he was finally elected to the Senate in 1944.

There were eight other congressional aspirants in the 1938 open primary, so it is not surprising that Taylor was ignored by the Idaho Democratic party. The former actor has said of his initial campaign, "I am sure that I was the only person in the world who had faith that I would eventually achieve my ambition."[2]

Although Taylor had set his sights on a seemingly impossible goal, he attempted to be practical in achieving that goal. Working with the tools at hand, he relied on his cowboy band, his radio program, and his nightly performances throughout southeastern Idaho. For more effective campaigning, a platform, equipped with loudspeakers, was constructed on the roof of the family Ford. The troupe would roll into a community and start entertaining right on "Main Street." According to Taylor, "The band would raise enough hell to attract a crowd, and then I would make my talk."[3]

The Glendora Ranch Gang continued to hold their daily sessions at KSEI. Taylor would use this radio time to announce the schedule of their political rallies and dances. Unable to restrain himself, he occasionally delivered short political speeches over the air. After some complaints from the listening audience, the station management persuaded him to confine his activities "to songs and schedules—no politics."

As a campaign gimmick, Taylor organized the "Cockle Burr Club of Southern Idaho." Members of the organization received a picture of Glen, Dora, and Arod and pledged themselves, "solemnly" no less, to support Taylor in his bid for the congressional nomination. In return, Taylor pledged himself to do "my best, stick on the job, and not sit on my Cockle Burr." He signed the back of the picture-card as the "Grand Cockle Burr."[4]

Taylor finished fourth, but his greatest fear, that the electorate would think he was a joke, disappeared when he obtained 6,742 votes. According to Taylor, "I found out that some people would actually vote for me. And that was a big step forward."[5] This was the only election in nearly twenty years in which the Idaho Democratic party could afford to ignore Taylor.

After the 1938 election, Taylor returned to the routine of the radio show and the Western band. Following a performance at the small entertainment-starved community of Pingree, Taylor told the school principal that he was preparing himself to run for the United States Senate and intended to do so at the appropriate time.[6] Fate gave Taylor an opportunity to seek a Senate seat sooner than he had anticipated. Senator William E. Borah, the famous Idaho legislator, died on January 19, 1940, and the Republican governor, C. A. Bottolfsen, appointed a former United States Senator, John Thomas, to fill the vacancy until an election could be held later that year.

Idaho Democrats believed John Thomas was politically vulnerable. Thomas had been defeated in the Democratic landslide of 1932, and since his defeat had resided in California. The Senate seat of William E. Borah, unattainable for Democrats for thirty-four years, suddenly seemed within reach. The party leaders hoped to give the voters a choice in the primary between two safe regular Democrats, but they failed to realize that Glen Taylor harbored political ambitions which far exceeded finishing fourth in the 1938 congressional race.[7] He announced his candidacy for the Senate in March 1940 and began to campaign immediately.

[1] *Pocatello Tribune*, June 9, 1938. See also *Lewiston Morning Tribune*, July 1, 1938. Hereafter cited as *Lewiston Tribune*. *Idaho Daily Statesman* (Boise), August 7, 1938. Hereafter cited as *Idaho Statesman*.

[2] *Cong. Rec.*, 79th Cong., 1st sess., 1945, 91, pt. 8:10498.

[3] Interview with Glen H. Taylor, June 14, 1967.

[4] Interview with Henry Fletcher, August 25, 1967.

[5] Karl M. Schmidt, *Henry Wallace: Quixotic Crusade 1948* (Syracuse: Syracuse University Press, 1960), p. 57. Out of nearly 50,000 votes cast, Taylor's 6,742 constituted approximately 14 percent.

[6] Brigham D. Madsen to writer, August 8, 1967.

[7] Interview with Robert Coulter, former Idaho Democratic party chairman, September 14, 1967. Coulter, a very witty and sarcastic gentleman, literally despises Glen Taylor. He did not like Taylor, Taylor's philosophy or methods, and is quick to admit it.

Relying heavily on his limited study of economics, Taylor promised to carry his bid for election to every county of the state to answer questions and discuss the "people's corporation." A Taylor speech usually included a plea for the cause of the common man and an attack on anyone with collected wealth. During the depression years, the Populist approach of berating the bankers, the wealthy, and the profit system was not uncommon and appealed to a large element of the population.[8]

Repeatedly the Idaho liberal called for the abolition of the profit system and "cutthroat competition." In an early speech he asked for "a plan, the object of which could be to produce plenty for all the people, and not profits for the few."[9] Taylor believed that international and national difficulties were caused by the profit system: "European democracies are in a sad plight because of the profit system. . . . The profit system has been dead and waiting to be buried since the settling of this country."[10]

In 1940 Taylor was somewhat critical of Franklin D. Roosevelt's attempts to solve the depression problems, because, according to Taylor, the Roosevelt program kept the "profit system going by the artificial means of borrowing and everyone knows that borrowing cannot be continued forever."[11] However, the Idaho Democrat conceded that Roosevelt's programs had done a great deal to provide relief for the little man. Consistently denying that he was not a supporter of Roosevelt, Taylor categorized himself as "for Roosevelt all along and in many respects ahead of the President."[12]

The campaign devices Taylor used in 1940 differed only in degree from his initial campaign. Because he had to cover the entire state in the 1940 senatorial race, instead of just the Second Congressional District as he had in 1938, he left the Ranch Gang in Pocatello. "At first I tried to take my whole gang of musicians," he recalls, "but found that to be unsatisfactory, so we did the campaigning by ourselves."[13] By "ourselves" Taylor meant him-

[8] William E. Leuchtenburg, *Franklin D. Roosevelt and the New Deal* (New York: Harper and Row, 1963), pp. 179-82. Leuchtenburg discusses the appeal of Huey Long, Francis Townsend, and Father Charles Coughlin. Also see Arthur M. Schlesinger, Jr., *The Politics of Upheaval* (Boston: Houghton Mifflin, 1959), pp. 15-28.

[9] *Idaho Pioneer* (Boise), March 20, 1940.

[10] *Lewiston Tribune*, June 21, 1940.

[11] Ibid.

[12] Ibid., August 25, 1940.

[13] *Pocatello Tribune*, August 14, 1940.

self, Dora, and Arod. They drove throughout the state, holding impromptu open-air meetings. From the public-address system mounted on a platform atop the car, Arod would sing several songs to attract a crowd; then Taylor would join in musically before he veered off into politics. The Taylor family slept in their car during the entire campaign. They usually ate canned vegetables, fruit Mrs. Taylor had canned, and hard-boiled eggs. At each stop they collected small sums of money from the crowd that gathered at the car and used the money to buy enough gasoline to take them to the next town. Young Arod, five years old, summed up the campaign when he said, "I entertained them, Daddy spoke to them, and Mother collected the money."[14] According to Taylor, Arod sang more than 2,000 times during the 1940 primary campaign.

Taylor's opposition in the 1940 primary came from George Donart, a lawyer from Weiser, and Judge James R. Bothwell of Twin Falls. To many expert observers, it seemed to be a contest between Donart and Bothwell, because the "cowboy" entertainer from Pocatello was considered either a joke or a crass opportunist using the political campaign to advertise himself and his band and to make money.[15] No one seemed to give Taylor a chance in the 1940 primary, but he slipped by the two veteran politicians, receiving 18,984 votes of a total of 53,064 votes cast. When he won, an Idaho newspaper reported that his "victory will rank among startling upsets with that of D. Worth Clark in the [1938] primary over . . . Senator James P. Pope."[16]

Taylor's victory created frustration for many lifelong Democrats. Robert Coulter, the state's Democratic party chairman, viewed Taylor as an opportunist and not a Democrat. The veteran chairman was convinced that Taylor's independent stance, together with his extreme liberal philosophy, would only hurt the party.[17] Owen Stratton, a Salmon physician, resigned as Lemhi County chairman in 1940 when some party leaders supported Taylor, because Stratton claimed that he had accepted "the chairmanship

[14] Ibid.

[15] *Lewiston Tribune*, July 21, 1940, and August 11, 1940. See also *Idaho Pioneer*, August 9, 1940.

[16] *Idaho Statesman*, August 14, 1940. Idaho, Department of State, "Abstract of Votes at Primary Election, August 12, 1940," *Biennial Report of the Secretary of State*, 1939-1940 (Boise), appended to p. 94. Clark had defeated New Deal Senator Pope in part because of the Roosevelt purge of 1938. In the off-year elections, Roosevelt had campaigned actively for New Deal liberals. This created a voter backlash which led to the defeat of many liberals.

[17] Interview with Robert Coulter, September 14, 1967.

[with] the distinct understanding and agreement that I was not to support Mr. Taylor." Stratton's admission that the state party organization had originally encouraged its county chairmen not to support Taylor created further tension. Stratton announced that his biggest objection was that Taylor was not a Democrat and "I do not like his methods and principles."[18] The relationship between Taylor and many of the Democratic party regulars in Idaho remained strained throughout Taylor's career, in part because of his lone-wolf tactics.

A realist, Taylor understood why the party regulars were not pleased by his victory in the primary, but the hostility of the press dismayed him. The *Idaho Free Press* reacted to the victory with editorials demanding a change of the direct primary law: "Many Democrats who thought they knew their party intimately are flabbergasted over the nomination of Glen Taylor for senator. . . . They scratch their heads and wonder how come? The answer is simple. The direct primary."[19] The *Pocatello Tribune* asked the people of the state to "take a thoughtful note of the inefficiency and utter absurdity of the state's primary law and do something about it."[20]

These attacks on Idaho's primary law were obviously aimed at Taylor. One paper sarcastically suggested that perhaps the Democrats "have learned that the thing to do is pin a hill-billy badge onto the candidate for . . . senator, put an accordion in his hands and send him out with a soundtruck."[21] A more favorable view of Taylor's victories was expressed in neighboring Oregon. The *Portland Oregonian* backhandedly stated that "maybe Taylor is the best man in the Democratic party. There is no reason why a cowboy singer shouldn't be."[22]

Taylor developed a basic dislike for Idaho newspapers following the 1940 primary, and he maintained that feeling for the rest of his political career, especially during the bitter, hate-filled campaigns of 1946 and 1950. The twelve largest newspapers in Idaho, Taylor recalls, were "all against me but one—and it was neutral."[23]

18 *Lewiston Tribune*, October 15, 1940.
19 *Idaho Free Press* (Nampa), August 15, 1940.
20 *Pocatello Tribune*, August 18, 1940.
21 Ibid.
22 *Oregonian*, August 16, 1940.
23 Taylor to author, December 11, 1967. The paper neutral toward Taylor was the *Lewiston Tribune*, which was ordinarily favorable toward the New Deal and the Democrats. However, when Taylor bolted the party in 1948,

Faced by the lack of party support and adequate financing, Taylor conducted his 1940 general election campaign just as he had the primary. He continued to drive from town to town in his "sound car" with Dora and Arod. Late in the campaign, the senatorial candidate, nearly out of money, resorted to an unusual method of securing funds. On September 24, he inserted the following advertisement in the *Pocatello Tribune*: "We need some campaign funds. Must be no strings attached. Anything over a dollar, I'll repay double, if I'm elected. If I lose—nothing. Will be home, Wednesday, September 25th only. Your friend, Glen Taylor."[24] The advertisement caused political and legal repercussions throughout the state. Politicians in both parties speculated that Taylor's candidacy might be declared void if an investigation were held, but the incident blew over.[25]

Attempting to use the fund-raising incident to establish a rapport with the public, Taylor told a McCall audience that he refused to follow the usual political procedure of "sneaking up a back alley on a dark night, accepting a few hundred dollars from a representative of some big utility and . . . giving them a mortgage on every waterfall in Idaho to square accounts."[26] At Nampa, Taylor asserted that he could have plenty of money if he would only compromise his principles: "I've had offers of campaign contributions if I'd just slip a little and forget what I have said before. I didn't take them." He promised his potential constituents, "I will hoof it and hitch-hike from town to town before I will take that kind of money."[27]

The fact that Taylor was seeking the Senate seat recently occupied by the dignified William E. Borah provided Taylor's opponents with a marked contrast they used to advantage. The *Idaho Pioneer*, a Boise weekly, reported that it was impossible to "feature Idaho telling the nation that the best it can do for a man to fill the great Borah's shoes is a sweet singer, wholly uneducated and wholly unfitted."[28]

Combining the Taylor-Borah contrast with a charge that Taylor

---

the *Tribune* became hostile as well. After 1948 all papers were openly defiant toward Taylor.

[24] *Pocatello Tribune*, September 24, 1940. The advertisement was accompanied by a picture of Taylor wearing a mammoth white cowboy hat.

[25] *Idaho Statesman*, October 1, 1940.

[26] Ibid., October 17, 1940.

[27] Ibid., October 1, 1940.

[28] *Idaho Pioneer*, October 18, 1940.

was pro-Communist, the *Idaho Pioneer*'s Frank Burroughs claimed: "It's plainly a choice between Communism on the one side and Americanization on the other side. . . . Taylor is not a good citizen, because this nation has no use for Stalin-dictated Communism. . . . I just cannot feature this illiterate strolling player taking Borah's place in the nation's greatest assembly."[29] Some Republicans bitterly accused Taylor of basing his entire philosophy on *The People's Corporation,* which Eugene M. Lerner, a Boise Republican, considered to be "full of statements which go Adolf Hitler and Joe Stalin one better."[30]

In answering these accusations, Taylor charged his political opponents with attempting to brand him as a Communist "because I don't own a string of banks and because I urge better distribution of the nation's vast wealth. . . . Simply because I see the need for more help to the small businssman, the farmer and the poor people on relief and on WPA, Republican state headquarters has attempted to smear me with red."[31]

Although definitely an underdog in 1940, Taylor received the endorsement of many local followers of Dr. Frances Townsend and Idaho's labor leaders because of his announced support of Townsend's proposal that every citizen over sixty receive two hundred dollars per month, increased social security benefits, national health insurance, and higher minimum wages. But the backing of these groups was not enough. Thomas defeated him by nearly 14,000 votes while Roosevelt carried the state by 35,000.[32]

The election result was a tremendous personal defeat for Taylor. "They just had too much money for me," he concluded, adding a slap at some of Idaho's Democratic party leaders: "Two years ago, I slipped on the first rung of the ladder because of inexperience, and this time I fell from the top rung because it was 'well greased' with corporation money and there were quite a few termites working on it with no regard for the rank and file of the party."[33]

[29] Ibid., November 1, 1940.

[30] *Lewiston Tribune,* October 29, 1940. Lerner's statement putting Stalin and Hitler in the same camp is typical of the response to Taylor by his opponents. Rarely did they approach his proposals intelligently; they attempted to brand him instead. Governor C. A. Bottolfsen and A. M. Goff, a Moscow Republican, also accused Taylor of being communistic.

[31] *Idaho Statesman,* November 1, 1940.

[32] Idaho, Department of State, "Abstract of Votes at the General Election, November 5, 1940," *Biennial Report of the Secretary of State,* 1939-1940 (Boise), appended to p. 94. Thomas received 124,535 votes to Taylor's 110,614.

[33] *Pocatello Tribune,* November 6, 1940.

Democratic party officials figured that Taylor's political career was finished following the 1940 election. They did not exclude the possibility that Taylor would try again, but many leaders, such as Robert Coulter and Charles C. Gossett, believed that Taylor's style and message would be stale by 1942 when Thomas had to run for election again.[34]

After his defeat Taylor, as a patriotic and a political gesture, considered joining some branch of the military service, as most of his band had done; because of his age and a bad back, however, he decided to find work in a defense plant. He tried the Naval Ordnance plant in Pocatello, where he applied for a job as either a truck driver or a carpenter, and was told by the personnel director to fill out an application blank. Taylor later recalled: "I shoved the paper across the counter. The man looked at it and said, 'Glen Taylor. Are you the man who ran for the Senate?' I said, 'Yes.' He said, 'Well, Mr. Taylor, we have nothing suitable for you.'" Although Taylor explained that he was not asking to manage the plant but simply wanted a job, the manager insisted he had nothing suitable. "I saw what the score was. He thought I wanted to put on a silk hat and a pair of gloves and be a gentleman."[35] Unable to find work, Glen Taylor left Idaho and went to California, where most of his family now lived. He became a sheet-metal worker at a munitions factory near San Francisco.

While in California, Taylor confined his political activities to a few letters to Idaho friends, but he experienced an ideological transformation concerning foreign policy. Although Taylor was a near isolationist during the 1940 campaign and often spoke against involvement in a European power struggle, by November of 1941 he was convinced that Hitler had to be destroyed. Ten days prior to Pearl Harbor, he sent Roosevelt a telegram suggesting that "if we must fight, better to fight abroad than to subject our women and children to the horrors of a war at home."[36] Later Taylor used this telegram to play down the charge that he had been a total isolationist prior to the war.

[34] Interviews with Robert Coulter, September 14, 1967, and Charles C. Gossett, September 15, 1967. Both men still exhibit a genuine dislike for Taylor and admitted that they could not view their old enemy objectively.

[35] *Cong. Rec.*, 79th Cong., 1st sess., 1945, 91, pt. 7:9128.

[36] See *Lewiston Tribune*, November 11, 1942. A reproduction of this telegram was used by Taylor in an advertisement shortly before the 1942 election. The original could not be located among Roosevelt's papers at the Franklin D. Roosevelt Library, Hyde Park, New York. Hereafter cited as Roosevelt Papers.

Returning to Idaho in the spring of 1942, Taylor announced his candidacy for the Senate. He campaigned alone during the primary because Paul John, the Taylors' new baby, was hardly old enough to endure the rigors of extensive travel by car. Since the family had saved only a few hundred dollars, Taylor planned to economize. Boarding a bus, he stopped in Boise and told the press, "Dora and I decided we could save rubber and gas if, instead of using our car to campaign, I were to saddle up and ride around the state."[37] He knew that this idea was a political gimmick, but felt it would give him much-needed publicity.

In Coeur d'Alene, northern Idaho, Taylor bought a dapple gray Arabian horse and a saddle for $150. Wearing a huge white broad-brimmed hat of the Tom Mix variety, Taylor rode from house to house and chatted with the people. He did not conduct formal political meetings, but in the evenings, if he happened to be in a town, he would hold a street-corner rally.[38] Every day Taylor mailed penny post cards to the wire agencies and press services. He enjoyed reporting on his progress: "Left Coeur d'Alene July 4 and made 30 miles to Worley in 8½ hours and stopped at every house. Haven't loped [galloped] the horse yet. Had him shod here." At Tensed he wrote: "The West still lives on. Two days and two nights out of Coeur d'Alene and haven't been able to spend a cent to feed or bed my horse or myself."[39] From Moscow he wired ahead to Lewiston that he would be "coming down the mountain at high noon." He also reported a disabling accident: "Lacerated right palm opening barbed wire gate to farmer's lane. Unable to shake hands for two days. Can think of no worse calamity to befall a candidate."[40]

When Taylor arrived in Lewiston, he was described as "tanned and dressed in high-heeled cowboy boots, Levi's, and a big hat." The saddle-sore campaigner had tied to his saddle a length of garden hose given him by a farmer, an automobile floor mat presented him by two motorists whose tire he had helped fix, a rubber doll he had purchased from a farmer's daughter for eight cents, and a fan belt he had found along the road. He rode down

[37] *Idaho Statesman*, October 1, 1940.
[38] Interview with Taylor, June 14, 1967.
[39] *Lewiston Tribune*, July 8, 1942.
[40] Ibid., July 9, 1942. It is thirty-three miles from Moscow (elevation approximately 2,500 feet) to Lewiston (elevation 730 feet). The last ten miles are switchbacks leading down to Lewiston, which is located at the junction of the Snake and Clearwater rivers.

Lewiston's Main Street and told the crowd which gathered, "I'm not making any speeches. . . . I'm just goin' through the country saying hello to the folks."[41] After trading his sore-footed mount for a new steed, Taylor left Lewiston and rode to Grangeville, where his wife met him with a trailer and they continued to southern Idaho.

In the 1942 race, Taylor ran against four Democrats, including Owen T. Stratton, who bitterly called him a "goddam Pettifogging demagogue."[42] Taylor's four opponents took turns requesting that the other three withdraw from the race so that Taylor could be defeated. They realized that the larger the field, the greater Taylor's chances, yet none of them would pull out, even though party leaders and newspapers continually urged this action.[43]

Taylor's personality, his economic theories, and his biennial candidacy were the only real issues in the primary. Since he won with barely half as many votes as he had received two years earlier, this victory was unsatisfying. The meager showing—10,249 votes, or 32 percent of the total 32,098 votes cast—was attributed partly to the large field and partly to voter apathy. Again the newspapers held the Idaho primary responsible for the nomination of Glen Taylor. The *Idaho Daily Statesman* called Taylor a man who was "absolutely unspeakable," a "perfect blank."[44] The *Pocatello Tribune* commented, "it is not fitting that the senator from Idaho should pick a banjo and sing cowboy songs as an argument for his fitness as a national legislator."[45]

Although Taylor had won his party's senatorial nomination for the second time, he was still an alien in the eyes of regular Democrats. After the 1942 primary, he finally realized that in order to win a Senate seat he had better try to work with the state Democratic party organization, primarily because it would provide better financing and more favorable press coverage. Considering it impossible to work with Robert Coulter, Taylor tried to defeat the state party chairman at the convention.[46] Taylor's candidate was beaten badly and the Coulter-Taylor split widened.

Following the convention, Taylor met with the state party

41 Ibid., July 10, 1942. The ride from Coeur d'Alene to Lewiston is approximately 110 miles and from Lewiston to Grangeville slightly less than eighty.
42 "Showman and Scholar in Idaho," *Time* (August 10, 1942), pp. 23-24.
43 *Idaho Pioneer*, July 10, 1942. See also *Lewiston Tribune*, July 12, 1942.
44 *Idaho Statesman*, August 16, 1942.
45 *Pocatello Tribune*, August 16, 1942.
46 *Idaho Statesman*, August 29, 1942.

leaders and he decided to campaign along more conventional lines. Minus his traditional trappings of horse, saddle, and trailer, he traveled with other Democratic candidates throughout the state. One editor, who felt that Taylor was losing votes every day because of the change, characterized the new Glen as "more serious-minded, and to tell the truth, much less attractive. Glen got his votes via the banjo and horseshoe route, and . . . will have to hold them that way."[47]

Throughout the 1942 campaign, which coincided with the dramatic early stages of the Second World War, Taylor proclaimed that war was caused by unchecked competition of "greedy corporations," contending that a lasting international peace could be obtained only when these corporations were eliminated.[48] He claimed that he was "a peace-loving man who believes in cooperation and arbitration between men and nations" and that his advocacy of a "people's corporation" made him a true believer in world peace and internationalism.[49]

A bitter opponent of the military establishment, Taylor believed that the United States should do away with a large standing army. He favored a volunteer army of citizens over a regular army "because when you get a big army on hand, history shows that someone always wants to put it to use. We don't want that to happen here."[50] Despite these views, he did send a letter to Roosevelt during the 1942 campaign advising the president to open a second front in Europe.[51]

In 1942 Taylor's economic philosophy, campaign tactics, and personality again came under attack from conservative Democrats, the press, and, naturally, the Republicans, all of whom branded him as a jester, a buffoon, and an opportunist.[52] Although these attacks were less vicious than in 1940, the change of emphasis from communism to socialism may be explained by the fact that the United States was now allied with the Soviet Union in the Second World War. W. Scott Hall, a veteran Idaho legislator, told a Salt Lake City audience that Taylor was not "a Democrat and members of that party know it. Judging from his public utterances, Taylor

[47] *Idaho Pioneer,* September 25, 1942.
[48] *Idaho Statesman,* July 20, 1942.
[49] *Lewiston Tribune,* July 14, 1942.
[50] Ibid., September 10, 1942.
[51] Glen H. Taylor to Franklin D. Roosevelt, July 30, 1942. Official File, Roosevelt Papers.
[52] *Idaho Statesman,* August 16, 1942.

is a Socialist."[53] Another Republican, J. L. Eberle, accused Taylor of harboring "Socialistic and Communistic crackpot ideas" and promised to "call attention to his [Taylor's] ideas of bureaucratic socialism."[54]

A group called the Idaho Businessmen's Committee was formed, and it circulated letters containing the substance of the attacks on Taylor. He replied to their charges with a declaration that "the whole thing is based on false representation and misstatements" and observed that the signatures on the letter read "like a Republican roster."[55] One Idaho political commentator, Ernie Hood, felt that the criticism of Taylor had been so "petty that it would do [him] more good than harm."[56]

Once again, however, Glen Taylor suffered a defeat at the polls, this time by less than 5,000 votes. In a press release, he admitted that he was "sadly disappointed . . . by the trend established nationally," obviously referring to the gains made by the GOP at the polls in 1942. The twice defeated senatorial candidate foresaw a "commercialized peace treaty with big business placing the cross of exploitation for profit upon the backs of whole peoples." But, Taylor concluded, "I am not giving up my fight for a better world. Emphatically I am not."[57]

Taylor returned to California and again obtained work in a defense plant as a sheet-metal worker. Spending considerable time in self-evaluation after his three unsuccessful campaigns, Taylor reached some basic conclusions. He realized that because of his radical economic views, he was invariably going to be branded a Communist. His Populist technique of dramatizing economic issues and reducing them to simplicities was successful enough to win the Democratic party's nomination in the Idaho primary, but to win a Senate seat he would have to make some basic changes—of style and emphasis, not alterations of philosophy.

Even before the close of the 1942 campaign, Taylor had begun to alter his techniques, partially because he traveled with George Curtis, the Democratic secretary of state of Idaho. Curtis, a former Rhodes scholar, admired both Taylor's philosophy and technique, perhaps because the intellectual Curtis himself had

53 Ibid., October 12, 1942.
54 Ibid., October 24, 1942.
55 Ibid., October 31, 1942.
56 Ibid., November 1, 1942.
57 Pocatello Tribune, November 5, 1942, p. 1. Taylor received 68,989 votes to Thomas's 73,353, a losing margin of 4,364.

difficulty communicating with the common man. Taylor and Curtis, because of their diverse educational and economic backgrounds, made an interesting combination; they worked well together and learned from each other. Curtis had faith in Taylor's native ability and intelligence, but he believed Taylor's endless energy needed to be effectively channeled. The polished Curtis, who later would work for Taylor in Washington, helped sell him to the more refined segments of Idaho's electorate. Under Curtis's influence, by 1944 Taylor had replaced his cowboy hat, chaps, and boots with a business suit. Knowing that Taylor's speeches and past record would still keep him on firm ground with the common people, Curtis hoped a new image would create the momentum to carry Taylor to victory.[58]

Although Taylor modified his techniques, he continued to capitalize on two positive political assets—his ability as an orator and the ease with which he met people. Vardis Fisher, the Idaho novelist, called Taylor "one of the greatest speakers of our time. I listen to Glen every time I get a chance, not because he ever says anything, but because he says nothing superbly."[59] Because of his long acting career, Taylor had an amazing facility for memorization. He took pride in the fact that he could deliver his speeches without ever referring to notes. Usually starting his campaigns in small communities, Taylor practiced and experimented with his main speech until, by the time he reached Idaho's larger population centers, his delivery was nearly perfect. Also as new issues were raised, he would incorporate them in his text.[60]

Taylor's oratory was at its best when he evoked emotion by enumerating the devils at work against the common man. He directed his attacks not only at Wall Street, bankers, and anything which "smelled" of Eastern financial interests, but also at such large Idaho corporations as the Idaho Power Company and Morrison-Knudsen, the huge Boise-based construction company. He added the *Idaho Daily Statesman* and the *Pocatello Tribune* to his list of villians because of their opposition to him and his reforms. In short, if the voters wanted to know whom to be against, Taylor provided an answer.[61]

[58] Interview with Merle Wells, November 2, 1966. Dr. Wells, historian of the Idaho State Historical Society, was a close friend of the late George Curtis.

[59] Quoted in Crichton, "Idaho's Hot Potato," p. 64.

[60] Interview with Glen H. Taylor, June 14, 1967.

[61] Interview with Sam H. Day, editor of the *Intermountain Observer*, September 15, 1967.

Glen Taylor enjoyed speaking, but he relished shaking hands even more. His formula was never to start a lengthy conversation with anyone. "You can agree on ninety-nine percent of the things," he said, "but you will end up arguing about the one percent and the guy will only remember that one thing and vote against you."[62] He moved in square-dance fashion, from one person to the next, grabbing each person's hand, shaking it vigorously, and announcing: "I'm Glen Taylor. I'm running for the United States Senate. If you don't know anyone you'd rather vote for, I'd appreciate your vote."[63] Quick and effective with this technique, Taylor went where people were congregated, whether at a church social or a saloon.

George Donart, who had run against Taylor in 1940, introduced him to a Weiser audience in 1944 by relating the following anecdote:

The first time I ever saw Glen Taylor I was over in Burley campaigning for the U.S. Senate against Mr. Taylor. I had seen all of the precinct committeemen and the county chairman. I was standing on the corner wondering what to do next. I looked down the street and here came a fellow with a white cowboy hat on and he was shaking hands with everybody. He rushed to me, stuck out his hand, and said, "I'm Glen Taylor. I'm running for the Senate and I'd appreciate your vote." Well I opened my mouth to tell him that I was also a candidate for the Senate, but before I could say anything, he was shaking hands with the tenth fellow down the street.[64]

Taylor tried to get his friend George Curtis, who was running for the gubernatorial nomination in the 1944 primary, to use a similar technique. They would start together in a town, with Taylor introducing himself and Curtis to the first person they met. The vibrant Taylor would go up and down the street meeting most of the residents and return to find Curtis "arguing about vivisection with the first damn guy we met." Curtis told Taylor that he just could not walk off and leave people.[65]

Glen Taylor had another "new look" by 1944. One of the reasons he had worn a huge cowboy hat in his early campaigns was that he was losing his hair quite rapidly, a fact brought

[62] Interview with Glen H. Taylor, June 14, 1967.
[63] Ibid.
[64] Ibid. Taylor told this story as he remembered it.
[65] Ibid.

strikingly to his attention during the 1942 campaign. When he and Dora had stopped at a service station Taylor went to buy soft drinks. Upon returning, he asked the attendant how much the gas cost and was told, "Your daughter already paid for it." Overlooking the compliment to his wife and rather shaken, Taylor decided to do something about his appearance. Using an aluminum pie tin, a piece of felt, and human hair, he molded his first toupee. When he returned to Idaho from California in 1944, Taylor had not only a business suit, but a new head of hair and new optimism.[66]

Taylor officially announced his third candidacy for a United States Senate seat on April 17, 1944. For the first time in his career he wrote a platform, a detail usually left to the party, and sent copies of it to 300 members of the Idaho American Federation of Labor.[67] In it he called for a united effort to win the war, and he strongly advocated an international organization with sufficient force to maintain peace in the world. Taylor's domestic program, based on Gillette's economics and Roosevelt's New Deal, called for full employment legislation after the war and protection for small businessmen through the control of monopolies and trusts.[68] Taylor also proposed more farm and business cooperatives, increased federal aid for Idaho reclamation projects, and sixty dollars at sixty years of age for senior citizens. The platform concluded with a reminder to Idaho voters: "I have accepted no political job. My sole interest in politics is to help bring about a more stable economic system and to do what I can to prevent further wars by removing the causes, chief of which is International Competition for markets and raw materials by corporations and cartels."[69] With a different image and a familiar platform, Taylor set out for the third time in quest of the Democratic senatorial nomination.

Senator D. Worth Clark, the Democratic incumbent, was opposed in the 1944 primary by John W. Cornell and James H. Hawley, two Boise lawyers, as well as by Taylor. (It is not uncommon for members of the incumbent's party to challenge the officeholder in an Idaho primary.) Clark had defeated Senator James Pope, an ardent New Dealer, in the 1938 primary. Now, because of his

---

[66] Ibid.

[67] Taylor to August Rosqvist, April 22, 1944. Political file, August Rosqvist Papers, Idaho State Archives, Boise, Idaho. Hereafter cited as Rosqvist Papers.

[68] Undated mimeographed platform, Rosqvist Papers.

[69] Ibid.

consistent opposition to Roosevelt in both domestic and foreign affairs, Clark was considered politically vulnerable.[70]

Although Taylor's opponents were warned not to underestimate the two-time senatorial loser, as late as two weeks before the election most political forecasters were predicting a close race between Clark and Hawley. Some observers felt that Taylor's candidacy had not shown the vigor and spark of his previous campaigns.[71] H. H. Miller, a noted Idaho political analyst, wrote that Taylor would probably finish third behind Clark and Hawley. In the last ten days prior to the election, Miller had reversed his original opinion that Taylor was the principal threat to Clark's reelection. The argument that Taylor was slipping was based on the contention of democratic leaders that he had tried twice, and twice had lacked the necessary punch to win in the finals.[72] The *Idaho Daily Statesman* reported that Taylor, "from all indications, is no factor in the primary unless the vigorous Clark-Hawley campaign splits the intelligent vote."[73] When some of the leaders of the railroad brotherhoods came out for Cornell, it appeared that Taylor might slip to fourth.[74] Taylor calmly asserted, "I have my votes. . . . Let Hawley and Clark fight it out. The more their votes are split, the better off I am."[75]

Taylor drove throughout the state with either George Curtis or, after school was dismissed in May, with Dora and the boys. His speeches followed his platform very closely and almost invariably included a prophecy that "a change is coming"—an economic change of such magnitude that it would alter the American system. According to Taylor, the only way to assure that it would be peaceful instead of violent and the only way to preserve democracy and the freedom of the common man to own and operate a place of business or a farm, was to elect men to office who believed in change—men who would not try to hold back the tide.[76] Taylor proclaimed that true liberal leadership would keep the nation from going too far to the left or to the right, and he opposed violence or dictatorship as a means of accomplishing social reform. As a dedicated liberal he "honestly felt" that "we can learn and

---

[70] Interview with Robert Coulter, September 14, 1967.
[71] *Idaho Pioneer*, June 2, 1944; *Idaho Falls Commoner*, June 2, 1944.
[72] *Lewiston Tribune*, June 4, 1944.
[73] *Idaho Statesman*, June 11, 1944.
[74] *Lewiston Tribune*, June 4, 1944.
[75] *Idaho Statesman*, June 10, 1944.
[76] *Lewiston Tribune*, May 31, 1944.

profit by the example of what has been achieved by planning in Russia."[77] The guitar-playing, singing candidate had become a more refined, orthodox campaigner, but Taylor's economic convictions, acquired during the bleak depression years, were still evident.

One of the closest elections Taylor was ever involved in was the 1944 primary. The day after the election, the incumbent, Clark, led by 202 votes, but as the backcountry precincts slowly reported, Taylor gained on Clark. Within two days, Taylor led by fourteen votes. When the official canvass was conducted, Taylor was declared the winner by 216 ballots. He had manager to capture barely 33 percent of the vote.[78]

Taylor's third successful bid for the Democratic senatorial nomination caused the customary blasts against the Idaho primary law, but many reporters humbly admitted that they had misjudged the persevering former actor. Frank Burroughs, editor of the *Idaho Pioneer,* wrote that his "guess that Glen Taylor had faded was not a very bright one. This prognosticator's head is still whirling trying to figure out why a bunch of Democrats would vote for Glen for senator."[79] Another observer believed that Taylor would have won by a greater margin but for the fact that "by abandoning his picturesque hat, his horse, and his vaudeville show [he] had lost a lot of supporters."[80] One newspaper viewed Taylor's victory as definite assurance that Governor C. A. Bottolfsen, the Republican senatorial nominee, would win easily in November, and prophesied that the Democratic candidate "would make a suitable sacrificial lamb to serve Bottolfsen. Taylor has played the next-best November part so often."[81]

The victorious Taylor announced, "I have shown that I can get votes with the quietest sort of campaign. I reserve the right in the future to sing, use a sound system, wear my cowboy hat, or ride a horse."[82] He said that he had conducted an orthodox campaign to prove that "my critics were wrong when in the past

[77] Ibid.
[78] Idaho, Department of State, "Abstract of Votes at the Primary Election, June 13, 1944," *Biennial Report of the Secretary of State,* 1943-1944 (Boise), appended to p. 94. Taylor received 10,711 votes and Clark 10,495 out of a total of 32,228 cast.
[79] *Idaho Pioneer,* June 16, 1944.
[80] *Lewiston Tribune,* June 18, 1944.
[81] *Idaho Statesman,* June 18, 1944.
[82] *Idaho Statesman,* June 27, 1944.

they have said that I had to exploit my family or resort to ballyhoo and trick publicity stunts to get votes."[83]

The unique feature of his campaign for the Senate after the primary in 1944 was the change in attitude of the Democratic party in Idaho. Robert Coulter, who had had enough of Taylor, resigned as state chairman, and his replacement, David L. Bush, told Taylor, "Glen, I want to reiterate that I am for you."[84] Taylor quipped, "The state committee decided to come in and help me this time. . . . They probably figured the only way to get rid of me was to elect me."[85]

Taylor firmly fastened himself to Franklin D. Roosevelt's coat-tails and prepared to ride to victory with the Democratic president. Although he had been critical of Roosevelt in 1940, he assumed the role of Idaho's defender of the president in 1944. At Rigby, in southeastern Idaho, the senatorial candidate compared Roosevelt and Dewey and what he felt were the basic philosophies of the two major parties: "When human values and property values clash, the democrats would resolve the problem in terms of human beings, and the republicans in terms of property."[86] Offering a simple comparison, Taylor said, "The democrats say that the primary business of government is to safeguard and improve the conditions of life of all the people. . . . The republicans say that the first business of government is to safeguard and improve the conditions of property, private property."[87] Taylor claimed that this difference in political philosophies was why Roosevelt had maintained the support of the masses.

Foreign affairs was a keen and important issue in this election. By the fall of 1944, it was apparent that the Allies would win the war. Winning the peace presented a different problem. Taylor advocated the formation of an international body dedicated to preserving world peace. He blamed the isolationist leaders in the Republican party for the mistakes made after World War I and for keeping the United States out of the League of Nations: "At that time they promised to give us a better plan to preserve peace than the League of Nations. But they haven't given us anything at all."[88] Taylor told the voters of Weiser, "If I am elected senator,

83 Ibid.
84 *Lewiston Tribune,* July 1, 1944.
85 Crichton, "Idaho's Hot Potato," p. 64.
86 *Lewiston Tribune,* October 11, 1944.
87 Ibid.
88 *Idaho Statesman,* October 19, 1944.

I will not only 'stand ready' to vote for a plan to preserve peace. I will never rest . . . until such a world organization is in being."[89]

At a public meeting sponsored by the League of Women Voters in the Boise Hotel, Taylor followed his opponent, Governor Bottolfsen, on the program and was cheered loudly as he mounted the stand. He ignored the microphone used by the governor and left his notes on the podium. Taylor, like the hero in a melodrama, walked back and forth across the stage dramatically pleading his cause. Judging his audience accurately, he assumed that the mothers and wives present wanted the war to end and hopefully looked forward to an era of peace. He reminded his listeners that he had two small sons who would be "prime cannon fodder if history repeats itself in another 25 or 30 years." He promised that his first order of business in the Senate would be consideration of a plan to "preserve peace in the world, imperfect though it may be, and if I have the high honor of casting my vote in favor of it [an international organization] . . . I would feel repaid."[90]

During the campaign, Taylor also discussed issues that would be of special interest to Idahoans. His concern for the economic underdog was still evident, but it was presented with less militancy. Instead of emphasizing what was wrong with America, the senatorial candidate laid stress on how much Roosevelt had accomplished. He found the farmers trying to outdo each other "telling stories of how, during years of the Democratic administration they . . . had come back from the brink of disaster and foreclosure to the point where foreclosure is almost unheard of."[91]

In a debate with Bottolfsen, Taylor strongly supported the Kilgore-Murray bill, which was being discussed in Congress. This bill proposed authorization of thirty-five dollars a week unemployment compensation for war workers. Accusing Bottolfsen of opposing such federal aid, Taylor argued that "since the big financiers take money out of Idaho and into Wall Street and then are taxed by the federal government, I want to bring all the federal money into Idaho possible."[92] According to Taylor, Idaho would be in line for federal aid for postwar projects if it had "representation in Washington . . . sympathetic with the purposes of the Democratic administration." It was late for Idahoans to get in on the federal

[89] Ibid., October 26, 1944.
[90] Ibid., November 5, 1944.
[91] Ibid., August 16, 1944.
[92] Ibid., September 5, 1944.

projects planned to take up the slack in employment during the period of reconversion, but not too late if they had "at least one senator to look after the state's interests."[93] Strongly convinced that Idaho's future development depended on federal projects, and especially on a Columbia Valley Authority modeled on the successful Tennessee Valley Authority, Taylor included that proposal in his 1944 campaign speeches.

Taylor's most potent political ammunition was provided by Governor Bottolfsen when the latter in effect vetoed the Senior Citizens' Grants Act. This act had been passed by initiative on the 1942 Idaho ballot and provided a monthly pension of sixty dollars plus other benefits for everyone over sixty-five. The Republican majority in the legislature repealed the act and Bottolfsen signed the repeal measure. Late in the campaign, Taylor made an issue of Bottolfsen's "rejection of the people's will."[94] Townsendites, laborers, and farmers waited for Bottolfsen's reply, but the governor remained silent.

The Taylor candidacy received support from many Idaho Democrats in 1944 for the first time. Former Governor C. Ben Ross publicly announced in mid-October that Taylor "would give us the best service and make the best senator. I honestly believe that."[95] He joined Taylor for the last two weeks of the campaign. Ross, who had lost the gubernatorial race to Bottolfsen in 1938, was extremely sarcastic and cutting in his attacks on the governor, especially when he discussed the Senior Citizens' Grants Act: "Bott didn't want to veto that bill because he knew all you people would be mad—but he wasn't quite man enough to stand up under pressure of the big interests."[96] Charles C. Gossett, the Democratic candidate for governor, James H. Hawley, George Donart, and George Curtis, all supported Taylor. His new image, and the primary victory he had won with it, had at last given him a certain respectability among many Democratic leaders.

Taylor also received support from the Independent Voters League of Idaho and from the Committee for Political Action of the Congress of Industrial Organizations, both considered by many Idahoans to be left-wing organizations. The Independent Voters League launched an anti-Bottolfsen campaign, while the Political

93 Ibid., September 28, 1944.
94 *Lewiston Tribune*, October 29, 1944.
95 Ibid., October 17, 1944.
96 *Idaho Statesman*, October 3, 1944.

Action Committee simply worked for Taylor as a prospective friend of labor in Washington. When the *Idaho Daily Statesman,* a strong supporter of Bottolfsen, criticized Taylor for accepting aid from such left-wing groups, the Independent Voters League came to Taylor's defense. It ran a newspaper advertisement quoting an editorial in the August 9, 1942, issue of the *Statesman* which had urged the selection of William Detweiler over Bottolfsen in the Republican primary. The editorial had labeled Bottolfsen as "timid and faltering" stating he was afraid of political consequence and "more interested in himself than in good government."[97]

Viciously attacking Taylor on many subjects in 1944, the *Statesman* continually belabored the point that the Democratic candidate was not a resident of Idaho and that he was an opportunist who returned to Idaho only when there was an election. According to the *Statesman,* Taylor's residence in California between 1940 and 1942, and again between 1942 and 1944, proved that he was a poor financial manager, had no experience in government, had no executive ability, and did not know Idaho's problems. The editorials also discussed Taylor's economic theories, his acting career, and his political ideology and concluded that the state was fortunate that Bottolfsen was in the race. The *Statesman* claimed that Donart, Ross, Curtis, and the other Democrats who were supporting Taylor had betrayed their ideals for political expediency.[98]

The Republican state party chairman, S. L. Thorpe, told Idaho Democrats they were the victims of the "greatest instance of opportunism in the history of the state." Using many of the same arguments as the *Statesman,* Thorpe said that Taylor made his living outside of Idaho and "resides in the state only long enough to conduct his biennial campaigns."[99] Thorpe and J. L. Eberle, a Boise attorney, both attacked Taylor for what they called "pro-Communism." Eberle called Taylor a Communist who is "being financed by the political action committee of the C.I.O."[100] Quoting from earlier Taylor speeches concerning "the people's corporation," Thorpe concluded, "If the foregoing isn't Communism . . . what definition can be put on Communism?"[101]

97 Ibid., November 2, 1944.
98 See the following editorials in the *Idaho Statesman:* September 2, 5, 13, 19, October 17, 19, 24, and November 1.
99 *Idaho Statesman,* October 12, 1944.
100 *Lewiston Tribune,* October 26, 1944.
101 *Idaho Statesman,* November 3, 1944.

Answering the charges against him in a Boise speech two days prior to the election, Taylor told the throng assembled on the Capitol building steps: "I had been a resident six years when he [Bottolfsen] came in 1910. . . . During all the years the republican candidate was making such a success of his newspaper, I was constantly traveling Idaho . . . learning first hand the problems . . . of Idaho."[102] He reminded Republicans that Senator John Thomas had also spent most of the time between 1933 and 1940 in California. Taylor discussed the charge of communism only once, in a speech at Burley. He chastised Thorpe and Eberle for trying to discredit every "liberal and social measure and man by calling it communistic. Again it is a straight steal from Hitler who cried 'Bolshevik' at everybody who opposed him."[103]

On election eve, Taylor urged the reelection of Roosevelt and criticized the Republican campaign assaults on himself. He used the words of Horace Greeley, uttered in 1872, to describe how he felt during the campaign: "At times I have been in doubt as to whether I was running for the Senate or the penitentiary."[104]

Early Wednesday morning, November 8, it was apparent that Idaho's new junior senator would be Glen H. Taylor. Taylor ran behind both Roosevelt and the new governor, Charles C. Gossett, but his victory was substantial. The final vote was 107,096 for Taylor to 102,373 for Bottolfsen.[105] A grateful Taylor thanked his supporters and expressed happiness over "the confidence shown in me by the people of Idaho."[106] Referring to Governor Jimmy Davis of Louisiana and Senator Lee "Pappy" O'Daniel of Texas, the happy victor laughingly asserted that he had been the first of the "cowboy singers" to enter the political arenas, but "the last to get elected."[107]

Slightly more than eight years had passed since Taylor decided to enter politics and he had finally won. His victory represented a compromise, not of principles, but of techniques. He realized the importance of identifying with Franklin D. Roosevelt's image as well as with Roosevelt's reforms. Taylor still believed in the

---

[102] *Lewiston Tribune*, November 5, 1944.

[103] *Idaho Statesman*, October 31, 1944.

[104] *Pocatello Tribune*, November 6, 1944.

[105] Idaho, Department of State, "Abstract of Votes at the General Election, November 7, 1944," *Biennial Report of the Secretary of State*, 1943-1944 (Boise), appended to p. 94.

[106] *Lewiston Tribune*, November 9, 1944.

[107] *New York Times*, November 10, 1944, p. 13.

economic theories of Chase and Gillette, but he had conducted a campaign designed to bring political success rather than create controversy.

On Monday morning, December 11, 1944, Glen and Dora Taylor, with their two small sons, left for Washington, D.C. Taylor told reporters before he departed: "I hold the down to earth people of Idaho as my personal acquaintances. I intend to do everything I can in Congress to help them. . . . By bringing new industries to Idaho, by protecting the little fellow from the big fellow and by working for an international organization that will mean peace, . . . I intend to be a good senator."[108]

One of Taylor's supporters, eighty-six-year-old Mrs. Anna B. Littlefield, who lived in Clarkston, Washington, across the Snake River from Lewiston, Idaho, was worried about the new senator-elect. She wrote to President Roosevelt requesting that he look after Taylor.

My dear President I am one of your old standbys Mrs. Anna B. Littlefield . . . and I want you to know one of my adopted family Glen H. Taylor is now member of U. S. Senate from Idaho. I sure worked for him as for you thru many campaigns and won out to my hearts content. So want you to be a real father to that youngster he is a fine young man. You will won't you? And make him at home and may God bless you in this hour of turmoil but I am sure all will be well and our trust in such as Glen H. Taylor and your own loyal self is not misplaced.[109]

[108] *Salt Lake Tribune,* December 12, 1944. The Salt Lake City dailies, the *Tribune* and the *Deseret News,* which publish Idaho supplements, had large Idaho circulations. Often, when Taylor was in southern Idaho, the Salt Lake papers provided better coverage than the Idaho papers.
[109] Anna B. Littlefield to Franklin D. Roosevelt, January 3, 1945, President's Personal File SC-L, Roosevelt Papers.

III. *Fair Deal Senator*

Glen Taylor's first major struggle in Washington was not over labor legislation, reclamation projects, or civil rights, but concerned housing. Because of the desperate wartime housing shortage, Taylor was unable to find suitable housing for his family. John J. Halsey, secretary of the Senate, heard about the freshman legislator's dilemma and invited the press to meet Taylor on the Capitol steps on January 3.[1] Taylor was persuaded to put on his Stetson, strum his guitar, and sing for the reporters and photographers. The tune was "Home on the Range," but the words were clearly Glen Taylor's:

> O, give us a home, near the Capitol Dome,
> With a yard where the children can play.
> Just one room or two—Any old thing will do,
> We can't find a pla-a-ce to stay.[2]

The story of this Capitol-steps concert was circulated widely by the national press. Washington realtors flocked to Taylor's assistance and took the new arrivals into Washington's most elite neighborhoods, but Taylor refused to pay "merely to be elite." Balking at $250-a-month rent, the Taylors bought a home in the southeast section of the city for $15,000. "That's a fearful lot of money, . . . but not as much as $250 a month [in rent] for six years," Taylor said. The family moved in, and Taylor put his wife on his office staff to help pay for it. As for nepotism, the new senator met the issue head-on: "Mrs. Taylor works in my office. She always has worked with me, as everybody in Idaho knows. In fact, if she weren't working too, I would despair of making ends meet."[3]

After Taylor's initial Washington performance, an Idaho newspaper reported that the "great radio personality who is about to represent us in such splendid fashion in the halls of Congress will probably demand a microphone in the Senate for his eloquent periods."[4] Taylor may have read the editorial; shortly afterward, in an interview with a reporter, he criticized the acoustics of the Senate chamber: "Visitors see a senator making a speech and the other senators are paying no attention to him. That's because they can't hear him."[5]

Following this unorthodox beginning, the new senator from Idaho immediately began his fight for the common man. Taylor considered himself a New Deal Democrat and believed that he had a mandate from Idaho voters to support Franklin D. Roosevelt's policies in war and peace. His first speech on the Senate floor, delivered as a supporter of Roosevelt, concerned confirmation of the appointment of Henry A. Wallace as secretary of commerce. Wallace, the former vice president, had been dumped by the Democratic leaders at the 1944 convention who considered him too liberal to be chosen as a possible successor to Roosevelt. An ardent New Dealer, Wallace was offered the cabinet post as appeasement, but there was considerable opposition to his appointment among Republicans and southern Democrats. Conservative fears that Wallace would attempt to maintain federal control of business after the war were perhaps justifiable. There is no doubt that Wallace wanted to curb the activities of corporations.

The day Wallace's name came before a Senate committee, Taylor wrote a short note assuring the former vice president of his support. Predicting a big fight, Taylor's main fear was that the Senate would strip Wallace of any meaningful authority. He suggested introducing a bill that would increase Wallace's authority and then working out a compromise that would preserve the status quo. The former troubador even jokingly suggested, "If the situation gets too bad I may have to take out the banjo again."[6]

[1] Kyle Crichton, "Idaho's Hot Potato," *Collier's* (June 30, 1945), p. 64.

[2] *New York Times,* January 4, 1945, p. 36. Later Taylor described his feelings about singing on the Capitol steps: "Frankly, I wanted to back out. . . . I turned the thing over in my mind. I didn't want to disappoint all the newspaper fellows. I knew that the stuffed shirts wouldn't like it but the ordinary people with a sense of humor would get a laugh out of it. So I went ahead— I was never going to be a favorite of the stuffed shirts anyway." Quoted in the *Citizen,* April 1948.

[3] Richard L. Neuberger, "Cowboy on Our Side," *Nation* (August 24, 1946), p. 210. Mrs. Taylor still works with her husband at their Taylor Topper plant in Millbrae, California. In fact, when the writer visited Glen Taylor, Mrs. Taylor was acting as receptionist.

[4] *Pocatello Tribune,* January 5, 1945.

[5] Crichton, "Idaho's Hot Potato," p. 64.

[6] Glen H. Taylor to Henry A. Wallace, January 25, 1945; 53,963M; Henry

Taylor attended some of the hearings and penned a congratulatory letter referring to Wallace's appearance before the committee: "It did my heart good the way you handled yourself and the grand ovation . . . was very gratifying to me as it must have been to you."[7] Wallace reciprocated a few days later: "It is most gratifying to see such courage and definiteness of purpose in a young senator."[8]

The Senate debated the Wallace appointment during the last days of February 1945. At times the discussion was heated and tempers nearly exploded. Republican Senator Alexander Wiley of Wisconsin had just concluded a tirade against Wallace and the New Deal when Taylor rose to deliver his maiden Senate address: "It is with considerable humility and with some trepidation that I rise to contribute a few words to this discussion. It is, I believe, thought that a newcomer should keep his seat for a time until he has become better acquainted with the procedures of . . . the Congress. . . . However, I am somewhat vexed at having to sit here and listen to all the reverberations from the other side of the aisle with nothing emanating from this side. . . . I think this may be a good time for me to practice a little bit."[9]

Taylor proceeded to deliver a pro-Wallace and pro-New Deal speech. Emphasizing how much the New Deal had done for Idaho and how much could still be done, Taylor gave Henry Wallace much of the credit for the New Deal's accomplishments. Taylor claimed that during the war international combinations of industrial capital were receiving government favors and reaping substantial profits. He ended his address by telling his colleagues, "I would rather have Henry Wallace, with all his idealism and love of mankind—which seems to be a crime in the eyes of some—than one of the fierce troglodyte animals with tremendous power and no social brains."[10] After a lengthy debate, Wallace was confirmed. It is ironic that Taylor's first Senate speech was delivered in support of the Democrat who later was to lead Taylor out of the Democratic party.

Apparently Taylor admired the new secretary of commerce and wanted to meet him. One of Wallace's assistants, in a memo to

A. Wallace Papers, University of Iowa Library, Iowa City, Iowa. Hereafter cited as Wallace Papers.

[7] Ibid.

[8] Wallace to Taylor, February 5, 1945; 36,121M, Wallace Papers.

[9] *Cong. Rec.*, 79th Cong., 1st sess., 1945, 91, pt. 2:1609.

[10] Ibid.

the secretary, reported that the junior senator of Idaho was seeking an appointment and that Taylor was a "good, solid, citizen, quiet and unassuming, who admits he knows nothing but Idaho, but wants to learn. . . . Taylor based his campaign on Wallace ideas."[11] Subsequently Taylor was invited to a luncheon at the Commerce Department.

Three weeks after Wallace's confirmation, Taylor rose to defend Aubrey W. Williams, whom Roosevelt had nominated to be Administrator of the Rural Electrification Administration. Calling the formidable opposition to Williams "an attempt to stab the President in the back," Taylor castigated the Republicans and southern Democrats for "pushing pins under the toe nails of the President, and trying to irritate him at a time when the fate of the world is resting in large part upon his capable shoulders."[12] Despite Taylor's earnest plea, the Senate refused to confirm Williams. He was the last Roosevelt appointee Taylor had the opportunity to defend.

Roosevelt's death on April 12, 1945, brought Harry S. Truman into the White House. Truman and Taylor had become acquainted during the three short months that Truman presided over the Senate as vice president. Their offices in the Senate Office Building were in the same area, and they had often walked to the Capitol building together. Later, when writing to Truman, Taylor referred to himself as "Your former neighbor SOB."[13] Taylor considered Truman "very likeable and a personal friend."[14] Shortly after Truman's ascension to the presidency, when Taylor and his Democratic senatorial colleagues visited him at the White House, and the senators were applauding, Taylor explained to reporters, "Harry told us how much he loved us and we enjoyed it."[15] Nearly two months later, Taylor wired Truman, inviting the president to join him in the "Gem state" for a period of relaxation. "Dear Harry— Would you honor the state of Idaho . . . by spending a day or two as my guest. . . . No speeches no banquets. . . . I want to go fishing and am looking for another common plug to enjoy the good time. . . . You are doing a swell job. Everybody is pleased."[16]

[11] George M. Reynolds to Wallace, May 4, 1945; 42,277M, Wallace Papers.

[12] *Cong. Rec.*, 79th Cong., 1st sess., 1945, 91, pt. 2:2611.

[13] Telegram, Taylor to Harry S. Truman, June 11, 1945, President's Personal File (hereafter cited at PPF) 1626, Harry S. Truman Papers, Harry S. Truman Library, Independence, Missouri. Hereafter cited as Truman Papers.

[14] Interview with Glen H. Taylor, June 14, 1967.

[15] *Daily Worker* (New York), April 24, 1945.

[16] Telegram, Taylor to Truman, June 11, 1945, PPF 1626, Truman Papers.

Truman wired back that he would be unable to accept, but said that he would "take a rain check."[17] Unfortunately, because of subsequent developments, this friendship would become strained.

Taylor hoped that Truman would continue the reform measures of the New Deal as soon as the war ended, and Taylor's concern was shared by many of his Democratic colleagues in the Senate. On July 31, 1945, thirteen senators, most of them liberals, met at a luncheon and mapped plans for enacting postwar legislation. Denying that they had discussed President Truman's alleged drift toward the right, the group claimed their purpose was to see what liberal bills could be passed early in the fall. This group, which included Glen Taylor, wanted the resumption of federally sponsored reclamation projects, housing for veterans, controls on possible inflation, increased social security benefits, and full employment legislation.[18]

Actually, Truman was as interested as the liberal Democratic senators in reviving the New Deal and he incorporated many of their suggestions in the legislative program which he sent to Congress on September 6, 1945, only four days after the Japanese formally surrendered. Calling for the demobilization of the armed forces as soon as possible, a return to peacetime production, and the continuation of price, rent, and wage controls in order to prevent inflation, Truman also requested, in his 16,000-word message, full employment legislation and a Fair Employment Practices Commission. Later he added health insurance, prepaid medical care, federal aid to education, the nationalization of atomic energy, and the development of the St. Lawrence Seaway.[19] In essence, Truman's September proposals were the core of his Fair

17 Telegram, Truman to Taylor, June 14, 1945, PPF 1626, Truman Papers.

18 *New York Times*, August 1, 1945, p. 20. Other Democrats in the group were Claude Pepper, Florida; Harley M. Kilgore, West Virginia; Warren Magnuson, Washington; Hugh B. Mitchell, Washington; Theodore F. Green, Rhode Island; Scott W. Lucas, Illinois; Brien McMahon, Connecticut; Edwin C. Johnson, Colorado; James M. Mead, New York; Olin D. Johnston, South Carolina; Abe Murdock; Utah; and Elbert Thomas, Utah. The luncheon was allegedly called by Kilgore and Pepper; Alben Barkley, senate majority leader, was not invited.

19 Harry S. Truman, *Public Papers of the President*, 8 vols. (Washington: Government Printing Office, 1965), 1:263-309. Hereafter cited as *Truman Public Papers*. Truman's message on domestic affairs quieted the fears of the liberals temporarily. Taylor joined the president and about seventy other guests for a weekend at Annapolis shortly after Truman's September 6 speech. At the informal gathering which included highballs, cards, and horseshoes, Taylor and Truman were defeated at horseshoes, 21-20, *New York Times*, September 23, 1945, p. 37. No scores were recorded for highballs or cards.

Deal program of domestic reform. Taylor and other liberals were heartened by these legislative suggestions, and the Idaho senator felt that he could successfully carry out his pledge to the "little man" as long as Truman continued to follow Roosevelt's path.

But President Truman's legislative program did not receive such an enthusiastic reception in Congress as a whole. Robert Taft of Ohio led the opposition in the Senate; Joseph Martin of Massachusetts and Charles Hallack of Indiana, in the House. Republicans complained that Truman was trying to "out-deal the New Deal."[20] Conservatives claimed he not only was determined to carry on the social-welfare tradition of Roosevelt but also was attempting to use his wartime economic powers to perpetuate government dominance over private enterprise.

Consistently supporting Truman's domestic program during the early part of Truman's presidency, Taylor and his liberal colleagues attempted to act rapidly on some of the proposed legislation. The Murray-Wagner Full Employment bill was one of the first bills to reach the floor of the Senate. Although he thought the bill was limited in its scope, Taylor believed that it would have psychological value, if nothing else. Comparing the unemployment bill with the act creating the Federal Deposit Insurance Corporation, sponsored by the New Deal, he said there was nothing in that law which stated "Your deposits are insured unless something else happens so we cannot take care of this obligation." It proclaimed, "Your deposits are insured up to $5,000, and regardless of whether or not we deserve it, the people have confidence in the Congress of the United States."[21]

According to the Idaho senator, the people would have confidence in a bill that said, "There will be a job," and then made sure that jobs were available. To insure employment for all the nation's unemployed, Taylor wanted Congress to take the same type of positive action that had pledged all the national resources to winning the war. Concluding with a verbal jab at the Republican opposition for taking the teeth out of the bill, the freshman senator said: "When I see . . . measures like this watered down, frankly, my hopes are not very high."[22]

Later, Taylor offered an amendment to the Murray-Wagner bill

20 Joseph Martin, *My First Fifty Years in Politics* (New York: McGraw-Hill, 1960), p. 178. See also Cabell Phillips, *The Truman Presidency* (New York: Macmillan, 1966), p. 104.

21 *Cong. Rec.*, 79th Cong., 1st sess., 1945, 91, pt. 9:9127.

22 Ibid., p. 9129.

which appealed to the disciples of Francis Townsend. In a statement to the press, the Idaho senator explained that his amendment was designed to provide an income for the "aged sufficient to enable them to maintain a decent and healthful standard of living and to promote the retirement from the labor force of older citizens."[23] Eventually an employment bill was passed in what Taylor considered an "emasculated" form.[24]

In October of 1945 the Idaho Democrat went to Los Angeles to speak before a CIO-organized convention on full employment. After his speech, the senator was served with a writ filed by his former wife, Pearl, now Mrs. Kenneth Nitkowskie of Los Angeles, for past support of their daughter, Olive, who was now over twenty years of age. Her complaint declared that Taylor had deserted her and had failed to provide her with common necessities.[25] Taylor, who was in California for only one day had to return to Washington, turned the case over to attorneys. He was later absolved of the charges, but certain Idaho Democrats still claim that the resultant whispering campaigns in "straight-laced" southern Idaho hurt Taylor politically.[26]

Taylor returned to Washington a bit ruffled, but he arrived in time to help Truman with a legislative battle over extension of the Office of Price Administration (OPA). One of the most controversial of the wartime agencies, OPA was responsible for setting and enforcing price and rent ceilings, and Truman believed that controls were still necessary to avoid an inflationary spiral. Republicans such as Taft and Kenneth S. Wherry of Nebraska were adamantly opposed to extension, but Taylor, supporting Truman, told the Senate, "If we were to abolish the OPA at this time we would simply surrender to uncontrolled inflation."[27] Before adjourning its 1945 special session, Congress grudgingly granted a six-months reprieve to OPA.

When Congress reconvened in January 1946, Truman asked for

[23] *New York Times*, September 20, 1945, p. 19.

[24] *Cong. Rec.*, 80th Con., 1st sess., 1947, 93, pt. 4:4266. The best account of the ill-fated Full Employment Act is Stephen K. Bailey, *Congress Makes a Law: The Story behind the Employment Act of 1946* (New York: Columbia University Press, 1950). Perhaps one redeeming feature of the Act was the establishment of a Council of Economics Advisors.

[25] *New York Times*, October 4, 1945, p. 25.

[26] Interview with Robert Coulter, September 14, 1967. Coulter referred to southern Idaho because it is heavily Mormon; he believed that although Taylor was neither tried nor convicted, the charge alone hurt him.

[27] *Cong. Rec.*, 79th Cong., 1st sess., 1945, 91, pt. 9:11706.

a full additional year of authority to regulate prices and to ration scarce commodities. The president promised to relax the controls, item by item, as supply and demand leveled off. According to one observer, the ensuing committee hearings on the extension of OPA constituted one of the greatest "carnivals of mass lobbying and political manipulation Washington had ever seen."[28] Opposition to OPA was led and directed by the United States Chamber of Commerce and the National Association of Manufacturers (NAM), which united to spend millions on newspaper, magazine, and radio advertising against OPA. Truman was dismayed more by "distorted editorials and slanted headlines" than by the vast amounts of money spent by these groups. The administration countered with the testimony of top labor leaders and spokesmen for consumer groups.[29] The Truman administration, however, did not present a united front concerning OPA. There was fierce opposition from Secretary Clinton Anderson of the Agriculture Department and from John Snyder, director of the Office of War Mobilization and Reconversion. Faced with internal disruption, Truman did not support OPA adequately.[30]

The extension of OPA was an issue that fitted Taylor's Populist-New Deal philosophy precisely. He viewed the OPA conflict as a battle between the "haves" and the "have-nots" and told his fellow senators that the question boiled down to whether the "people of America are willing to sacrifice temporary, unexpected, speculative gains for the general welfare."[31] In a Washington radio address, Taylor denounced the Republicans and "some" Democrats who "want to pawn the future of America for greedy profits now." He made the point that if the new OPA bill was burdened with amendments the country would have price control in name only.[32] Two weeks later, Taylor told a meeting of the New Council of

28 Phillips, *The Truman Presidency*, p. 107. The best account of the OPA struggle is Harvey Mansfield et al., *A Short History of the O.P.A.* (Washington: Government Printing Office, 1947).

29 Harry S. Truman, *Memoirs*, 2 vols. (New York: Doubleday, 1955), 2:206. Hereafter cited as Truman, *Memoirs*.

30 For descriptions of this interdepartmental difficulty, see Allen J. Matusow, *Farm Policies and Politics in the Truman Years* (New York: Atheneum, 1970), Chapter 3, "Agriculture and the Death of O.P.A."; and Barton J. Bernstein, "The Removal of War Production Board Controls on Business, 1944-1946," *Business History Review* 39 (Summer 1965):243-60. See also Mansfield, *A Short History of the O.P.A.*, pp. 82-94.

31 *Cong. Rec.*, 79th Cong., 2d sess., 1946, 92, pt. 3:3405.

32 *Lewiston Tribune*, April 15, 1946.

American Business, an organization of liberal businessmen, that the "reactionary group which has been filling the air with their pained outcries against price control is a small minority which is dominated by the giant monopolies."[33] Taylor castigated the NAM for fighting old age insurance, unemployment insurance, minimum wages, and a national health act and claimed that the entire history of the NAM was "a history of opposition to everything the people have wanted." He concluded with a denunciation of the Republican-business alliance which wanted, he said, "to abolish the price act or at least cripple it so that wild inflation can roar over the land unhindered."[34]

Truman had told Congress in January that for the purpose of orderly planning it was imperative that a new OPA bill be passed by April 1946, but the Senate launched a prolonged debate that was finally to produce a thoroughly mangled compromise bill late in June. The most cumbersome amendment was the Taft amendment, which provided that OPA could not issue any price schedules which did not reflect the manufacturer's profit on each item covered. This clearly created an administrative monstrosity.

As the Senate debated the compromise OPA bill, a group of pro-OPA demonstrators gathered at the Washington Monument, and Glen Taylor was invited to address the cheering crowd. For Taylor, facing such a throng was like the old days in Idaho, and he empathized with the consumers: "Buyers can wait for a more advantageous market, too. I need a new suit badly, but I am not going to buy one until prices come to a sensible level. . . . If, when you see me from the Senate Gallery, you think I look a little shabby, I want you to understand this: Glen Taylor is in uniform. He is wearing the uniform of the militant consumer who will pay reasonable prices, but who refuse to outbid each other in runaway inflation."[35] Taylor and his colleagues of a similar persuasion believed that OPA had to be continued intact and that any compromise would be disastrous, but their efforts were doomed to failure.

In a last-ditch attempt to extend the existing OPA until February 1, 1947, Taylor joined Senators Wayne Morse and Claude Pepper in a short filibuster, in which he told the Senate that the compro-

33 Ibid., April 27, 1946.
34 Ibid.
35 *Daily Worker*, June 25, 1946. Among others who spoke at the OPA demonstration were Congressmanwoman Helen Gahagan Douglas, Robert Nathan, and Orson Welles.

mise OPA bill was "absolutely inadequate and will lead to inflation."[36] When the bill was passed, he urged Truman to veto it because it "is a gigantic hoax upon the American people. . . . It is the exact bill which the lobby machine of the NAM and Chamber of Commerce had hoped for."[37] Taylor believed that Truman would veto the bill because it removed livestock, meat, poultry, milk, grain, dairy products, foodstuffs, tobacco, petroleum, rents, and many other items of great importance to the consuming public from price control.

When the compromise bill finally was presented to the president late in June, Truman was faced with a dilemma. He could sign the new OPA bill and have the responsibility of checking inflation without the necessary tools, or he could veto the bill and watch all price controls go out of the window on June 30. Dramatically, Truman chose to veto the bill, and Taylor supported this decision because, he said, "I want real price control."[38]

Within a few days after the end of OPA, the anticipated inflationary spiral began. In New York City veal cutlets went from fifty cents a pound to ninety-five cents, and milk rose from sixteen cents a quart to twenty cents. Consumers went on strike in a number of areas, and agitation for a new OPA increased, with Glen Taylor as an active participant.

Monopolizing the Senate floor on July 11 and July 12, Taylor discussed what he called "runaway prices." The Idaho Democrat, supplied with statistics by the New Council of American Business, revealed that in the week after OPA died, prices rose on the average of 11.1 percent. He claimed that it was the small businessman and the consumer who suffered during a period of rapidly rising prices and quoted Henry McCarthy, the director of the New Council of American Business who had written to Taylor pessimistically, "We do not face the OPA-less future with confidence, as the full-page ads of the NAM assume. We are worried. We are worried about our businesses, and our country. . . . We urge the Congress to continue the Government's price stabilization program for 1 year, without emasculating amendments."[39]

A new OPA bill was whipped through Congress. However, in many ways it was a carbon copy of the bill Truman had vetoed,

---

[36] *Cong. Rec.,* 79th Cong., 2d sess., 1946, 92, pt. 6:6830.
[37] *Idaho Statesman,* July 14, 1946.
[38] *Lewiston Tribune,* July 14, 1946.
[39] Henry L. McCarthy to Taylor, July 10, 1946, quoted in *Cong. Rec.,* 79th Cong., 2d sess., 1946, 92, pt. 7:8636.

and Taylor was aware that the new bill would also be "toothless." When Republican Senator Homer Capehart of Indiana suggested that America return to the private enterprise system that he said had made America great, Taylor, with flashbacks of the depression racing through his mind, said that Capehart was advocating the "system which almost ruined America." Taking a verbal jab at Capehart and the GOP, he added, "In those dark days when Mr. Hoover was exemplifying rugged individualism for us, I have heard farmers and businessmen say, 'We are not going to stand for this much longer.' "[40] He concluded with a gloomy warning that "if we kill price control, . . . if we permit it to die, our private enterprise system, which senators on the other side of the aisle so vociferously champion, may be on the way out."[41]

Reluctantly Truman signed the new bill despite all its obvious defects. The president was sure that he had made his point as to where the responsibility for high prices lay. About all that remained of the OPA was the formal capacity to decontrol prices; it had little authority to enforce any controls.[42]

Truman, in January of 1946, had stated that "of the three major components which make up our standard of living—food, clothing, and housing—housing presents our most difficult problem."[43] Taylor was convinced that without OPA rent ceilings and without low-cost housing many veterans and laborers would suffer immensely. The Idaho senator was appointed as a conferee on a bill designed to prevent speculation and excessive profits in the sale of housing. Advocating subsidies for builders in order to expedite construction, he also demanded price ceilings so that the low-income element of society could afford decent housing.[44]

An emergency housing bill was passed on May 22, 1946, which provided for the construction of 2.7 million homes for veterans. Truman called this act "the first effective legislation designed specifically to cope with the housing shortage."[45] However, Congress failed to respond to the overall housing crisis and refused to take prompt action on a proposed permanent law, the Wagner-

[40] *Cong. Rec.*, 79th Cong., 2d sess., 1946, 92, pt. 7:8792.
[41] Ibid., p. 8973.
[42] Truman, *Memoirs*, 1:540.
[43] Ibid., p. 565. The best account of Truman's housing program is Richard O. Davies, *Housing Reform during the Truman Administration* (Columbia: University of Missouri Press, 1966).
[44] *Cong. Rec.*, 79th Cong., 2d sess., 1946, 92, pt. 3:3411, 3693.
[45] Truman, *Memoirs,* 1:565.

Ellender-Taft bill, which was designed to build fifteen million homes in the next ten years.[46]

Highly disturbed by the housing situation, Taylor in November 1946 wrote Truman, "A cold winter lies ahead. There will be widespread dissatisfaction with the lack of housing. The veterans want to know where you stand on the question. I urge you not to let them down."[47] The president replied to Taylor immediately, because housing was definitely one of Truman's top priorities.

I don't think there is anybody in the country more interested in the housing situation than I am but, as you remember, the Congress refused pointblank to give us an adequate Housing Act, just as they refused to give us an adequate Price Control Act, and they killed the Wagner-Ellender-Taft Bill in the House. Therefore, we are somewhat handicapped in an endeavor to get a housing program that will work. However, in spite of that we have built a million houses this year, which is a record.[48]

In February 1947, after the election of the Eightieth Congress, Republican C. O. Buck of Delaware, chairman of the Senate Banking Subcommittee, announced that he expected rent ceilings to increase 10 to 15 percent on new houses and housing newly opened to renters. After visiting Truman at the White House concerning Buck's proposal, Taylor reported, "the Chief Executive opposed a flat increase in rents and there are no ifs, ands, or buts, about it." Truman also told him, that every effort should be made to "implement machinery to take care of landlord hardship cases on their individual merits."[49]

As a member of the Committee on Banking and Currency, a rather unusual assignment for a senator with Taylor's economic theories, Taylor worked all spring of 1947 for the continuation of adequate rent control legislation. In April the committee reported on a bill which would gradually phase out control. Taylor and Robert F. Wagner of New York submitted a minority report which

[46] Davies, " 'Mr. Republican' Turns 'Socialist': Robert A. Taft and Public Housing," *Ohio History* 73 (Summer 1964):136-43. See Davies on the irony of the Wagner-Ellender-Taft coalition. The bill was finally passed in 1949, and although applauded by Truman, proved inadequate. Forced to declare a state of emergency, Truman authorized free importation of lumber into the country.

[47] Taylor to Truman, November 26, 1946, Official File (hereafter cited as OF) 63, Truman Papers.

[48] Truman to Taylor, November 29, 1946, OF63, Truman Papers.

[49] *New York Times*, February 12, 1947, p. 19.

disagreed with the proposed bill and urged continuation of rent control and the creation of local advisory boards to administer rent control on an individual basis.[50] The Taylor-Wagner proposals were ignored when the Senate debated the rent control bill during the summer of 1947.

Taylor fought for rent controls, as he had for the extension, because he believed controls were necessary to protect the little man from the profiteering of big business. Rent controls had been a vital part of the OPA, but when OPA expired in the spring and summer of 1947, rent ceilings were lifted in many areas. Taylor presented to the Senate a case study of what had happened when rent controls were removed in Twin Falls, in south-central Idaho. A family of four was required to pay $7 a day for an apartment that had formerly rented for $60 a month, and the rent on another small home surged from $30 a month to $100. Taylor also reported that eviction notices had increased astronomically in Idaho and in the nation.[51] The Idahoan stated that his main objection to the compromise bill was that it provided for decontrol rather than effective control. By proposing that the landlord and the renter, under the supervision of an advisory committee, should reach an agreement on a rent increase up to a mutually agreed ceiling, the bill, according to Taylor, would create chaos.

In a last-ditch effort to avoid the removal of rent controls, Taylor introduced a bill merely extending existing rent controls for another year as a substitute for the pending legislation. The Idaho senator included in his Senate speech on this bill a tirade against the domestic legislation passed since he had entered the Senate. Among other items, he listed repeal of the excess-profits tax, stripping OPA of its powers, failure to provide adequate housing, as well as cuts in appropriations for cancer research, reclamation projects, and the school lunch program—"and now comes the rent control." The Democrat from Idaho told the Senate that he wanted to disociate himself "from all these measures. I disapprove of them. I want no part of the credit, if any be due, for enacting them."[52] Taylor then concluded with a statement that the Republicans now had a plan to reduce the debt by increasing excise taxes, in other words, taxes that the little man has to pay: "We have reduced the income taxes on the big boys, we have reduced their excess-

[50] *Cong. Rec.*, 80th Cong., 1st sess., 1947, 93, pt. 4:4266.
[51] Ibid., pt. 5:6125, 6138-39.
[52] Ibid., p. 6140.

profits taxes; we have given them the carryback provisions. They are pretty well taken care of. Now we will pay the national debt by saddling it on the little everyday taxpayer, the man with a family."[53]

Taylor's substitute bill was easily defeated, but the persistent senator refused to give up. He told his colleagues that if the Rent Control Act of 1947 was passed, American renters would think they were protected, just as they had when the OPA was continued in an ineffective form in 1946. He announced that he would vote against the bill "in order to be honest with the people and tell them that we have left them to their own devices." However, the bill won approval easily.[54]

Taylor then issued a press release in which he urged Truman to veto the measure and "place responsibility for destroying rent control where it belongs, squarely on the Republican Congress." Taylor believed a better name for the Rent Control Act was the "rent decontrol and dehousing bill of 1947."[55] He also wrote a letter to Truman reiterating his request that the president veto the bill. Taylor told Truman that enforcement was impossible because "of lack of appropriations . . . and because state boards in nine cases out of ten will be composed of local real estate men." He finished the letter with an emotional plea for Truman to veto this "deceptive, misleading, and dishonest pieces of legislation."[56] The president signed the bill, but severely criticized it for lacking the provisions necessary to halt inflation.[57]

Prices continued to rise and the cost-of-living index soared astronomically. In December of 1947, after the country had been without effective price controls for nearly a year and a half, Taylor obtained radio time to discuss spiraling inflation. In typical Taylor fashion, he brought his wife to the studio and introduced her to the radio audience as a "very close student of market prices and cost of living, who, in my opinion, knows more about the subject than anyone I know."[58] After the Taylors briefly discussed

[53] Ibid.

[54] Ibid., pt. 6:7300.

[55] Ibid., pt. 12:A2971.

[56] Taylor to Truman, June 23, 1947, OF 63-A, Truman Papers.

[57] Truman, *Memoirs*, 1:540. Truman's official view of rent controls was similar to that of OPA but, faced with a conservative Congress, he could not deliver the reforms he desired.

[58] Radio talk by Senator and Mrs. Glen H. Taylor, American Broadcasting Company, December 4, 1947. Transcript, Glen H. Taylor File, Political Action Committee, AFL-CIO, Washington, D.C., p. 1.

examples of rising prices, Glen Taylor put his finger on why prices and the cost of living had increased. The answer was very simple: "Profits!" He then quoted from the November 1 issue of *Business Week,* a magazine that he said circulated among the "top crust of management": "Business this week was heading down the homestretch of the biggest year profitwise, in all its history. . . . U. S. corporations are probably going to wind up the year with a total income 50% or so above 1946."[59] Taylor proposed that the only way to halt inflation was to reinstitute price controls, but he glumly concluded: "I expect to see price controls fall by the wayside as they did in '46. . . . A real fearless price program is the only way we can avoid a depression."[60]

Taylor sincerely believed Harry Truman had presented a good program to Congress, although very little had been accomplished. He summed up what had happened to Truman's proposals in a Senate speech on July 1, 1947, in which he expressed his exasperation with legislative compromise. Taylor informed his colleagues that he "would rather take nothing than to take these bills that are dished out to us here which are so little better than nothing that one cannot tell the difference."[61] Taylor's dream of achieving great reforms for the common man was far from realization, and his work with labor legislation was to create further frustration.

Glen Taylor relied heavily on his wartime experience as a factory worker whenever labor issues came before the Senate. Proud of his union affiliation, Taylor paid "withdrawal" dues while he served in the Senate. In 1945 two amendments to the Selective Service Act were proposed by Democratic Senators Josiah W. Bailey of North Carolina and Chapman Rivercomb of West Virginia which would allow the government to draft workers for vital industries. Taylor spoke against the amendments, emphasizing that American laborers were willing to work even if they were not compelled to do so. He was not in favor of having anyone drafted, he said, but if someone had to be drafted, "We should draft the managers and those engaged in procurement and the allocation of contracts, those who have failed to have the materials brought to the factories on time. Certainly the workers have not been to blame."[62] Taylor warned the senators that coercion could bring rebellion.

[59] Ibid., p. 2.   [60] Ibid., p. 5.
[61] *Cong. Rec.,* 80th Cong., 1st sess., 1947, 93, pt. 6:8007.
[62] Ibid., 79th Cong., 1st sess., 1945, 91, pt. 2:1834-35.

A few days later, Taylor again spoke, claiming that drafting workers at home would have a disastrous effect on soldiers who were fighting to preserve freedom. Answering the accusation that he was disloyal to his own party, which sponsored the legislation, Taylor said, "If my brother were doing something wrong which I felt in my heart was wrong and I tried to dissuade him, I do not believe it could be honestly said that I am against him. I would be for him. I am for the administration."[63] The "work-or-fight" bill was subsequently defeated.

Taylor invariably supported unions in their disputes with management even though such support often conflicted with the Truman administration's attempts to hold the line on wages. He backed Walter Reuther's United Automobile Workers in their lengthy strike against General Motors in 1945–1946 because he despised the bigness of General Motors. Demanding that huge corporations should publicize their profits, Taylor hoped that the disclosure of "excessive profits resulting from too-high prices and two-low wages" would result in the "payment of higher wages and the cutting of prices."[64] Taylor adhered to the union position that the UAW-GM conflict was a lockout, not a strike. A compromise was eventually reached and the auto workers returned to the assembly lines.

Throughout Taylor's term in the Senate, he consistently supported all minimum wage increases. Truman asked for an increase in minimum wages as part of the Fair Deal, and Congress complied with a boost to sixty-five cents an hour. Taylor supported the raise, but he felt this action was insufficient, especially because farm labor was not covered. He introduced an amendment to the Fair Labor Standards Act which would have extended to farm laborers the benefits of minimum wages and maximum hours, but the amendment was defeated.[65]

In a Senate speech on the minimum wage, Taylor discussed the excess profits of certain industries. He asserted that the

[63] Ibid., pt. 3:3068. An excellent account of this proposal to draft workers is Albert A. Blum, "Deferment from Military Service: A War Department Approach to the Solution of Industrial Manpower Programs" (Ph.D. diss., Columbia University, 1953).

[64] *Cong. Rec.*, 79th Cong., 1st sess., 1945, 91, pt. 9:11388. See Bernstein, "Walter Reuther and the General Motors Strike of 1945-46," *Michigan History* 49 (September 1965):260-77, for a more comprehensive discussion of the strike.

[65] *Cong. Rec.*, 79th Cong., 2d sess., 1946, 92, pt. 3:3194.

tobacco industry's profits had been $154 million in 1944, while 59 percent of the tobacco workers were making less than sixty-five cents an hour. "Sixty-five cents an hour times 40 hours is $26 a week. Could any Senator live on that? Would he expect anyone he knew to live on that? And yet, $26 a week is more by many dollars than 34 percent of the nonagricultural workers . . . receive in any week of the year."[66] For big industry to accumulate so much in profiits was repugnant to Taylor, who demanded an economic, social, and political leveling of society.

Taylor chastised the "profit-seeking few" who would rather have "wealth themselves than let the wealth be fairly distributed among the millions of those who are in need." He concluded with a sentence reminiscent of the ideas of Chase and Gillette. "Until every American is able to buy and consume the products of American industry and thus assure full production and full employment throughout our economy, we will constantly be faced by the fearful specter of mass unemployment, depression, crises, and permanent chaos."[67]

A devastating series of strikes swept the nation during 1946. Restrained from striking during the war because of the Smith-Connally Act and other antistrike programs, workers were itching to get their fair share of the lush pie being served after the war. In all, over four million workers were on strike at one time or another in 1946. The UAW was joined by the packinghouse workers, electrical workers, railroad workers, coal miners, and others.

Taylor refused to deviate from his pro-union position. He voted against the Lea bill, which was specifically aimed at James C. Petrillo, president of the AFL-affiliated American Federation of Musicians. Admitting that Petrillo was guilty of certain dictatorial actions, Taylor claimed that the legislation would hinder the activities of all members of the musicians' union.[68] Taylor was so upset by the overwhelming support for the Lea bill that a month later he told his colleagues that they had made "a jackass of themselves . . . in passing the Lea bill."[69]

[66] Ibid., pt. 2:2495.   [67] Ibid., p. 2496.
[68] Ibid., pt. 3:3093. Petrillo attempted to control personally all his union members' performances on radio. According to Taylor, the Lea bill put performers at the mercy of the broadcasting industry. He received a telegram from Frank Sinatra, Bing Crosby, Bob Hope, and other Hollywood stars urging him to vote against the Lea bill.
[69] Ibid., pt. 5:5520.

Taylor was appalled by what he considered Truman's high-handed activities in threatening to draft railroad workers, or use the army to operate trains, if they carried out their threat to strike in May 1946. In another major labor dispute, Taylor, who favored less arbitrary methods, joined Wayne Morse and Claude Pepper in an appeal to provide opportunities for mediation between John L. Lewis's coal miners and the mine owners. Although he did not approve of Lewis's iron-fisted control over the United Mine Workers, Taylor's sympathy rested with "the American coal miner who stands before us, grim-faced and over-worked, underpaid, poorly nourished, horribly housed."[70] When the miners' strike reached its fortieth day, Truman seized the coal mines in the name of the government but granted the miners many of their wishes.[71]

Early in 1946, Taylor had engaged in a semifilibuster against the Case bill, which he believed discriminated against the working man. The bill excluded the secretary of labor from all mediation proceedings and also from a new coordinating board. Taylor believed the proposed board would prolong collective bargaining and thus force the laborers to make concessions. When Truman vetoed the Case bill, Taylor's faith in the chief executive's liberalism was reconfirmed.[72]

Taylor told the Utah State Democratic convention during the summer of 1946 that the recent wave of strikes had not been "caused by a lack of labor laws. They have been caused by failure to pass adequate social legislation."[73] On the same trip through the West, he reported to an Idaho Falls audience that "President Truman had presented a fine program to Congress, but nothing has been done about it."[74] When Taylor returned to the nation's capital, he joined Truman in another losing battle—the struggle against the Taft-Hartley Act.

After the Republicans had captured the Senate in 1946, Taylor sarcastically said that he was glad the Republicans had won. He had, he said, "always envied . . . Taft and Kenneth Wherry because they have never had to formulate a constructive program. As a

[70] Ibid., pt. 4:5172. Joel I. Seidman, *American Labor: From Defense to Reconversion* (Chicago: University of Chicago Press, 1953), is a concise account of the pressing labor difficulties facing the nation after World War II.
[71] Truman, *Memoirs*, 1:553.
[72] *Cong. Rec.*, 79th Cong., 2d sess., 1946, 92, pt. 5:5841.
[73] *Salt Like Tribune*, June 9, 1946.
[74] *Lewiston Tribune*, June 9, 1946.

minority they only criticized."[75] It is doubtful that there was a personal animosity between Idaho's Glen Taylor and Ohio's Robert Taft, but their ideological and political differences were so glaring that a clash between the two was inevitable after the 1946 election.

Early in 1947 Taylor reproved Taft, the chairman of the Joint Committee on the Economic Report, for failing to provide workable alternatives to the recommendations contained in Truman's Economic Report. The president had urged the passage of Fair Deal legislation and the enactment of more social reforms, including a more flexible National Labor Relations Act. When Taft made a statement to the effect that Truman's report was "highly controversial," Taylor characterized it as a lazy answer and criticized Taft for evading the issues. In a press release, a copy of which was sent to the president, Taylor said, "surely Mr. Taft does not expect to avoid controversy in the Senate. It is desirable that fundamental differences be aired in public and that the public know exactly where each party stands." In conclusion the Idaho Democrat gibed at Taft's presidential ambitions: "If a clear cut position on so many matters involves personal embarrassment to Mr. Taft's candidacy for other office, he should not have accepted this chairmanship."[76] Pleased by Taylor's actions and remarks, Truman wrote, "It seems to me that you 'hit the nail on the head' which I highly appreciate."[77]

Labor legislation became a prime issue in 1947, in part because of John L. Lewis's repeated defiance of the government during the previous year. This defiance, together with the mass strikes of 1946, had strengthened antilabor forces. The Taft-Hartley bill, which reached the Senate floor in May 1947, was a product of a ten-man Senate-House conference committee. Among other things, the bill proposed that industry-wide strikes, the closed shop, sympathy strikes, mass picketing, and strikes by government workers be made unlawful. The unions were made liable for damages inflicted while striking, and union leaders were required to take a loyalty oath. The president was empowered to obtain injunctions against strikers in interstate transportation, communications, or public utilities.[78]

[75] Ibid., November 6, 1946.
[76] Taylor press release, Taylor to Truman, February 4, 1947, OF 396, Truman Papers.
[77] Truman to Taylor, February 7, 1947, ibid.

Glen Taylor, consistent with his past record, vehemently opposed the Taft-Hartley measure. In a speech to the United Labor for Progress at Louisville, Kentucky, Taylor told the crowd of 2,400 that the "drive against labor unions is in truth a drive against the living standards of the entire American people." He declared that the proposed legislation was "an all-out offensive against trade unions."[79] A few days later, in a Senate speech, Taylor openly accused the Republican-dominated Eightieth Congress of trying to "turn the clock back and repeal all social advances made in the Roosevelt period."[80]

The Idaho Democrat then joined other liberal senators in repeated futile attempts to amend the Taft-Hartley bill. Since this bill made it mandatory for unions to vote on the last offer of an employer, Taylor proposed an amendment requiring management to poll all the shareholders in order to ascertain whether they were willing to accept the last offer of the union.[81] Naturally the Taylor amendment was rejected as a joke, but Glen Taylor was serious. Although the former sheet-metal worker admitted that both organized labor and management were guilty of abuses, his decision to vote against the Taft-Hartley bill was for a rather simple, yet truly humanitarian reason: "I shall vote against it because I value human rights over property rights—and because I place the welfare of all the people above the narrow, selfish interests of a few monopolies."[82] The bill passed, 68–24, in June 1947.

Truman vetoed the bill on June 20, and the Senate attempted to override his veto the same day. Taylor, Wayne Morse, Claude Pepper, and Harley M. Kilgore combined their efforts in a filibuster that, according to Taylor, would give "the American people time

---

[78] *Cong. Rec.*, 80th Cong., 1st sess., 1947, 93, pt. 2:2436-37. The best account of the Taft-Hartley fight is A. Alton Lee, *Truman and Taft-Hartley* (Lexington: University of Kentucky Press, 1966).

[79] *Salt Lake Tribune*, March 10, 1947. Taylor also claimed that Taft-Hartley could destroy the labor movement and lead to chaos. Under this act, he asserted, it would be virtually impossible for national union officers to hold their unions together. *Daily Worker*, May 7, 1947.

[80] *Cong. Rec.*, 80th Cong., 1st sess., 1947, 93, pt. 2:2614.

[81] Ibid., pt. 4:4896. Among other senators opposed to Taft-Hartley were Wayne Morse, Claude Pepper, Harley M. Kilgore, James Murray of Montana, Elbert Thomas of Utah, William Langer of North Dakota, Dennis Chavez of New Mexico, Robert Wagner of New York, Alben Barkley of Kentucky, and Sheridan Downey of California.

[82] Ibid., p. 5003.

to read the President's veto message and listen to the President on the radio and form their own conclusions."[83] Morse added that both the employers and employees in America should have an opportunity to respond to the veto of the Taft-Hartley Act by letting their representatives in Washington know their desires.[84] The filibuster lasted throughout the weekend, with Taylor speaking from Friday at 6:55 P.M. to 3:15 A.M. the next morning, in what might be called the swing and graveyard shifts.

On Monday, June 23, the four senators ended their filibuster, permitting the Senate to vote on the veto. Pepper of Florida, the leader of those wishing to sustain the veto, granted Taylor five more minutes prior to the final vote. Taylor used the time to cite petitions he had received during the weekend and to offer an interesting compromise to the southern Democrats. Taylor, who was pushing for full civil rights in the South at this time, appealed to his southern colleagues to sustain the president's veto of the Taft-Hartley Act. In return, Taylor said, "we want to advance the cause of the colored people, we insist that progress be made, but we do not insist on a revolution overnight in this matter."[85] The Senate and the House overrode Truman's veto, and Taylor wrote the president later that evening, "Just returned from the floor on the labor veto. Sorry. We did the best we could."[86] A month later Taylor cosponsored a bill to repeal Taft-Hartley, but it failed also.[87]

Taylor's consistent support of Fair Deal measures endeared him to liberals throughout the nation, but he was frustrated by the Fair Deal's lack of success in handling pressing domestic problems. After three years in the Senate, Taylor felt that the common man was still left wanting, and he continued to work for reform legislation which he considered to be in the social-welfare tradition of the New Deal and the Fair Deal.

Taylor also wanted to give the people a greater hand in, and control over, government, so he sponsored a constitutional amendment to abolish the electoral college and, with Wayne Morse, cosponsored a bill to require members of the legislative, judicial, and executive branches of government to file statements on the

[83] Ibid., pt. 6:7380.
[84] Ibid., p. 7383.
[85] Ibid., p. 7534.
[86] Taylor to Truman, June 23, 1947, OF 63-A, Truman Papers.
[87] *Cong. Rec.*, 80th Cong., 1st sess., 1947, 93, pt. 7:8818.

amount and sources of their personal income. The Idaho senator also proposed that the voting records of all senators, together with an explanation of the issues, be published and distributed to the people.[88] In short, although Taylor believed the Fair Deal had not succeeded in its original intent, he continued to work for domestic reforms which he hoped would make America a better place for all its citizens.

[88] All these proposals, and Taylor's speeches in support of them, can be found in the *Congressional Record*. For the amendment to abolish the electoral college, see *Cong. Rec.*, 80th Cong., 1st sess., 1947, 93, pt. 2:1961; for the bill concerning personal income, ibid., 2d sess., 1948, 94, pt. 1:605; for the voting records of senators, ibid., 79th Cong., 2d sess., 1946, 92, pt. 6:7811-12.

IV. *Equality for Black America*

Glen Taylor's concern for "the common man," or "the underdog," was genuine and may be traced to the ideals of his preacher father, as well as to his own experience during the depression. His consistently liberal voting record reflected a desire to help the underprivileged economically, politically, and socially. Taylor was not politically motivated in the sense that he was trying to appeal to Idaho constituents merely to insure his own reelection. As a matter of fact, nothing testifies more clearly to the sincerity of Glen Taylor's liberalism and humanitarianism than his record on labor legislation and civil rights, especially the latter. Since Idaho was primarily agricultural rather than industrial, he had very little to gain politically from support of labor legislation, or from support of civil rights measures, when there were approximately 500 blacks in the entire state.

One of Taylor's earliest debates in the Senate dealt with the issue of black equality. Senator Theodore G. Bilbo of Mississippi had announced that he opposed the nomination of Aubrey Williams as Administrator of the Rural Electrification Administration. The Mississippi senator, like James Vardaman, Ben Tillman, and other southern senators, had risen to power by advocating total segregation, by keeping the ballot from the black citizen, and by preaching a hate-filled doctrine of a master race.[1] Biblo reminded Williams's supporters that "the publishers and editors of all the Republican Negro newspapers in Philadelphia . . . endorsed Aubrey Williams."[2] Leaping to his feet, Taylor demanded to know what Bilbo's remarks had to do with the nomination of Williams and what difference it made if "the colored newspaper editors of Philadelphia are endorsing him. They are Americans. . . . I certainly object to having brought up on the floor of the Senate the question of whether a man is red, black, or white."[3] The veteran Mississippi senator put down the freshman from Idaho by asking him, "What do they know about Negroes in Idaho?"[4] Bilbo and Taylor never forgot this early confrontation, and nearly two years later, when

Taylor introduced a resolution to deny Bilbo his Senate seat because of racism, they would tangle again.

In the late session of 1946, by resorting to a filibuster, southern senators succeeded in blocking a proposal designed to give permanent status to the Fair Employment Practices Commission (FEPC), a wartime agency. Truman had adopted FEPC as part of his domestic legislative package, but the president was not committed to full civil rights.[5] During the filibuster, Taylor periodically secured the floor to speak out on civil rights for blacks. After Millard Tydings declared that most senators would "move out of a hotel if a colored man came in and sat down," the Idaho Democrat responded by stating: "I may say that I live one block from the colored section."[6] Taylor's response, although true, was rather extreme, but he wanted it understood that he was not a racist.

At a press conference, Taylor called for all-night sessions or any other measures necessary to break the filibuster and to force a vote on the bill for a permanent FEPC. In discussing the filibuster, the Idaho senator said, "This is not democracy, this is rule by a small minority. . . . I hope that those who really believe in democracy will stand by their guns and not yield to this legislative blackmail."[7]

In their filibuster against FEPC, the southern senators reverted to the pre-Civil War technique of claiming that southern Negroes were better off than their northern counterparts. Allen J. Ellender of Louisiana quoted statistics to show that among northern blacks there was a higher rate of incarceration for various crimes than among whites. Taylor responded quickly, telling Ellender that

[1] C. Vann Woodward, *The Strange Career of Jim Crow* (New York: Oxford University Press, 1966), pp. 67-109.

[2] *Cong. Rec.*, 79th Cong., 1st sess., 1945, 91, pt. 2:2618.

[3] Ibid. Although the term colored would not be used by a civil libertarian now, in 1945-1946, it was still a common and acceptable term.

[4] Ibid.

[5] Barton J. Bernstein, "The Ambiguous Legacy: The Truman Administration and Civil Rights," in *Politics and Policies of the Truman Administration*, ed. Bernstein (Chicago: Quadrangle Books, 1970), pp. 269-314. See also William C. Berman, "The Politics of Civil Rights in the Truman Administration" (Ph.D. diss., Ohio State University, 1963).

[6] *Cong. Rec.*, 79th Cong., 2d sess., 1946, 92, pt. 1:203.

[7] *Daily Worker*, January 25, 1946. The *Daily Worker*, a long-time advocate of full equality for all races, applauded Taylor frequently on his civil rights stand. Taylor's statement concerning filibusters is ironic, especially since he frequently used the device to suit his own purposes.

if he would do more research, he would undoubtedly find "that many more underprivileged whites are convicted of crime than are white people who have greater advantages."[8] Taylor's sociological plea for tolerance and understanding fell on deaf ears. The FEPC issue was temporarily shelved, but the Idaho liberal refused to give up the fight.

During the summer of 1946 Taylor capitalized on Senator Bilbo's extreme racism in order to renew his struggle for civil rights. On June 26 Taylor dramatically called the attention of the Senate to "an incident which reflects seriously on the integrity of this body, and which therefore should be thoroughly and quickly investigated."[9] Taylor requested that the Senate's Committee on Privileges and Elections investigate the campaign for reelection being conducted by Bilbo in Mississippi. The Idaho senator accused Bilbo of infringing upon the civil rights of Negroes by encouraging "racial discrimination at elections."[10] It was Taylor's contention that Bilbo should be given an opportunity to clear his name if the charges were false, but, if the charges were true, he warned, "Ours is the duty . . . of passing on the credentials of our Members, and we cannot disregard charges such as these without serious loss of prestige."[11]

At the committee hearing held on July 1, Taylor presented a brief composed of newspaper reports and quotations from Bilbo's speeches and admonished the Committee on Privileges and Elections to do their duty: "The American people in every city in the country are reading these reports in the newspapers. They are observing that the United States Senate is completely unruffled and unperturbed. . . . We must take action to assure that every qualified citizen and voter will be permitted to cast his ballot for Federal officials. . . . I ask your committee to give full force to the provisions of the Constitution and laws of the United States."[12] Taylor believed that the Senate could no longer turn its back on the problem of election practices of its members. "We cannot duck it, we cannot avoid it. It is before us."[13]

Asking the committee to gather all the facts while the evidence

<hr/>

[8] *Cong. Rec.*, 79th Cong., 2d sess., 1946, 92, pt. 1:964.
[9] Ibid., pt. 6:7541.
[10] Ibid.
[11] Ibid. According to a *Daily Worker* article of July 4, 1946, Bilbo had been elected by 7 percent of the adult voting population.
[12] *New York Times*, July 2, 1946, p. 48.
[13] Ibid.

was still available, Taylor also expressed his belief that President Truman should send troops to Mississippi to protect the blacks' right to vote "if this is the only way that their rights can be assured."[14] His suggestion to use troops in the South had hardly been heard since the days of Reconstruction.

During December 1946 Taylor's brief was used before the Special Committee to Investigate Senatorial Campaign Expendiutres. The Mississippi senator, appearing before the committee, admitted that he had asked "every redblooded American who believes in the superiority and integrity of the white race to get out and see that no nigger votes."[15] The Mississippi demagogue also called Clare Boothe Luce "the greatest nigger-lover in the North—except Old Lady Eleanor Roosevelt. Yep: Old Lady Roosevelt is worse. . . . In Washington she forced our southern girls to use the stools and the toilets of damn syphilitic nigger women."[16] Regarding the Mississippi literacy test, Bilbo proclaimed: "The circuit clerks are under oath to protect the provisions of the Constitution, and if there is a single man . . . serving in this important office who cannot think up questions enough to disqualify undesirables; then write Bilbo . . . and there are a hundred good questions which can be furnished."[17] Dramatically Bilbo reported what two Jackson policemen had found when they broke into one of the Negro meetings: "Northern niggers teaching them how to register and how to vote."[18] Ironically Bilbo condemned the voting of eighty blacks in a municipal election at Pass Christian as "one of the most damnable demonstrations of demagoguery in our Southland."[19] When Bilbo, holding Taylor responsible for the investigation, later told his constituents that the Idaho senator lived in a black residential district in Washington, Taylor retorted, "there was no racial question involved. . . . I simply got a house in a section where I could afford the rent."[20]

After four days of hearings in December, Bilbo was cleared by the special investigating committee. The majority report stated that Bilbo was guilty of departing "from ordinarily accepted good taste," but that he was not guilty of discrimination or denying

14 Ibid.
15 U. S., Congress, Senate, Special Committee to Investigate Senatorial Campaign Expenditures, 1946, *Hearings, Mississippi*, 79th Cong., 2d sess., 1946, pp. 7-11.
16 Ibid.   17 Ibid.
18 Ibid.   19 Ibid.
20 *New York Times*, June 29, 1946, p. 34.

the Negro in Mississippi of the right to register to vote. The report concluded: "Considerable of the more vituperative remarks uttered by Senator Bilbo in his campaign we deem to be justifiably directed at the attempted and unwarranted interference with the internal affairs of the state of Mississippi by outside agitators, seeking not to benefit the Negroes but merely to further their own political ends."[21] Although the committee was finished with the Biblo case, Glen Taylor was not.

When the Republican-dominated Eightieth Congress convened in January 1947, it was widely suspected that some senators were going to attempt to keep Bilbo from taking his seat until the entire Senate had had an opportunity to review his case. Homer Ferguson of Michigan, a Republican, was appointed to "bar Bilbo at the door." On January 3, the first day of the session, the Republicans were gathered shaking hands and slapping backs. After sixteen years as the minority party in Congress, the GOP was in control. On the opposite side of the aisle, the Democrats were subdued and silently waiting for the Republicans to make a move against Bilbo.

The recently elected senators were sworn in alphabetically. After Raymond E. Baldwin of Connecticut took the oath of office, the clerk called the name of Theodore G. Bilbo. Just as the "Bil" was pronounced, a shout reverberated across the Senate Chamber. The flustered secretary of the Senate recognized Idaho's Glen Taylor, who solemnly announced, "I send to the desk a resolution to which I wish to address myself."[22] After Ferguson and Kenneth Wherry of Nebraska had requested parliamentary inquiries, raised points of order, and attempted to introduce substitute legislation, the Taylor resolution was read. Accusing Bilbo of violating the civil rights of American citizens and of delivering war contracts to friends in exchange for gifts and compensation, Taylor's resolution called for a further investigation and asked that Bilbo be denied his seat until the inquiry was completed.[23]

Following the reading of the resolution, Taylor delivered a hard-

[21] U. S., Congress, Senate, Special Committee to Investigate Senatorial Campaign Expenditures, 1946, *Report, Mississippi*, 80th Cong., 1st sess., 1947, pp. 1-23. The vote was 3-2. The Democrats, Allen Ellender of Louisiana, Elmer Thomas of Oklahoma, and Burnett R. Maybank of South Carolina voted to seat Bilbo, and the Republicans, Styles Bridges of New Hampshire and Bourke Hickenlooper of Iowa, voted against it.
[22] *Cong. Rec.*, 80th Cong., 1st sess., 1947, 93, pt. 1:7.
[23] Ibid., p. 8.

hitting speech against intolerance and racism. Although he was frequently interrupted by Bilbo's southern colleagues and some Republicans, Taylor held the floor for an hour. Interestingly, on this issue he found himself allied with his Republican opponents Taft, Wherry, and Ferguson.

Taylor warned the senators, "We . . . are not only on trial collectively, we are on trial individually. For a statement was issued to the press asserting that if Mr. Bilbo were refused his seat, he would expose the foibles of other members of the Senate. . . . I for one do not fear the threat of retaliation. The sound of the rattling skeleton in the closet does not intimidate me."[24] While Taylor spoke, a scowling Bilbo stalked into the Senate chamber, spotted Taylor, and advanced toward him. During the rest of Taylor's speech, Bilbo sat at his elbow glaring up at him.[25]

Undaunted, Taylor never paused: "Bilbo . . . has toured . . . his state stirring up racial hatred, inciting white to hate black and causing black to hate white." Taylor admitted that race relations were a complex problem which would require patience and good will, but it was important, he told the senators, "that we move forward; that we do not turn back the clock."[26]

Taylor then told his colleagues that while the Constitution gives the Senate the power to pass upon qualifications of its own members, "that power should be used sparingly . . . and it would be extremely unwise for this body to set itself up as a self-righteous arbiter of the personality, the politics, or the morals of the man . . . duly elected to office."[27] The Senate could claim no right to censor the views of members, according to Taylor, and it should not "question the will of the electorate freely and fairly expressed. But intimidation and violence cannot masquerade as free speech; indeed they destroy the freedom of the electorate."[28] In Taylor's words, "at this moment the honor and prestige of the Senate hang in the balance. . . . Will . . . the Senate . . . have the courage to face this issue squarely?"[29] "Will the code of the cloakroom . . . prove to be a higher law than the Constitution of the United States?" he asked.[30]

Turning to the brief that he had prepared, Taylor read the press

---

[24] Ibid., p. 8.
[25] "That Man," *Time* (January 13, 1947), pp. 21-22.
[26] *Cong. Rec.*, 80th Cong., 1st sess., 1947, 93, pt. 1:12.
[27] Ibid., p. 8.   [28] Ibid.
[29] Ibid., p. 9.   [30] Ibid.

reports of many of Bilbo's campaign utterances. The unanimity of
the press reports and the character of the reporters were not the
only warranty of their authenticity, said Taylor. Bilbo's "failure
to deny, repudiate, correct, or attempt to rectify these reports
would . . . constitute a virtual adoption of the language quoted."[31]
From Taylor's point of view, an even more severe indictment was
that Bilbo knew that the mere appearance of his statements in
Mississippi newspapers would intimidate thousands of qualified
voters and would incite thousands of hoodlums. Still, Bilbo had
made no attempt to deny any statement until he appeared before
the Senate investigating committee in December, with five lawyers
at his side.[32]

Taylor then trained his oratorical battery on the Ku Klux Klan,
its philosophy, and Bilbo's alleged membership in it:

Is the white robe and hood the uniform of a debating society? Is it
the costume of a discussion group? Or is it the mask of the . . . Klan,
a secret organization which has committed more crimes under cover
of darkness than any other organization in the Nation's history, an
organization which from its inception has been dedicated to the op-
pression of Negroes, to an attempt to reduce them to the status of
animals, to the denial of their franchise by beatings, bloodshed, torture,
mayhem, threats, coercion, and murder?[33]

Taylor openly accused Bilbo of taking the solemn pledge of
membership in the Klan, citing a radio speech in which Bilbo
had admitted membership and said "once a Klansman, always a
Klansman."[34]

Quickly Taylor returned to the Senate's role in upholding the
Constitution: "No amount of acquiescence can wither the great
fourteenth and fifteenth amendments to our Constitution. . . . No
amount of indifference can expunge the statutes which protect the
civil rights of all our people. The dust of connivance can obscure,
but it cannot tarnish, the bright gold of our free institutions."[35]
It was not Taylor's purpose at the moment to brush the dust away.
He did not propose that the Senate embark on a series of inquiries
into elections in all states to determine whether the constitutional
mandates were being observed.

Taylor, however, recognized a familiar underlying issue in the

[31] Ibid., p. 10.   [32] Ibid., p. 11.
[33] Ibid.   [34] Ibid.
[35] Ibid.

Bilbo case—the typical southern demagogue who exploited southern whites. Taylor emotionally told the Senate and a packed gallery that a man like Bilbo did not offer the poor whites what they needed—"prosperity, nourishment, clothing, food, and education" —but instead offered them "the delicious sense of feeling superior to someone else, the cheap thrill of membership in a master race, the joy of kicking someone else around."[36]

With Bilbo sneering up at him, Taylor chastised the Senate, including himself, for ignoring the "mess in our own backyard." Admitting that it was easier to ignore a problem than to "probe around in the muck," Taylor said, "It remained for Mr. Bilbo to force us to sit and smell it; it remained for Mr. Bilbo to rub our noses in it."[37] He then added: "What a hypocritical and blasphemous gesture we would witness today, if Mr. Bilbo were to stand in our midst and place his hand on the Holy Bible and swear fealty to democratic institutions, to free elections, to the rights of citizens."[38] Drained by the speech, Taylor sat down, and the glowering Bilbo stalked out of the Senate chamber.

Taylor's address elicited enthusiastic applause from the galleries and from a few senators. Bilbo cackled to reporters, "The greatest joke of the Eightieth Congress is that a cowboy named Taylor stole the whole Republican show."[39] Later, Bilbo was reported to have said, "Taylor ain't got no sense. He's just a nut. He goes around playing a fiddle with a hillbilly band."[40]

Harold L. Ickes, the "Old New Dealer," now a newspaper columnist, called Taylor's address "A great speech, one that will reverberate throughout the country for a long time."[41] Another Washington columnist, Marquis Childs, applauded Taylor's "boldness and courage. . . . Taylor showed on the very first day of the new session that it is not essential for the Democratic party to collapse like a worn out accordion."[42]

A delegation of young southerners of both races expressed their gratitude to Taylor, and the Southern Negro Youth Congress distributed thousands of copies of Taylor's speech. The Idaho Democrat told his visitors, "Don't be discouraged. At one time the majority in this country wanted to stay under the British King.

---

[36] Ibid., p. 13.   [37] Ibid., p. 11.
[38] Ibid., p. 12.
[39] *New York Times,* January 4, 1947, p. 3.
[40] *Daily Worker,* January 11, 1947.
[41] *Washington Evening Star,* January 15, 1947.
[42] *Washington Post,* January 8, 1947.

The minority had to convince them that freedom was desirable. Most worthwhile causes have started with a minority."[43]

After Taylor had relinquished the floor, the Republicans, somewhat halfheartedly, submitted their own resolution to prevent Bilbo from taking his seat. A southern filibuster, which lasted the rest of the day, attempted to keep the Senate from enacting any legislation until Bilbo was seated. Georgia's Senator Richard Russell ironically commented that the "anti-Bilboites, of which Sen. Taylor is the leftwing . . . are just taking up time."[44] Allen Ellender added that Taylor and the Republicans were playing "putrid politics" and were out to capture the "Nigger not Negro vote."[45] Minority leader Alben Barkley of Kentucky achieved a compromise by tabling all motions concerning the seating of Bilbo until the Mississippi senator recuperated from a scheduled second cancer operation.[46] It was known that Bilbo was very sick and that in a previous operation part of his jaw had been removed. The Mississippian died later that year, and the Taylor resolution was never brought before the floor of the Senate.

Taylor's action in regard to Senator Bilbo must have further encouraged the political migration of Negroes from the party of Lincoln to the party of Franklin Roosevelt which had gradually been taking place. By 1948, however, Taylor was attempting to lead the black Americans out of the Democratic party and into the Progressive party. On February 23, 1948, Taylor announced his candidacy for the vice-presidency on the third-party ticket. One of the reasons for his schism with the Democratic party was his conviction that Truman's Fair Deal was not going far enough to help the Negro.[47]

During the remainder of his term in the Senate in 1948, Glen Taylor continued to work for Negro equality. The fact that schools and public facilities in the nation's capital were segregated aggravated Taylor. When the New York City superintendent of schools, William Jansen, canceled a trip to Washington, D.C., for fifty-one outstanding students because four were blacks and would be subjected to segregation, Taylor praised the school official's action. In a Senate speech, Taylor said that it would be "impossible

[43] *Daily Worker*, January 12, 1947.
[44] *Cong. Rec.*, 80th Cong., 1st sess., 1947, 93, pt. 1:103.
[45] *Ibid.*, p. 104.
[46] Ibid., p. 108.
[47] The complete details of Taylor's decision to run for the vice-presidency as a Progressive are discussed in Chapter 7.

to destroy segregation in the United States until it was abandoned at the seat of our Government."[48] The same day he introduced legislation which would require the integration of the public schools in the District of Columbia.[49]

Because of Taylor's sympathetic stand on civil rights, he received many letters from black Americans concerning injustice in the South. In March 1948 Taylor read to the Senate a letter from an official of the National Association for the Advancement of Colored People, who was also a union director, describing the murder of a Louisiana Negro, Ray C. Brooks, by a police officer. The Idaho Democrat pleaded with the Senate to enact effective antilynching legislation and to provide the necessary funds for enforcement. He called on Attorney General Thomas Clark and President Truman to investigate all lynching cases and to offer protection for "colored Americans in the South."[50] The coalition between the southern Democrats and conservative Republicans, however, was strong enough to prohibit passage of effective civil rights legislation, even an antilynching law.

According to the Idaho senator, the armed forces and federal agencies would be the logical places to start cracking the segregation barrier, and he attacked both the military and civilian agencies for paying lip service to civil rights, but never supporting effective legislation. Throughout his 1948 vice-presidential campaign, Taylor enumerated specific bills which the Senate had failed to enact. Antilynching and anti-poll tax proposals, as well as a Fair Employment Practices Commission bill, were all tied up in various committees. Believing that the only recourse was for the president to take positive action, he urged Truman to use his executive power to lead the nation in guaranteeing full civil rights for all American citizens.

Especially after he had left the Democratic party, Taylor was extremely critical of the president for not providing the necessary vigorous leadership. During a 1948 Senate speech Taylor blasted Truman viciously: "The President has had the power to abolish segregation and disciminination in the armed services. He has failed to do so. He has had power to abolish discrimination and segregation in Federal employment simply by issuing an Executive order. He has failed to do so." The small things that Truman had done were attacked for being totally inadequate. "He has had

[48] *Cong. Rec.*, 80th Cong., 2d sess., 1948, 94, pt. 5:5901.
[49] Ibid.   [50] Ibid., pt. 3:2927.

the power to recommend the setting up of an effective civil rights division within the Department of Justice, instead of a small and ineffective section on civil rights. He has failed to do even that simple thing."[51]

Taylor ended this speech by emphasizing how foreign nations had seized upon the United States' poor civil rights record for propaganda purposes, using it to denigrate American democracy. He claimed it was hypocritical to "set ourselves up as a model for a democratic rights and privileges of which we boast before all the world," although Congress and the president had failed to provide increased civil rights for the black American.[52]

Taylor's criticism of Truman's civil rights record was, in some respects, unduly harsh. His view of presidential power, especially in the political context, was somewhat unrealistic. Truman was not insincere; he had hoped to move in the direction of increased civil rights, but realized the political consequences if he did it by executive decree. After the 1948 Democratic convention, in which a strong civil rights plank was adopted, the Truman administration attempted to implement some of the suggestions of liberals, but effective civil rights legislation was still blocked by the coalition of southern Democrats and conservative Republicans. Adequate legislation would not be passed until the 1960s.[53]

The same alliance of southern Democrats and conservative Republicans also helped to prevent Taylor's dream of obtaining a Columbia Valley Authority for the Northwest from becoming a reality. By insisting on a strong civil rights legislation, Taylor alienated the very senators whose votes he needed to secure a CVA. He also alienated the chief executive, Truman, who had originally proposed a CVA as part of his Fair Deal package. Although these actions may suggest that Taylor was a poor politician, they testify to the sincerity of his dedication to racial equality.

[51] Ibid., pt. 6:7254.
[52] Ibid., p. 7253.
[53] Bernstein, "The Ambiguous Legacy," p. 301. Bernstein claims that the Democrats retreated from this 1948 platform when they discovered it was impossible to deliver the promises. It is interesting to note that Taylor also attempted to better the living conditions of another Idaho minority, the Basques. See *Cong. Rec.*, 80th Cong., 1st sess., 1947, pt. 2:1617. The Basques, mostly farm workers and sheepherders, were threatened with massive deportation, and Taylor attempted to halt Justice Department proceedings.

V. The Columbia Valley Authority

Glen Taylor considered a Columbia Valley Authority an unfulfilled part of the New Deal. The Roosevelt administration had authorized construction of dams at Grand Coulee and the Cascade Rapids (Bonneville Dam) on the Columbia River. The Bonneville Power Act had passed Congress in 1937, and Roosevelt hoped that the Bonneville Power Administration would result in lower rates for consumers and at the same time curb the high profits of private utilities.[1] Less than one week after Truman took office, he informed Interior Secretary Harold L. Ickes that the new administration intended to pursue the Roosevelt course regarding the development of the Northwest and suggested that Ickes prepare a CVA bill for his approval.[2]

A difficult problem which confronted Ickes was the impossibility of coordinating the policies and activities of the Army Corps of Engineers, the Interior Department's Bureau of Reclamation, and the Bonneville Power Administration. Above all Ickes wanted to avoid unnecessary duplication and competition. Ickes decided that a CVA based on the successful TVA formula was the best solution. In November he wrote to Truman urging the president to send "to the Congress your specific recommendations for the establishment of a Columbia Valley Authority."[3] Truman's suggestions for the CVA were encompassed in a bill which was almost an exact duplicate of the act creating TVA. The bill was introduced by Senator Hugh Mitchell of Washington in late 1945, but because of strong opposition, it never left the committee room.[4]

Glen Taylor worked for a unified development of the Columbia and its tributaries. According to Taylor, the CVA would provide the needed coordination between the conflicting federal agencies, state governments, and local authorities. Many Oregon and Washington groups, publicly announced their support of CVA, but there was very little response from Idaho.[5] Taylor believed that his constituents feared CVA because the private power combine was conducting a mass propaganda compaign, telling the Idaho farmers that a CVA would take away their individual water rights.[6] Idaho lacked the experience of Washington and Oregon with BPA and public utility districts, mainly because the Idaho Power Company had a virtual monopoly on the distribution of the hydroelectric energy produced in the state. Although Congress turned its back on CVA in 1945, Taylor decided to make an issue of the proposed legislation by returning to Idaho to campaign in the midterm elections of 1946.

The death of Republican Senator John Thomas in 1945 had created a vacancy in Idaho's congressional delegation. Governor Charles C. Gossett, a Democrat, resigned, and the new governor, Arnold Williams, appointed Gossett to the Senate. Gossett returned to Idaho in 1946 for the purpose of winning the Senate seat in his own right. Firmly convinced that Gossett had done the voters of Idaho a tremendous injustice by having himself appointed to the Senate, Taylor announced his support of George Donart.[7] Coming to Idaho in June, Taylor announced that it was impossible to work with Gossett because the latter was a tool of the "vested interests

[1] Arthur M. Schlesinger, Jr., *The Politics of Upheaval* (Boston: Houghton-Mifflin, 1959), pp. 377-79.

[2] Harry S. Truman to Harold L. Ickes, April 21, 1945, OF 360, Truman Papers. Truman's quick endorsement of CVA indicates that he considered the project of prime importance. It is also apparent from David E. Lilienthal, *The Journals of David E. Lilienthal*, 2 vols. (New York: Harper and Row, 1964), 2:3-7, that Truman believed a CVA bill could be passed quite easily at that time.

[3] Ickes to Truman, November 23, 1945, OF 360, Truman Papers. Ickes was a veteran of many organizational disputes. See Richard Polenberg, "The Great Conservation Contest," *Forest History* 21 (January 1967):13-23. Polenberg discusses Ickes's attempts in 1938 to bring TVA into the Interior Department, as well as the controversies between the National Park Service and the Forest Service.

[4] *Cong. Rec.*, 79th Cong., 2d sess., 1946, 92, pt. 6:7059-60. See also Wesley C. Clark, "Proposed Valley Authority Legislation," *American Political Science Review* 40 (February 1946):62-70; and Henry C. Hart, "Valley Development and Valley Administration in the Missouri Basin," *Public Administration Review* 7 (Winter 1948):1-11.

[5] The official files of the Truman Papers (OF 360, OF 360-A) contain materials dealing with the Columbia Valley Authority. There are many telegrams and letters from groups supporting CVA, but none from Idaho.

[6] *Idaho Statesman*, November 1, 1946. Taylor found it almost impossible to convince southern Idaho farmers, who had willingly subordinated their individual rights to cooperatives and irrigation companies, that a centrally controlled valley authority would adequately protect their rights.

[7] *Lewiston Tribune*, January 9, 1946. Even when he was not a candidate, Taylor's intrusion in Idaho Democratic primaries, every two years since 1940, would contribute to his own eventual downfall.

in Boise," which included the Idaho Power Company, a bitter opponent of CVA.[8] Taylor's actions split the unstable Democratic party prior to the primary, as Donart's candidacy took a back seat to the Taylor-Gossett controversy.

Taylor's move to dump Gossett succeeded when Donart won the primary by a slim margin, so Taylor immediately pounded a plank into the party platform calling for a CVA. Many Democrats throughout the state were distressed not only because Taylor was determined to saddle himself to the party but also because they believed he had moved the party closer to his "socialistic views."[9] The CVA issue precipitated the old Republican charge, this time by T. W. Smith, the state chairman, that Taylor was a Communist, "whether he realized it or not." The *Idaho Daily Statesman* accused Taylor of giving "comfort to the Communist cult" by his advocacy of planned economy in the form of CVA.[10] Henry Dworshak, the Republican candidate, charged Taylor with sponsoring the Civil Rights Congress, which was supposedly a Communist-front group, but had nothing to do with CVA.[11]

Returning again to the state in September and remaining until the election, Idaho's controversial senator told his constituents that if everyone, including Republicans, could go to Tennessee and see what TVA had accomplished, there would be little opposition to CVA. At Lewiston, Taylor asserted that CVA was "the biggest issue of the campaign," and he promised new jobs and new industries for Idaho if a CVA became a reality.[12]

When Wayne Morse, a supporter of CVA, campaigned for Republicans Dworshak and Henry P. Cain, who was running against Senator Hugh Mitchell in Washington, Taylor was irate and contradictory. The Idaho Democrat accused Morse of "prostituting the liberal reputation he has built up." He continued his tirade against Morse with an implied warning to the Oregon senator: "I am afraid . . . he has not learned the lesson of Theodore Roosevelt, George Norris, . . . and Bob LaFollette [Jr.], whom Republicans voted down as too liberal."[13]

Shortly before the election, Taylor joined Democratic Senators

---

[8] Ibid., June 1, 1946.
[9] Interview with Robert Coulter, September 14, 1967.
[10] *Idaho Statesman*, July 28, 1946.
[11] Ibid., September 24, 1946.
[12] *Lewiston Tribune*, October 1, 1946.
[13] Ibid., October 7, 1946. Robert LaFollette, Jr., had just been defeated by Joseph McCarthy in the Wisconsin Republican primary.

Warren Magnuson and Hugh Mitchell of Washington, and James Murray of Montana, in a declaration announcing their support for regional development for the Northwest, which included valley authorities for the Columbia and Missouri river systems. In short, Taylor and his colleagues attempted to obtain a mandate on this issue from the voters of the Northwest in the 1946 election.[14]

Less than two weeks before the election, Taylor observed that the voters seemed to be favoring the status quo rather than the liberal senators. In desperation, Taylor launched bitter attacks on the Idaho Power Company, on Morrison-Knudsen, the large Boise-based construction firm, and on Boise's *Idaho Daily Statesman*. In a Boise speech, Taylor accused Idaho Power and Morrison-Knudsen of having interlocking directorates and of using each other to obtain prime contracts, especially for the construction of dams. The *Statesman* was denounced as a pure propaganda organ and was accused of suppressing any news favorable to liberals.[15] Taylor gave the same speech over three radio stations, and the *Statesman* sued all the stations, as well as Taylor, for libel, demanding damages of $100,000. The suits were later settled out of court for one dollar from each station, because there was no proof that the paper suppressed information favorable to Taylor.[16]

Like most other Democrats throughout the nation, the Idaho Democrats suffered a resounding defeat in November 1946. Donart was beaten badly and two of Taylor's closest Senate allies, Hugh Mitchell and Utah's Abe Murdock, both advocates of CVA, lost their Senate seats. Persistent as usual, Taylor announced that he would "probably be back campaigning again on the issue of a Columbia Valley Authority."[17]

Taylor had a tendency to become short-tempered when he was aroused. His reaction to Donart's defeat is a good example. On election night, Taylor was stopped in the Boise Hotel by Ray McKaig, a long-time Idaho Republican farm leader and Taylor enemy. McKaig, according to Taylor, called him an obscene name in front of Mrs. Taylor. "Instinctively my fist shot out," Taylor stated, "but I pulled the punch and hit his chest." McKaig hit Taylor twice in the face, and the senator, although his nose

14 Ibid., October 21, 1946.
15 Ibid., October 26, 1946.
16 *Idaho Statesman*, October 31, 1946. The radio stations were KIDO (Boise), KESI (Pocatello), and KID (Idaho Falls). Many other stations canceled the speech for fear of being sued also.
17 *Cong. Rec.*, 80th Cong., 1st sess., 1947, 93, pt. 6:7383.

was bleeding, counterpunched with a combination that floored the sixty-year-old Republican and broke his jaw. "I have taken defeat before," Taylor said, "and I can take defeat as well as anyone, but I can't take that."[18] The liberal senator returned to Washington nursing a sore nose, a battered reputation, and a badly defeated CVA, yet within a few short weeks he was again participating in the fight for development of the Columbia River.

Taylor shared President Truman's expectations of the worst from the Eightieth Congress. Nearly all Fair Deal proposals, including reclamation projects, were either slashed or ignored by the Republican-dominated Congress. In the Senate the Idaho Democrat joined with Magnuson and Morse in repeated efforts to curb Republican-sponsored budget cuts aimed at reclamation and related projects. They were concerned about projects already under way as well as CVA, but they failed to halt the Republican economy drive.[19]

In the spring of 1947, Taylor helped sponsor bills which would develop the Missouri Valley and the St. Lawrence Seaway. He believed these measures would provide an adequate test run before he and his liberal colleagues tried CVA again. The Missouri Valley Authority proposal suffered the same fate as had CVA in 1945 and 1946, but the St. Lawrence Seaway received enough support to carry it beyond the planning board.[20] Taylor was encouraged and believed that with a well-planned educational program, the CVA could become a reality.

Unable to develop a successful educational program, Taylor resorted to belittling the Republican party in the eyes of the voters whenever reclamation and conservation were issues. When it was suggested that Boulder Dam be renamed Hoover Dam in honor of the former president, Taylor used the opportunity to deliver a sarcastic tirade against the traditional Republican view of public power. Pointing out that Hoover had vetoed the first Muscle Shoals bill, a forerunner of the act creating TVA, the Idaho Democrat proposed that if the dam's name were changed to

---

[18] *Idaho Statesman*, November 8, 1946. According to Taylor's administrative assistant, Foy Blackburn, McKaig had precipitated the incident by saying, "There sure are a lot of sons-of-bitches getting whipped tonight and I know one more who will get licked in 1950." Interview with Foy Blackburn, June 15, 1967. This was one of the few times that Taylor resorted to physical violence, and it hurt him politically, especially because of the age difference between the two men.

[19] *Cong. Rec.*, 80th Cong., 1st sess., 1947, 93, pt. 2:1436.

[20] Ibid., pt. 4:4856.

Hoover Dam, Lake Mead should be renamed Harding Lake, and the spillway should be called the Albert Fall Spillway. He concluded by suggesting that Boulder City be renamed Hooverville, even though the local chamber of commerce might resent the connotation of the name, remembering the many "depression Hoovervilles."[21]

The Idaho senator also attacked the Republican majority leader in the Senate, Robert Taft of Ohio. When the Republican-controlled House cut the Interior Department budget recommendations of the president by more than 40 percent and Taft approved this action, Taylor accused the Ohio senator of attempting "mass desecration of the West and its resources." Specifically the Idahoan feared that the cuts would halt progress on the Anderson Ranch Dam above Boise and delay construction of the Palisades Dam on the south fork of the Snake River.[22]

True to his word, Taylor joined Murray, William Langer, Lister Hill, and John Sparkman in introducing a new CVA bill on July 16, 1947. The bill was patterned after the one which had been introduced by Taylor and Mitchell in the Seventy-ninth Congress. Taylor issued an explanatory statement setting forth the need and reasons for a CVA, and he denied that individual water rights would be destroyed under the proposed authority and that private enterprise would be injured.[23] There were three significant differences in the new proposal, as compared with its predecessor, the so-called Mitchell bill. Taylor and his associates attempted to break down their opponents' argument that CVA would be "Washington, D. C. controlled," by stipulating that two of the three CVA directors be natives of the Northwest. Their bill also provided for an advisory committee with at least sixteen of the twenty-four members from the CVA region. Finally the new bill would authorize the transfer of all existing federal dams and projects in the Columbia watershed to CVA in order to avoid competition among federal agencies. Concluding with a summary of how the nation would benefit from CVA, Taylor's statement listed greater food production; more hydroelectric power; expansion of industry; conservation of forests, soils, minerals, water, and recreational facilities; and development of the navigational possibilities of the Northwest's river systems. The Idahoan pleaded with his colleagues "not to delay. Let us fulfill our obligations to the future."[24]

[21] Ibid., pt. 3:3841.   [22] Ibid., pt. 4:4373.
[23] Ibid., pt. 7:8997.   [24] Ibid., p. 8999.

The 1947 version of the Columbia Valley Authority met the same fate as its predecessors. Naturally Truman and Taylor blamed the Eightieth, or as the president called it, the "Do-Nothing" Congress. Later, during the 1948 campaign, Truman would tell a Seattle audience, "Bonneville and Grand Coulee mark a fine beginning. But we must have more dams if that mighty stream is to be effectively harnessed for useful purposes." Pointing an accusing finger at Congress, Truman exclaimed, "Congress threw us backward when it cut the appropriations for this work."[25] CVA advocates hopefully awaited the Eighty-first Congress to try the CVA issue again.

The president again called for the establishment of a CVA in his 1949 State of the Union speech.[26] He then sent letters to the Interior, Agriculture, and Army departments asking the various secretaries to work together for an acceptable CVA bill. Each department head was urged to take into account "the characteristics and needs of the region" and to place these over their own departmental interests.[27] Extremely pleased by Truman's persistence, Taylor planned once more to initiate CVA legislation as soon as possible.

However, opposition to the CVA was growing simultaneously with the renewed liberal attempt to pass the valley authority act. Five western governors, A. G. Crane of Wyoming, Douglas McKay of Oregon, C. A. Robins of Idaho, Arthus B. Langlie of Washington, and Vail Pittman of Nevada, sent telegrams to Truman in January and February 1949, voicing their opposition to CVA.[28] Various irrigation districts throughout the region sent petitions urging that the CVA be tabled. Most of these groups were concerned about their individual water rights and believed a powerful valley authority would destroy them.[29] Taylor still maintained that the real opposition to CVA came from private power companies and

25 Speech, Harry S. Truman, Seattle, Washington, June 10, 1948, OF 360, Truman Papers.
26 *Truman Public Papers*, 1:1-7.
27 Truman to Julius A. Krug, Secretary of the Interior, January 13, 1949, OF 360-A, Truman Papers. Secretary of Agriculture Charles Brannan and Army Secretary Kenneth Royal also received letters.
28 Telegram, Vail Pittman to Truman, February 3, 1949, ibid. The telegrams and letters from the other governors are attached to the Pittman correspondence. The governors feared that each state would have only a small voice on the administration board.
29 Louise Keefer to Truman, March 17, 1949, ibid. Mrs. Keefer was secretary of the Progressive Irrigation District, Idaho Falls, Idaho. Her group's opposition is typical of that found in this file.

from business organizations connected with, or dependent upon, private power companies. These groups were accused by Taylor of financing CVA opponents on the local level.[30]

Hugh Mitchell, the former Washington senator who had sponsored the original CVA bill in 1945, was elected to the House in 1948. In a letter to the president, Mitchell complained that the real villains aligned against CVA were the various agencies of the executive branch. The Washington legislator claimed that the Bonneville Power Administration, the Army Corps of Engineers, and the Bureau of Reclamation were cutting the throat of CVA. Each agency, according to Mitchell, realized that a TVA-type authority in the Northwest would replace it in developing the region.[31]

When Interior Secretary Julius A. Krug testified in support of CVA before the House Public Works Committee, he claimed that the existing agencies were "just too bound by red tape and inefficiency to do a total job." Krug told the committee that a CVA would give the people of the region a much greater measure of participation than they enjoyed under the existing agencies.[32] It was for this reason that Taylor had incorporated, in his 1947 bill, provisions which would give the region a greater voice in the administration of the valley authority.

On April 13, 1949, Truman asked Congress to pass legislation which would weld together "the many federal activities concerned with the region's resources" into a CVA. This Truman proposal suggested that legislation be based on planning already completed and on the large construction program already under way on the Columbia River and its tributaries.[33] A bill was formally introduced five days later in the Senate. Among the many sponsors of the

[30] *Cong. Rec.*, 80th Cong., 2d sess., 1948, 94, pt. 7:8282. Robert Tininenko, "Middle Snake River Development: The Origins of the Hells Canyon Controversy, 1947-1955" (M.A. thesis, Washington State University, 1967), pp. 90-115, lists the ways in which Idaho Power worked with irrigation groups, mine owners, and the forest industry to combat the proposed federal dam at Hells Canyon.

[31] Hugh B. Mitchell to Truman, March 28, 1949, OF 360-A, Truman Papers.

[32] Julius A. Krug, statement before the House Public Works Committee, June 22, 1949, Papers of Joel D. Wolfsohn, Assistant Secretary of Interior, Truman Library. See also Polenberg, "The Great Conservation Contest," pp. 13-23, for a discussion of Ickes's plan to reorganize the executive agencies. The plan was defeated, in part because of the lobbying of the competing agencies.

[33] Truman, message to Congress, April 13, 1949, Clark Clifford File #3, Truman Papers.

CVA legislation were Taylor and two freshmen senators, Lyndon B. Johnson of Texas and Hubert H. Humphrey of Minnesota.[34] Writing Krug the same day, Truman expressed the hope that the CVA which he had recommended to Congress would "be authorized at an early date."[35] Thus, the two opponents of the 1948 campaign, Truman and Taylor, once again fought together for CVA.

Glen Taylor persisted in his attempt to bring the CVA closer to reality, but the bill languished in the Public Works Committee. In a Senate speech delivered on August 25, 1949, he recalled the depression years and prophesied that a CVA would remove poverty and want from the Northwest, but in an affluent era few northwestern residents believed that poverty existed. Taylor's views on the opposition to CVA were much simpler than those of Mitchell and Krug. True to his past philosophy, the Idaho liberal blamed it on the eastern-owned private utility companies, and he accused the private power organizations of playing the anticommunist tune at its highest pitch. According to Taylor, all the anti-CVA propaganda was "designed to show that CVA is socialistic."[36]

After a summer of prolonged congressional hearings featuring a parade of witnesses testifying for and against the CVA, it became apparent to Truman that passage of the CVA bill was impossible in the first session of the Eighty-first Congress. On August 30 the president wrote Krug that he wanted congressional action on CVA postponed until the next session. Truman called for a report from the competing agencies and decided to wait and review these reports.[37]

By February 1950 Truman was again ready to push ahead for a CVA. Taylor, now a member of the Interior and Insular Affairs Committee, felt that he was in a position to help get the president's proposal out of committee and before Congress. Through Director of the Budget Frank C. Pace, Truman instructed Oscar L. Chapman, the new secretary of the interior, to push for the authorization of CVA by Congress as early as possible in 1950, so "that orderly plans for the construction and budgeting may be laid out."[38]

---

34 *Cong. Rec.*, 81st Cong., 1st sess., 1949, 95, pt. 4:4740.
35 Truman to Krug, April 18, 1949, Charles S. Murphy File, Truman Papers.
36 *Cong. Rec.*, 81st Cong., 1st sess., 1949, 95, pt. 9:12204-6.
37 Truman to Krug, August 30, 1949, OF 360, Truman Papers.
38 Frank C. Pace to Oscar L. Chapman, February 1, 1950, U. S., Congress, Senate, Committee on Interior and Insular Affairs, *Hearings, Columbia River Basin*, 81st Cong., 2d sess., 1950, pp. 90-92.

Chapman wrote Vice President Alben Barkley, urging him to use his influence in the Senate to obtain favorable action on the reclamation projects in the Columbia Basin. Chapman's letter, which placed top priority on approval of individual projects, gave CVA secondary emphasis. Chapman, however, admitted that the establishment of a CVA constituted the best method of permanent administration for the Columbia Valley and he strongly urged favorable action on it. He concluded, "consideration of the method of permanent administration, however, need not and should not deter us from taking action now to implement desirable physical developments in the Pacific Northwest."[39]

Chapman's willingness to compromise was apparently sanctioned by Truman, and each reclamation and power project was discussed and debated on its own merits. But Taylor refused to give up on CVA. Believing that the CVA was necessary in order to provide the cheap power needed to entice industry to come to Idaho and believing that authorization of CVA was still possible, the Idaho Democrat decided to campaign on that issue when he ran for reelection in 1950.

Liberal hopes for a Columbia Valley Authority modeled on the successful TVA prototype died, however, after 1950. The Chapman concept that the success of individual reclamation projects was more important than central administrative authority prevailed. The post-1950 controversies, as typified by the Hells Canyon project, were fought over whether private utilities or the federal government should construct dams and distribute power. Taylor still believes that a CVA would have performed economic miracles for the entire Northwest, especially for Idaho. According to him, relative prosperity after the war destroyed the chances for a CVA. "If the depression would have continued, there is little doubt that we would have had not only a CVA, but a Missouri Valley Authority and many other similar projects."[40]

Although Taylor doggedly had pursued the goal of a CVA for six long years, he also proposed and supported individual reclamation, flood control, and building projects. The Kooshia native was, in part, responsible for the millions of federal dollars that were spent in Idaho for dams, electric co-ops, hospitals, schools, and roads. During his Senate term, nearly ninety million dollars of federal funds were appropriated for the Gem State.[41]

[39] Chapman to Alben Barkley, February 3, 1950, ibid., pp. 88-90.
[40] Interview with Glen H. Taylor, June 14, 1967.

Glen Taylor's persistent attempts to obtain a CVA were in harmony with his pledge to accomplish significant reforms for the common man. His decision to fight for a CVA in the 1950 campaign, despite the administration's determination to compromise, was another example of Taylor's willingness to sacrifice political considerations for an idealistic commitment. Taylor, however, did not lose his Senate seat solely because of his stand on CVA. Politically Glen Taylor was out of step with the times, and his dream of protecting Idaho's rivers, lands, and forests, while at the same time providing cheap power for Idaho's industrial development through CVA, died with his defeat in 1950.

Truman had openly advocated valley authorities throughout the first six years of his presidency, but he lacked the kind of sympathetic Congress which had helped Roosevelt secure such controversial legislation as the act creating TVA. Postwar America also was not characterized by the economic desperation of the New Deal years. Destined to follow the same course as many of Truman's other Fair Deal proposals designed as extensions of the New Deal, CVA suffered a fate similar to that of price controls, increase civil rights, attempts to provide cheap federal housing, federal health insurance, and extend unemployment insurance, most of which were either defeated or passed in emasculated form.

In viewing the total picture of immediate postwar America, Taylor believed that very little was accomplished domestically, the reason being that foreign policy occupied the position of top priority. Taylor was very much involved in attempting to bring permanent peace to the world, and this involvement started him on the path toward temporary political prominence.

---

[41] These statistics and descriptions of the specific projects are to be found in two Taylor campaign documents, "Man of the People" (1950) and "The Democrat" (1956). Documents are in the author's possession.

VI. *Taylor & the Cold War*

The Truman presidency is probably most remembered for its dramatic, but controversial, foreign policy. Included in those exciting eight years were the Truman Doctrine, the Marshall Plan, the Berlin airlift, the North Atlantic Treaty Organization, and the Korean War. It was Glen Taylor's reaction to Truman's Cold War foreign policy which caused him to seek a new political alternative. An intense dedication to the maintenance of peace during a period of history when the world seemed to be spiraling toward atomic destruction characterized Taylor's view of foreign affairs, a view that was to lead him away from Truman and the Democratic party in 1948.

Once asked what he considered the most important thing he did in the Senate, Taylor answered, "The resolution I introduced in 1945, which called for the establishment of a World Republic."[1] Taylor's emphasis can be explained by his concern for the fate of the common man and mankind generally. As Taylor often has said, "Like persons the world over . . . I did not bring my sons into this world to have them die in World War III."[2]

In order to avoid future wars, Taylor believed, it was necessary to eliminate economic competition among nations. He viewed colonialism and imperialism as the main threats to the maintenance of world peace.[3] It was his hope that an international organization or government could be instrumental in bringing an end to such economic rivalry.

Shortly after Taylor took the oath of office, at the time when Roosevelt was about to leave for his trip to the Crimea and the Yalta conference, the Idaho Democrat joined fifteen other freshmen senators in expressing support of the United Nations organization. The new senators, moreover, suggested the demilitarization of Germany and Japan and proposed to Roosevelt that the United States share "in the direction of and the responsibility for the settlement of this war and the maintenance of peace."[4]

Throughout 1945, Taylor anxiously watched as the two emerging world powers, the Soviet Union and the United States, drifted further apart. It became apparent to Taylor that despite ideological differences it was imperative for Russia and America to cooperate in order to maintain world peace. His primary concern was that another world war be avoided at all costs, even if it meant compromise on the part of the United States.

Taylor committed himself to work for a strong international peacekeeping organization, and throughout the spring and summer of 1945 he voted for all measures designed to strengthen the then developing United Nations. Although he was not personally involved in any of the preliminary UN meetings, Taylor sincerely hoped that the infant organization would provide the basis for lasting peace.[5]

Taylor, however, saw the United Nations as only a beginning. On October 23, 1945, the day that the United Nations officially came into being, Taylor rose from his Senate seat during the debate on a tax bill, addressed the chair, and asked for unanimous consent, out of order, to submit a resolution. With characteristic Taylor humor, the Idaho senator began by stating, "I dislike very much to interrupt consideration of the tax bill. On the other hand, it may be a welcome respite for the Senators to hear of something besides taxes for a few moments." He then made a brief statement about his proposal. "This is the first resolution I have introduced. Furthermore, it is a resolution which may be rather startling to some, and, to say the least, controversial. My proposal in the resolution is that the Senate go on record as favoring the creation of a world republic."[6] Taylor told the Senate that when the atomic bomb fell on Hiroshima, "the effect was something like that of a man turning around and seeing a grizzly bear on his tracks."[7] He used this analogy to convey his sense of urgency and to explain

---

[1] Interview with Glen H. Taylor, June 14, 1967.

[2] Glen H. Taylor, "Why a World Republic," *Free World* (December 1945), p. 27.

[3] Ibid., p. 30. The views Taylor espoused regarding the economic roots of war possibly can be traced to King Gillette's *World Corporation* (see pp. 123-37).

[4] Glen H. Taylor et al. to Franklin Delano Roosevelt, January 24, 1945, Crimean Conference File, Roosevelt Papers. Among the other signatories were J. William Fulbright of Arkansas, Warren Magnuson of Washington, Wayne Morse of Oregon, Homer Capehart of Indiana, and Leverett Saltonstall of Massachusetts.

[5] Taylor, "Why a World Republic," p. 27.

[6] *Cong. Rec.*, 79th Cong., 1st sess., 1945, 91, pt. 8:9987.

why, on the very day that the United States was entering an international organization such as the UN for the first time, he was asking his colleagues to consider a world republic.

The Taylor resolution asked the president to instruct the country's United Nations delegation to lay the groundwork for the formation of a world republic. Taylor's plan, which provided for a federated international organization, also called for eventual abolishment of armaments, the outlawing of military training and conscription, and prohibition of the manufacture of atomic weapons. The role of the United Nations would be to provide a police force to keep peace throughout the world. Comparing the Charter of the infant United Nations to the Articles of Confederation of the early American government, Taylor hoped the UN, like the loosely federated American states, would develop into a republic organized under a Constitution.[8] After briefly describing the structure of his proposed world republic, Taylor explained why he believed such an organization was necessary.

Speaking in what one reporter described as the "solemn tones of a preacher," Taylor passionately told the Senate that permanent world peace would not be found in more weapons and larger armies.[9] During these first frosty days of the Cold War, Taylor denied the familiar charge that it was impossible to get along with Communist Russia. He said that it was imperative for the United States and the Soviet Union to work together for peace, regardless of ideologies. Taylor concluded by quoting the statements of six atomic scientists, who all agreed that there was no possibility of permanently keeping the secret of the atomic bomb and that, unless some plan was devised which would prevent the manufacture of atomic bombs, the entire world would live in constant fear of sudden and violent death.[10]

Taylor's initial criticism of Truman's foreign policy came at approximately this time—late October 1945. Contending that Truman, since the use of the atomic bomb, had been sold on "another line— that of peace by force," the Idaho senator admitted he was worried. He feared that Truman's "so-called . . . advisors have persuaded him, apparently, that the most practical way to get along is to

---

[7] Ibid.   [8] Ibid.

[9] *New York Times*, October 25, 1945, p. 10.

[10] *Cong. Rec.*, 79th Cong., 1st sess., 1945, 91, pt. 8:9989. Taylor quoted Harold Urey, Robert R. Wilson, A. H. Compton, H. J. Curtis, Irving Langmuir, and Harlow Shapley.

frighten somebody."[11] Calling for empathy and introspection, Taylor stated, "We should put ourselves in the others' place. . . . Would we trust in their high intentions? No, if we're going to arm, others are going to." An armaments economy, said Taylor, is based on the industrialists' drive for greater and greater profits, and once an armaments race is underway, it is too late to stop.[12]

Actually Taylor had little hope that his resolution would be acted upon favorably. His only chance was that future events and the pressure of public opinion would influence the Senate to support Taylor's world republic. Although the proposal's chances for passage were slim, Taylor did believe the resolution would be sufficiently publicized to produce an immediate public reaction. In this regard, the Idahoan, who craved favorable publicity, was to be sadly disappointed.

Two weeks later, when Taylor again addressed the Senate concerning his world republic resolution, he admitted that he was extremely disappointed in the reaction to his earlier suggestion. What disturbed him most was that the press had hardly mentioned it. Somewhat bitterly Taylor reminisced about his first few days in Washington. "And I do not recall it too fondly—that when I first came to the Senate, members of the press asked me to go out on the Capitol steps and sing a song for them, . . . and they put my picture in every newspaper in the United States." By way of contrast, Taylor pointed out, "When I submitted the resolution calling for the creation of a world republic, I received very little mention in the newspapers. . . . In one Washington newspaper, in particular, I noticed a reference consisting of one sentence. . . . Next to the statement was a two-column wide picture of a man who had beat his wife on that same day."[13] Disgruntled, Taylor announced in the same speech that he would continue his efforts to bring about a world republic.

Within a few days Taylor renewed his attempt to obtain support for his plan. He wrote a letter, addressed it "To Whom It May Concern," and sent it out to various newspapers throughout the country. In the letter Taylor asked readers to write to the Senate

---

[11] *Daily Worker,* October 30, 1945. Taylor's remarks followed Truman's Navy Day speech of October 27, 1945. Truman had called for an open-door policy for trade throughout the world and demanded that democratic governments be established in the defeated nations.

[12] Ibid.

[13] *Cong. Rec.,* 79th Cong., 1st sess., 1945, 91, pt. 8:10497.

Foreign Relations Committee urging it to report favorably on the world republic resolution.[14]

In December Taylor wrote an article which was published in *Free World,* a monthly journal devoted to world cooperation. This journalistic endeavor was merely an elaboration of the speech he had delivered when he introduced the resolution. Taylor contended that wars were caused by the international political and economic rivalries created by the profit system and economic spheres of influence. He denied the contention that the world was too large for one republic and that economic spheres of influence were necessary. The freshman senator opposed the concept of economic spheres of influence on the grounds that they "have always been the prime ingredients of the witch's brew of suspicion between people."[15]

Persistently Taylor continued to work toward the creation of a world government. During a debate on the United Nations, Taylor interrupted Senator Thomas Connally after the veteran Texas legislator, chairman of the Senate Foreign Relations Committee, proclaimed, "We are not ready for a world government . . . we would be outvoted the first day." Taylor admitted that the United States should not surrender its sovereignty, "but we should be willing to yield enough sovereignty to a world government to insure peace in the world." Connally calmly cautioned Taylor to slow down. Agreeing that a world republic was conceivable, Connally told Taylor that it would take years to gain acceptance. In the meantime, Connally suggested continued work with the United Nations as he thought that would be a step in the right direction.[16]

Publicizing a world government occupied much of Taylor's time throughout the rest of his years in the Senate. By March 1946 the Idaho Democrat claimed to have mailed over 100,000 copies of his resolution in answer to requests received in his office.[17] Taylor now regrets that he was not an "organization man" while he was in the Senate. "If I had known how to organize," he says, "I would have got the World Federalists to help me." It seems strange that the World Federalists did not come to Taylor's assistance. However, instead of working with existing groups, the

---

[14] Ibid., p. 10498.
[15] Taylor, "Why a World Republic," p. 27.
[16] *Cong. Rec.,* 79th Cong., 1st sess., 1945, 91, pt. 8:10071.
[17] Ibid., 2d sess., 1946, 92, pt. 2:2720.

Idaho senator followed his own course, and his endeavors to raise support for a world republic ended in failure.[18]

Although Taylor reintroduced his resolution for the creation of a world government in 1948, 1949, and 1950, the proposal never received an impartial hearing. Taylor blames this lack of interest on the ideological Cold War which prevented nations from sincerely seeking peace. While he was the Progressive candidate for vice president in 1948, Taylor introduced a Senate resolution calling for a meeting between the president-elect of the United States and Joseph Stalin for the purpose of ending the Cold War. This proposed legislation also asked the two world leaders to select delegates to attend a world constitutional convention to be held in 1949.[19] This proposition too died in committee.

While Taylor pursued his unfulfilled dream of world government, he persistently worked for a stronger, more powerful United Nations. In July 1947 he cosponsored a concurrent resolution for the purpose "of making the United Nations capable of enacting, interpreting, and enforcing world law to prevent war."[20] The resolution was in part designed to combat the argument used by proponents of the Truman Doctrine, which Taylor bitterly opposed, that the United Nations was too weak to handle the Greek-Turkish situation. Arguing that the United Nations would only be as strong as its member states made it, Taylor said that the United States should lead the way in effectively correcting the weaknesses of the UN.

Taylor told the Senate, as he had in his earlier speeches on the world republic, that it was not impossible to get along with the Soviet Union and that America would never have peace with the Russians until it tried. The Idaho Democrat encouraged his government to take the initial step. "If Russia then refuses to cooperate in building a common security, we will know where we stand and we will know also that we have done all within our power to prevent the impending catastrophe."[21] Taylor believed that neither nation had tried very hard to find a solution to the Cold War and that there would be no lasting peace until they explored every possible road leading toward amity.

18 Interview with Glen H. Taylor, June 14, 1967.
19 *Cong. Rec.*, 80th Cong., 2d sess., 1948, 94, pt. 4:5173.
20 Ibid., 1st sess., 1947, 93, pt. 7:8506. Dennis Chavez of New Mexico, James Murray of Montana, Claude Pepper of Florida, and Olin Johnston of South Carolina joined Taylor in sponsoring this resolution.
21 Ibid., p. 8509.

Three weeks after the resolution designed to give the United Nations the power to keep the peace was introduced, Taylor joined Democratic Senators Dennis Chavez of New Mexico and Elbert Thomas of Utah in sponsoring legislation which would grant the UN power to ensure the peaceful use of atomic energy. Like the peacekeeping resolution, the atomic energy proposal died in committee.[22]

Taylor's greatest fight to strengthen the United Nations came in the course of the 1947 debate on whether or not the United States should send economic aid directly to Greece and Turkey. His opposition to Truman's proposal that the United States should unilaterally come to the aid of the established governments in Greece and Turkey drove the first significant wedge between Taylor and the Truman administration.

On Wednesday, March 12, 1947, Truman spoke to a joint session of the Congress assembled in the House chamber. He told the lawmakers that on March 31 Great Britain was going to pull out of Greece and Turkey. Hitherto Britain and the United States had shared a mutual responsibility to preserve the political integrity of the two Mediterranean nations. Now, according to the British, Communist guerrilla pressure threatened to overturn the existing government in Greece, and the collapsing British Empire was powerless to preserve the status quo. Truman requested $400 million for the tottering Greek and Turkish regimes. The president told Congress that the situation demanded immediate action and that the United Nations was not in a position to help. Although Turkey was mentioned as needing economic assistance, most of the Truman speech dealt with Greece. Truman reminded Congress that the Greeks were surrounded by totalitarian Communist regimes in Albania, Yugoslavia, and Bulgaria. The president believed it was necessary to send both military and civilian personnel to Greece in order to prevent the Communists from taking over. The philosophy of containment was formally enunciated as the president declared, "The free peoples of the world look to us for support in maintaining their freedoms."[23]

[22] Gar Alperowitz, *Atomic Diplomacy: Potsdam and Hiroshima* (New York: Simon and Schuster, 1965), points out that the period between 1945 and 1946 marked the height of America's confidence in atomic diplomacy. This very controversial volume contends that the United States attempted to use the atomic bomb as a means of forcing its intentions and desires on the Communist bloc. Whatever confidence Truman and his advisers had in atomic diplomacy was shattered before 1947.

The day before the Truman speech, Glen Taylor had written to Acting Secretary of State Dean Acheson that King Paul of Greece, "who represents only a small minority of Monarchists" in Greece, should be removed from the throne as a precondition to American aid. Taylor also suggested that democratic governmental reforms should be instituted, which would lead toward the formation of a "government that would be truly representative of all the democratic elements in Greece."[24]

Taylor opposed the Truman Doctrine initially because he believed that the United Nations should administer economic relief and that unilateral action on the part of the United States would severely cripple the effectiveness of the infant international organization. Taylor and Claude Pepper introduced a resolution which would provide money for Greece, but the money was to be given directly to the UN and administered by the international organization.[25] While the Senate debated the Greek-Turkish aid proposal, Taylor repeatedly entered the discussion either to speak or to read editorials which favored turning the problem over to the United Nations.

In a Senate speech on March 31, 1947, Taylor enumerated his

---

[23] *Cong. Rec.*, 80th Cong., 1st sess., 1947, 93, pt. 2:1980-81. For personal reflections on, as well as scholarly analysis of, the Truman Doctrine and the philosophy of containment, the following works proved especially helpful: George F. Kennan, *Memoirs* (Boston: Little, Brown, 1967), pp. 373-87; Walter LaFeber, *America, Russia, and the Cold War, 1945-1966* (New York: John Wiley, 1967), pp. 37-65; Ronald Steel, *Pax Americana* (New York: Viking Press, 1967), pp. 15-27; David Horowitz, *The Free World Colossus* (New York: Hill and Wang, 1965), pp. 69-96; Richard J. Barnet, *Intervention and Revolution* (Cleveland: World Publishing, 1968), pp. 97-127. Interestingly, most of these books basically agree with the Taylor criticism of the Truman Doctrine. Joseph M. Jones, *The Fifteen Weeks* (New York: Viking Press, 1955), is a good account of the pro-Truman Doctrine philosophy. The Truman-Marshall position is well known.

[24] *Salt Lake Tribune*, March 11, 1948. When asked where he obtained his information concerning conditions in Greece, Taylor claimed that most of it came from reading the newspapers and other reports that came from the chaotic nation. There were many journalists critical of the Greek regime. Columnists Arthur Crock, James Reston, and Seymour Frieden all opposed the Truman Doctrine proposal.

[25] *Cong. Rec.*, 80th Cong., 1st sess., 1947, 93, pt. 2:2869. Among those in the Senate who criticized the bypassing of the United Nations, was Republican Senator Arthur H. Vandenberg of Michigan, chairman of the Senate Foreign Relations Committee. *The Private Papers of Senator Vandenberg*, ed., Arthur H. Vandenberg, Jr. (Boston: Houghton-Mifflin, 1952), pp. 338-50. During the summer of 1947, by working through the United Nations, the United States tried unsuccessfully to solve the Greek crisis. See Cyril E. Black, "Greece and the United Nations," *Political Science Quarterly* 63 (December 1948), 551-68.

reasons for opposing Truman's Near East proposals. The Idaho senator reiterated his belief that the UN should be the force controlling the unstable Mediterranean situation. He then moved into a discussion of the issue of communism in Greece. According to Taylor, there were only a few thousand Communists in the mountains of northern Greece, and they were not supported by the Soviet Union. The Idahoan accused the Senate of being too timid to vote against the Truman proposal because it purported to fight communism. According to Taylor, reason and common sense went out the window when the word communism was mentioned. The administration's attempt to aid Greece and Turkey in the name of anti-communism was, to Taylor, an attempt to create unanimity by fear. Taylor, accustomed to the charge of being pro-Communist, told his colleagues: "We are in the same boat together; the Red hunt has got us all."[26]

The Idaho Democrat declared emotionally that he was willing to help democratic governments stay in power, but that Greece and Turkey were far from being democracies. Taylor then proceeded with a bitter and sarcastic attack on the proposed Truman Doctrine, the State Department, and the monarchy in Greece. Describing United States policy with an analogy, Taylor said, "The gallant warriors of the State Department, with their well-polished attaché cases bravely borne by well-manicured fingers, come riding down the caucus room like the gallant 300 who held the pass at Thermoplyae." In Taylor's opinion, it was ridiculous to say that the Truman proposal was going to save Greece from communism: ". . . the anti-Communist guise hardly fits . . . , for the Greek Government bears no relationship whatever to democracy, and it is not combating communism." Taylor then made a statement that hit at the core of United States postwar policy: "Indeed, for every Greek who was converted to communism by Russian propaganda last week, 100 have been converted to it by the present Greek regime, and by our State Department's insistence that the only alternative to that regime is communism."[27] He also blamed Britain's treatment of Greece during the war for driving many Greek nationalists into the mountain-based guerrilla camps.

Taylor not only opposed the Truman Doctrine because it circum-

[26] *Cong. Rec.*, 80th Cong., 1st sess., 1947, 93, pt. 3:2867. Taylor recognized the multiplicity of communist groups. Many reporters were vicious in their attacks on the Greek regime because of its lack of concern for the people.
[27] Ibid., p. 2868.

vented the UN and because it depended on what he felt was "red-baiting"; he also expressed distaste for the economics of such a plan. In his March 31 speech, Taylor asked if the proposed aid program was a humanitarian undertaking, or whether "we are doing it to pull British chestnuts out of the fire, to preserve British investments in Greece." He also expressed concern about whether such action would commit the United States to a policy of imperialism.[28]

Less than a week later, in a Washington radio speech, Taylor again discussed the administration's plan for Greece and Turkey. He claimed that the program, ostensibly aimed at aiding Greece and Turkey, involved an "oil-grab in the Middle East." According to the Idaho Democrat, the objective of the Truman Doctrine was not so much "food for the Greek people as oil for the American monopolies—the oil that lies in the great . . . lands just east of Greece and Turkey."[29] Concluding with a declaration that the Greek-Turkish aid plan involved a new American imperialism based on dollars and atom bombs, he expressed his fear that the American flag would follow America's dollars.

Unable to meet the March 31 deadline, as Truman had requested, Congress continued to debate the Truman Doctrine until late in April. Taylor was in part responsible for this delay. On April 11 he pleaded with his colleagues to turn the Near East affair over to the UN. He told the lawmakers that it was incomprehensible to him that the United States should spend millions "supporting the German Kings of Greece."[30] Four days later the troubled Idahoan, denying that he was an isolationist, delivered another long attack on the Truman Doctrine. Taylor accused Truman of attempting to browbeat the legislative branch into accepting the administration's analysis of the Near East situation. Noting that the deadline of March 31 had come and gone and nothing had happened, he asserted that the tense situation was caused not by ideological differences, but by economics. In support of this as-

---

[28] Ibid., p. 2866.

[29] *New York Times*, April 5, 1947.

[30] *Cong. Rec.*, 80th Cong., 1st sess., 1947, 93, pt. 3:334. According to Cyril E. Black, professor of history at Princeton University, senators such as Taylor, Pepper, and Kilgore, supported by many intellectuals, were more concerned about the United States' supporting reactionary regimes and embarking on a path of economic imperialism than they were about circumvention of the UN. Black believes the liberals were not pro-Communist or pro-guerrilla, but were sincerely concerned about America's future policy. Interview with Cyril E. Black, March 29, 1968.

sertion, he quoted from a Navy Department intelligence manual which stated, "all wars have been for economic reasons. To make them politically palatable, ideological issues have always been invoked."[31]

In the same Senate speech, Taylor maintained that all the talk about a Communist take-over was merely a fog bank blanketing the real economic issues. He again referred to the rich oil deposits of the Middle East and the fact that Britain's once powerful colonial empire was crumbling under the pressures of nationalism. He viewed the alleged Communist threat in Greece as minimal and in Turkey as nonexistent. "We are told that the 13,000 Greek guerrillas will sweep down on Athens; and the 120,000 men of . . . King Paul, aided by 10,000 British troops and equipped with the latest British arms, will be helpless before them. . . . We are told that the 13,000 will defeat the 130,000, and will establish a Communist dictatorship in Greece—even though it is admitted that most of the 13,000 guerrillas are not Communists."[32] Summarizing his opposition to the Truman Doctrine, Taylor declared that the United States was being asked to "underwrite backward regimes, intervene in a civil war, and jeopardize the peace of the world— mainly on the basis of hints and innuendos, broad generalizations, and half-truths."[33]

Taylor yielded the Senate floor to Edwin C. Johnson of Colorado, who proposed an amendment to the original Greek-Turkish aid bill to provide for an investigation of American oil interests in the Middle East.[34] Although Johnson's amendment was defeated, his attempt to differentiate between policy and oil diplomacy was praised by Taylor when he resumed his speech.

In concluding his speech, Taylor expressed fear that the Truman Doctrine would further divided the world into two ideological

[31] *Cong. Rec.*, 80th Cong., 1st sess., 1947, 93, pt. 3:3387.
[32] Ibid.
[33] Ibid., p. 3388.
[34] Ibid., p. 3398. A strong case can be made for the economic motivation of the Truman Doctrine. James Forrestal believed that the economic question was much more important than the political. See Walter Millis, ed., *The Forrestal Diaries* (New York: Viking Press, 1951), p. 410. See also Jones, *The Fifteen Weeks*, pp. 156-57. There was a clause in the original draft of the Truman Doctrine explaining the economic necessity for keeping Greece and Turkey in friendly hands. A brief analysis is to be found in Thomas G. Paterson, "The Quest for Peace and Prosperity, International Trade, Communism, and the Marshall Plan," in *Politics and Policies of the Truman Administration*, ed. Bernstein, pp. 91-97.

camps. According to Taylor, if the United States pursued the pattern set by the proposed Truman Doctrine, it would become involved in a worldwide "witch hunt." From now on, Taylor claimed, the United States would determine its allies by how loudly a nation claimed to fight communism. The Idaho liberal believed that Franco, Perón, and Chiang Kai-shek were rejoicing over the new turn of events in the United States. According to Taylor, if the United States was so willing to assist what he considered "reactionary regimes" (Greece and Turkey) in the name of anti-communism, the United States-Soviet split would continue to widen.[35] Finally, Taylor begged his colleagues to develop a degree of empathy. He asked them how they would feel if they were Russians and knew the United States was pouring millions of dollars into Greece and Turkey. What could be the reaction of the Russians except to bolster their defenses in the Balkans and in southern Russia? In Taylor's eyes, the future looked very dim, for he saw the two great powers pushing each other down the path to destruction. In spite of such grim warnings from Taylor and others, Congress approved the Truman Doctrine by a comfortable margin.[36] After the vote, Taylor glumly remarked to reporters, "I have never before seen so many members of Congress ignore the opinion of an overwhelming majority of the people."[37]

Although the battle over the Truman Doctrine was a significant round in the developing bout between Taylor and the Truman administration, there had been a series of minor conflicts earlier. So far as Taylor was concerned, the main point of contention was the executive branch's anti-Russian bias, which Taylor claimed was shared by the American press. Senator Claude Pepper, the liberal Florida Democrat, joined Taylor on numerous occasions in attempts to alter the official view toward the Soviet Union. Throughout 1946, these two senators, who were later accused of being either pro-Russian or anti-American, repeatedly called for increased efforts on the part of the two great powers to reach a *modus vivendi*.[38]

Following Winston Churchill's dramatic "iron curtain" pronouncement in 1946, Taylor, Pepper, and Harley Kilgore issued a joint statement criticizing the former British prime minister for

---

[35] Ibid., pp. 3404-7.
[36] Ibid., p. 2497. The final vote was 67-23.
[37] *Daily Worker*, April 23, 1947.
[38] Both Taylor and Pepper were confronted with these accusations when they ran for reelection in 1950.

attempting to destroy the unity of the postwar world. They announced that Churchill's speech would in effect "serve notice on Russia that the two English-speaking peoples had banded together to perpetuate the age-old game of European power politics."[39] Later Taylor claimed that Churchill's speech "did more to undermine our relations with Russia than any one thing that had occurred up to that time." Taylor blamed Truman for inviting Churchill to Fulton, Missouri, where the speech was delivered, and he cynically berated the former British prime minister for always trying to stay in the spotlight: "Certainly, after the damage he did to the hopes of mankind on that one day at Fulton, Missouri, he should have his belly full, he should be satisfied to rest on his laurels to his dying day."[40]

A month after criticizing Churchill, Taylor and Pepper again discussed American-Soviet relations on the floor of the Senate. The Idaho senator reminded the legislators that on several occasions he had tried to "point out that Russia is not all bad." He explained to the Senate, "I have found out through my lifetime that if I start saying bad things about a man and continue to say bad things about him eventually there will be a showdown."[41]

By the spring and summer of 1947, Taylor was convinced that the United States and the Soviet Union were rapidly moving toward such a confrontation. The Idaho liberal believed the danger of war would be enhanced by the United States' insistence on supporting totalitarian regimes because they were supposedly anti-Communist. The governments of Greece and Turkey exemplified this trend, according to Taylor. Another glaring example was Chiang Kai-shek in China.

Taylor, always a supporter of those he considered the underdogs, told the Senate that the future of China was with Mao Tse-tung and his followers, who were trying to overthrow the "reactionary

[39] *New York Times*, March 7, 1946, p. 1.
[40] *Cong. Rec.*, 80th Cong., 2d sess., 1948, 94, pt. 2:2488. Barton Bernstein, "American Foreign Policy and the Cold War," in *Politics and Policies of the Truman Administration*, ed. Bernstein, pp. 41-43, basically agrees with the Taylor assessment of Churchill's motives and of the effects of the speech. Most historians still view Churchill's remarks as an early recognition of an obvious situation and believe he should be credited with shocking the United States out of its lethargy. See John W. Spanier, *American Foreign Policy since World War II* (New York: Praeger, 1968), pp. 32-33; and Dexter Perkins, *The Diplomacy of a New Age* (Bloomington: Indiana University Press, 1967), pp. 26-27.
[41] *Cong. Rec.*, 79th Cong., 2d sess., 92, 1946, pt. 2:3859.

government of Chiang Kai-shek." According to Taylor, these people, like the guerrillas in the mountains of Greece, were fighting for a human cause similar to that "of the American colonists when they fought for and won freedom from tyranny in 1776."[42] Taylor emotionally explained that the moving force in China was not communism, but the "Chinese spirit" or nationalism. It was Taylor's belief that supporting Chiang would only ruin America's chances of aiding the oppressed millions of China. The government of Chiang was sinking because of corruption, not because of the Communist threat. Taylor agreed with Marshal Feng Yuh-siang, a non-Communist Chinese leader, who said that the leaders of the Chinese Nationalist government were using American foreign aid to line their own pockets.[43] Later events showed that Taylor's assessment of United States aid to China was at least partially sound.

In the summer of 1947, Taylor turned his foreign policy attack from Asia to Europe once again. Secretary of State George C. Marshall delivered the momentous address that launched the Marshall Plan on June 5, 1947, at the Harvard University commencement. Designed to aid Western Europe on its long road back to economic stability, the plan asked all Europe to join in this united effort.[44] The Soviet Union refused to participate in the Marshall Plan because, according to the Russian spokesman, the European nations then would become the economic satellites of the United States.[45]

Glen Taylor disapproved of the Marshall Plan for reasons similar to those he had voiced when he voted against the Truman Doctrine.

[42] Ibid., 80th Cong., 1st sess., 93, 1947, pt. 3:3702.
[43] Ibid., pt. 13:A4853. Marshal Feng Yuh-siang was living in the United States at the time; he opposed communism, but he also opposed Chiang Kai-shek. He became a supporter of Henry A. Wallace, and although he left the country in 1948, he wrote Wallace and wished the Progressive candidate well. Feng Yuh-siang to Wallace, July 30, 1948, 66631M, Wallace Papers.
[44] *Cong. Rec.*, 80th Cong., 1st sess., 93, 1947, pt. 12:A3248.
[45] *New York Times*, July 3, 1947, p. 4, notes the objections of Foreign Minister V. Molotov. The same objections were voiced by Andrei Vishinsky, chairman of the Soviet delegation to the United Nations; ibid., September 19, 1947, pp. 18-19. Both stated that the Marshall Plan was designed to enable the United States to dominate Europe economically. For a concise discussion of why the Marshall Plan was not feasible for the Soviet Union, see Paterson, "The Quest for Peace and Prosperity," pp. 98-102. Joseph Jones, *The Fifteen Weeks*, takes a very different view of the Marshall Plan, as does Robert H. Ferrell, *George C. Marshall* (New York: Cooper Square Publishers, 1966), pp. 111-34. It is viewed by these authors as a humanitarian attempt to rebuild war-torn Europe.

Admitting that Europe needed help in order to rebuild after a devastating war, Taylor believed the United Nations should administer the relief rather than individual nations. Speaking to reporters, he stated: "I am all for preventing the people of the world from starving. But our present program is not predicated on this but on gaining selfish political ends. The Hindus are starving, but there is no thought of aiding them, because there is no 'Communist threat' to worry us."[46] He also expressed fear that the Soviet Union would react adversely to the Marshall Plan by making Eastern Europe more dependent on the Soviet Union for economic survival.[47] The Marshall proposal did not reach the floor of the Senate until the spring of 1948. In the meantime, Taylor set out on a speaking tour of Idaho in October 1947 to see how his constituents felt about the new developments in foreign policy.

Idaho's Democratic senator spent less than a week in his native state, but in that short period of time he concluded that he had been following the right course. He was convinced that the people wanted peace above anything else. It was also his conviction that Truman's policies were leading toward war. In his Idaho speeches, Taylor accused the military, as well as large corporations, of fostering anti-Russian sentiment. In one speech he asserted, "They needed a villain and they picked on Russia." Theorizing that the military and the corporations wanted to keep tensions high and avoid war at the same time, Taylor claimed, "This way the generals can stay generals . . . and the corporations will get lucrative research contracts from the government."[48]

At the conclusion of the week in Idaho, Taylor decided to take his case to the people throughout the nation. To do this, the senator decided, he would resort to a prior technique—a horseback ride— this time across the country. He said his aim would be "to attract nation-wide attention to my crusade against our foreign policy that is provoking a third world war."[49] Taylor frankly told reporters, "I've spent most of my life on the stage and I realize that in order to attract attention to a voice which opposes our foreign

[46] *Daily Worker*, November 21, 1947. This paper is obviously biased, yet it was the only paper that gave Taylor's November 20 news conference significant publicity.

[47] *Lewiston Tribune*, October 5, 1947.

[48] *Salt Lake Tribune*, October 7, 1947. This Utah daily has a wide circulation in Idaho; because it is indexed, it is a handy research tool.

[49] Ibid., October 10, 1947.

policy, I must dramatize the issue."[50] In other words, by using this technique, Taylor knew that he could ensure full coverage by the press. If he went on a normal speaking tour and did nothing extraordinary, the newspapers might give him a paragraph or two.[51]

In order to avoid inclement weather, the expert campaigner traveled to Los Angeles late in October 1947 and announced that he would take the southern route across the nation. He left Los Angeles on October 27. Prior to his departure, the Idaho senator proclaimed to a crowd of four hundred people: "I am doing this to arouse the people on the most important question of our day—whether we shall remain at peace or go to war. . . . I am for peace!"[52]

As usual, Taylor included his family in his personal crusade. His wife, Dora, drove their 1946 Nash pulling a horse trailer. Taylor kept his horses in the trailer until they were within a few miles of a town; then he unloaded a horse, mounted, and rode into the city. Usually he explained the reason for his ride to the crowd: As a young senator, he said, his views were not as newsworthy as those of the elder statesmen; however, longevity did not mean accuracy. "I find though that almost without exception the elder statesmen are favoring a policy which I believe can lead only to atomic and biological war and ruin for our country and the world, whether we win or lose. . . . I must dramatize these issues. That is why I am going to cross the continent on horseback."[53] At each town there were reporters to discuss Taylor's ride and his crusade, and so he received the publicity he desired.[54]

There is little doubt that Taylor enjoyed this respite from Senate committee work. Before and after each speech, the Idaho senator uncased his guitar and sang Western songs for the crowd. Later he optimistically summarized his success: "The people came in droves. After every speech, I asked them to stand up and be counted if they agreed with me. They did, overwhelmingly. Well, I came back to Washington and decided to step out where I could do some good, maybe in putting the brakes on the drift toward war."[55] In fact, the farther Taylor rode, the more he became con-

---

50 *Lewiston Tribune,* October 21, 1947.
51 *Salt Lake Tribune,* October 10, 1947.
52 *Daily Worker,* October 28, 1947.
53 Ibid., October 21, 1947.
54 "Glen Taylor's Ride," *Newsweek* (October 24, 1947), pp. 26-27.
55 Gervasi, "Low Man on the Wallace Poll," *Collier's* (May 8, 1948), p. 16. As the 1948 election illustrated, Truman's foreign policies were quite popular.

vinced that America's foreign policy was not popular with the masses.

The ride came to an abrupt halt in central Texas when the president called Congress into special session.[56] Taylor was saddle-sore, but he was disappointed at not being able to finish the cross-country trek. In mid-November, he loaded his two horses into the trailer and returned to Washington. A few days later he was photographed wearing a large white Stetson and sitting astride one of his mounts, a sorrel, at the base of the Capitol steps. That evening he spoke to a crowd of a thousand people assembled in the Interior Department's Washington auditorium. Taylor told the crowd that "90-95 percent of the audience had stood" when he asked for a rising vote on whether he should continue his speeches denouncing the Truman administration's foreign policy. He then announced that if he could always have such success with his rides, the next time he "would ride an elephant."[57]

Although Taylor's horseback ride was indicative of his originality and his love of a crowd, there can be no doubt that he was sincerely concerned over foreign affairs. Taylor's opposition to Truman's foreign policy and his advocacy of a world republic were based fundamentally on his belief that World War III had to be avoided and that United States policy was heightening the chances of such an armed conflict. He was worried that the circumvention of the United Nations by both the Truman Doctrine and the Marshall Plan would weaken the new international organization and undermine chances for peace. His concern was shared by some liberals of both parties though most liberals strongly supported the Marshall Plan.[58]

Taylor's main complaint, however, was against the Truman administration's support of totalitarian regimes. These regimes, according to Taylor, were receiving American aid only because they claimed to be fighting communism. In a radio speech, delivered over New York City station WJZ, the Idaho senator contended that United States foreign policy was embarked on a disastrous course:

[56] Taylor apparently did not get all the publicity he craved. When he rode through the Dallas-Fort Worth area, the papers mentioned his coming but did not publish excerpts from his speeches. See *Dallas Morning News* and *Fort Worth Star Telegram*, November 1-10, 1947.

[57] *Salt Lake Tribune*, November 17, 1947. Taylor called, arranged, and conducted the meeting.

[58] Alonzo Hamby, "Truman and the Liberal Movement" (Ph.D. diss., University of Missouri, 1966), p. 179.

"The pathological fear and hatred of Russia . . . is leading some of our more affluent citizens to risk the extinction of mankind in a desperate effort to erase communism from the earth. . . . Our militaristic, Wall Street foreign policy is completely bankrupt. It has failed to make friends of Russia, and by its arrogant manner has cost us the friendship of practically every country on earth."[59]

The most significant result of Taylor's vociferous and continual criticism of the Truman foreign policy was that it made him attractive to a small group of liberals who were considering the formation of a third party late in 1947. The Communist party, which supported this liberal movement, also was impressed by Taylor. When Taylor returned to Washington following his horseback ride, therefore, he started another journey that would lead him into a new party.

[59] *Daily Worker,* November 6, 1947. In other speeches Taylor listed the nations whose democratic development the United States was hindering. He included the Philippines, China, Japan, Indochina, Indonesia, Greece, and most of Latin America. It was especially upsetting to him to have lend-lease aid used in Indochina and Indonesia to thwart popular revolutions against colonial rule by the French and the Dutch respectively; ibid., October 8, 1947; March 3, 1947; September 18, 1946. These addresses were delivered in Boise, Idaho; Grand Rapids, Michigan (Michigan State Democratic Party Convention); and Cleveland, Ohio (Mine, Mill, and Smelter Workers Convention). Taylor also believed that United States' ties with the oil-rich nations of the Middle East were encouraging economic imperialism.

VII. *Progressive Revolt*

On December 29, 1947, Henry A. Wallace formally announced that he would form a new party and seek the American presidency. He had resigned from the Truman cabinet in September 1946 at the president's request. The immediate cause of Wallace's fall was a speech he gave at Madison Square Garden in which he severely criticized the course of American foreign policy. Truman, to keep harmony in his official family, was forced to let Wallace out the back door, although he has said that he disliked doing it.[1]

Wallace, a mystical idealist, was convinced that his years as secretary of agriculture, secretary of commerce, and vice president had given him the experience needed to keep the nation from plunging into a disastrous war. The former editor of *Wallace's Farmer* considered himself the heir of Roosevelt's liberal policies and believed Harry Truman had betrayed those policies. Wallace, like Taylor, thought that cooperation with the Soviet Union, rather than distrust of the Russians, would bring peace to the world. Wallace's and Taylor's views of the Cold War were so similar that eventually the two disenchanted New Dealers were drawn together. Wallace needed someone of prominence who shared his hopes and beliefs to accept the second place on his presidential ticket, and Taylor's speeches and actions in the Senate made him attractive to Wallace.[2]

After Truman asked Wallace for his resignation, Taylor initially refused to take sides. Taylor's first speech in the Senate had been an appeal for the confirmation of Wallace as secretary of commerce.[3] After some consideration, following Wallace's dismissal, Taylor announced that he was in sympathy with Wallace on foreign policy issues. The Idaho senator reiterated his basic contention that world peace depended on cooperation between the United States and Russia.[4]

In retrospect, it is evident that Taylor took two positions in 1947 which convinced Henry Wallace and his backers that Taylor would be an asset to the new party. The first of these was Taylor's stand in opposition to the Truman Doctrine, the proposed Marshall Plan, and aid to China. The second was his repeated insistence that full civil rights be guaranteed for all Americans, including blacks and Communists.

Just ten days before Wallace formally declared his candidacy on a third-party ticket, Taylor asserted on the Senate floor that, in his opinion, American foreign policy was "going to go down in history as one of the most magnificent fiascoes the world has even seen."[5] The only possible benefit, Taylor said, was that "some hungry people will get some food out of it." The Idaho Democrat believed United States foreign policy had failed by giving money to "rotten, falling regimes," such as those of Greece and Nationalist China. According to Taylor, Chiang Kai-shek used the aid to secure his personal well-being with foreign investments. Taylor was convinced that appropriations "for China at this time are like pouring water down a rat hole, only we are pouring corn down the rat hole."[6]

The Idaho senator concluded his remarks with an emotional plea for understanding on the part of his senatorial colleagues: "I have searched my soul, I have gone over the facts, I have read the history books and studied the matter, and I cannot reach any other conclusion than that our foreign policy is going to be disastrous, it is going to make us the laughing stock of the world; we will have gotten in very deep and then will not be able to deliver on our fine promises. It will be a direct aid and comfort to the Communists and will help the spread of Communism."[7] Taylor said that he wished he could approve the Truman foreign policy, that it would be much more pleasant if he could "go along, instead of being practically alone in my criticism of it." Before his horseback ride, he said, he did not believe the American people were against the existing foreign policy, but afterward he was convinced of their opposition to it. In describing his dissenting position, he

---

[1] Truman, *Memoirs*, 1:615. Truman needed to keep the liberal wing, of which Wallace was a vociferous representative, in his camp. Obviously Wallace, who had been replaced by Truman in the vice-presidency during the last Roosevelt administration, had little positive feeling toward his new boss.

[2] Schmidt, *Henry A. Wallace: Quixotic Crusade* (Syracuse, N.Y.: Syracuse University Press, 1960), pp. 23-40.

[3] See Chapter 3, "Fair Deal Senator."

[4] *Salt Lake Tribune*, October 12, 1946.

[5] *Cong. Rec.*, 80th Cong., 1st sess., 1947, 93, pt. 8:11703.

[6] Ibid., p. 11704.

[7] Ibid.

referred to the joke about "the mother who witnessed her son taking part in a military parade, who said, 'They are all out of step but Jim.' I thought I was Jim."[8]

Taylor's consistent stand against the anti-Communist extremists had also endeared him to the Wallace supporters. The Idaho liberal had promised "to battle this [House] un-American Committee to a standstill" and had publicly announced his opposition to outlawing the Communist party.[9] He told a Manhattan audience that as soon as the United States outlawed the party it would go underground, thus becoming much more difficult to control and watch.[10] Frankly, Taylor admitted, "I cannot conceive of outlawing the Communist Party. . . . First it would be the Communists, then the Democrats, and even the Republicans."[11] The press repeatedly asked Taylor whether he would accept Communist support, and by late 1947 his answer was, "I'm not repudiating any support. Anyone who is going my way can come along as far as I'm going."[12] Later Taylor was asked if he would accept support and endorsement of the *Daily Worker,* the Communist party newspaper in the United States. He abruptly told the reporter that anyone could support him who wanted to—"That's something you can't help." Then the Idaho liberal summarized his feelings about the postwar "Red Scare" by exclaiming, "All this talk about Communists gives me . . . a pain."[13] These statements were to create trouble for him from the outset of his candidacy, because such declarations made it difficult for the average voter to judge him without bias.

Taylor felt he had no right to denounce anyone who exercised his American privilege of joining the political party of his choice, "so long as that party does not advocate the overthrow of our Government. I haven't seen any court convict anyone yet for joining."[14] Taylor had a legitimate concern about communism and how to control its spread, but the plan he proposed was neither a witch hunt at home nor direct involvement in foreign aid abroad.

[8] Ibid.

[9] *New York Times,* October 27, 1947, p. 26.

[10] Ibid., December 16, 1947, p. 41.

[11] *Daily Worker,* December 16, 1947. Taylor was addressing a meeting of the Independent Committee of the Arts, Sciences, and Professions—Progressive Citizens of America. Individuals within this group later played an important role in the formation of the Progressive party.

[12] MacDougall, *Gideon's Army* (New York: Marzani & Munsell, 1965), 1:186.

[13] *New York Times,* December 31, 1947, p. 2.

[14] Ibid.

He presented his solution in a November 1947 radio speech. "The Americans who do the most to block the spread of Communism are those of us who strive to protect civil liberty and insure decent incomes for the great majority of our people at home and who offer nondictatorial assistance abroad, through the instrumentalities of the United Nations."[15]

Henry Wallace believed that a United States Senator as the vice-presidential candidate on his ticket would add to the new party's appeal. There was an attempt to persuade Claude Pepper to accept the nomination, but the Florida liberal declined. The Wallace camp then turned all their persuasive forces toward Idaho's political maverick.[16] Two days before Wallace's own announcement of candidacy, Taylor admitted, "I have been tentatively approached and I am giving the matter consideration, but I do not expect to join."[17] Taylor did not leap at the offer. Nearly six stormy weeks would pass before he reached the final decision. The basic question he repeatedly asked himself was, "could a righteous cause overbalance a political future?"[18]

Harold Young, Taylor's distant cousin and Wallace's campaign manager, approached Taylor late in December to see if he would run with Wallace. Taylor then sent J. Albert Keefer, his administrative assistant, to Idaho to sound out Taylor's constituents. By the time Keefer returned, Wallace had made a formal offer to Taylor. Keefer told Taylor that, if he ran, his political career in Idaho was ended.

Taylor was mentally torn by the dilemma. On one occasion Wallace told Taylor, "You've got to join me. . . . You won't be able to live with yourself if you don't."[19] Frank McNaughton, a journalist and Truman biographer, wrote on January 2: "Taylor will finally decline. . . . Taylor will bow out with thanks. . . .

[15] Ann Rothe, ed., *Current Biography* (New York: H. W. Wilson, 1947), p. 630.

[16] MacDougall, *Gideon's Army*, 2:307. Throughout 1947 the most discussed potential Wallace running mate was Senator Pepper. People who wrote to Wallace and asked him to run usually mentioned Pepper or Taylor as a possible running mate. An example is Clarke A. Chambers to Wallace, March 14, 1947, C4453M, Wallace Papers. Chambers, of Berkeley, California, asked Wallace to start a third party; *Daily Worker*, April 14, 1947; ibid., June 30, 1947. The *Worker* later reported that former Assistant Attorney General John Rogge of New York was acceptable to Wallace; January 21, 1948.

[17] *Salt Lake Tribune*, December 30, 1947.

[18] Interview with Glen H. Taylor, June 14, 1967.

[19] Gervasi, "Low Man on the Wallace Poll," *Collier's* (May 8, 1948), p. 16.

About next weekend, if not sooner, Henry Wallace will be fishing around for another prospective running mate."[20]

One factor that Taylor considered thoughtfully was practical economics. A defeat in November would not hurt Henry Wallace financially, but if Taylor defected from the Democrats in 1948, his chances of being reelected to the Senate in 1950 were almost nonexistent. Mrs. Taylor was distraught because her husband lacked a profession to fall back on. A return to show business was impossible, and she asked her husband how they were going to educate their children if he was out of work. Reminding Dora that during their entire life together they had always managed, he added, "besides if there is an atom bomb attack, it doesn't make much difference if they are educated or not."[21]

On January 5, the press asked the Idaho senator whether or not he was going to run. His answer was, "I don't know." Then he explained that the question that concerned him was time: "If I thought we had time I would be willing to wait and work through the regular political machinery. But if I'm convinced that it's all said and done that they are going to get us into war, before another national election . . . , I'd take the great plunge and go with Wallace."[22] He even decided to consult historian Charles Beard in order "to get his ideas from the way history is going as to whether war is likely sooner or not."[23]

Keefer's trip to Idaho prompted many Idahoans, loyal to Taylor, to advise the senator to stay with the Democratic party and let Wallace go his own way. Joe R. Williams, Ada County Democratic chairman, attempted to persuade Taylor, during numerous January and February phone conversations, to remain a Democrat.[24] John Schoonover, a Boise banker, also encouraged the senator to stay with the party.[25] A member of the Idaho Democratic party State

[20] Frank McNaughton to Don Bermingham, January 2, 1948, Frank Mc-Naughton Papers, Truman Library.
[21] Interview with Glen H. Taylor, June 14, 1967. Dora Taylor opposed her husband's talking to Wallace backers. According to Taylor, his wife went through a period of great anguish concerning their future. During January 1948 she lost ten pounds.
[22] *Lewiston Tribune*, January 6, 1948.
[23] Jules Abels, *Out of the Jaws of Victory* (New York: Henry Holt, 1959), p. 34. According to Taylor, he did not consult with Beard: "I said I was going to, but he was gone someplace on a trip, abroad as I recall." Glen H. Taylor to the writer, June 27, 1968.
[24] Interview with Joe R. Williams, September 15, 1967.
[25] Interview with John Schoonover, September 14, 1967.

Central Committee, Sam J. Hyndman, told reporters that it "would be a tragic mistake for Senator Taylor to associate himself with the Henry Wallace third party." Hyndman claimed that Wallace's aspirations would only hurt the common man, whom Taylor had always wanted to aid. In Hyndman's opinion, Taylor's defection to the Wallace party would have a "harmful effect on Senator Taylor's own political future."[26] Charles Gossett, the former senator whom Taylor had helped to defeat in 1946, believed that Taylor was "just itching to run. All his statements tend in that direction."[27]

Taylor, still very much the actor, enjoyed the attention he was receiving from the press as the offer from Wallace dangled over his head. Throughout the last part of December and early January, Taylor met the press nearly every day, and each time he announced that his mind was still not made up. On one occasion, Taylor told reporters that a third party, to win his support, would have to be a "liberal party giving millions of politically displaced people who believed in Franklin D. Roosevelt a home to go to."[28] Finally it seemed that Dora, his advisers, and Idaho Democrats had influenced him to refuse the Wallace offer.[29]

Then a relatively minor event swung the balance in the other direction. Ironically, it was not foreign policy which eventually drove Taylor into the new party, but the dismissal of a New Deal Democrat. When the president requested the resignation of James Landis, chairman of the Civil Aeronautics Board, and a Roosevelt appointee, Taylor interpreted this action as further proof that Truman was betraying the Roosevelt mandate. On the day of the dismissal, Taylor claimed, he had written a letter of refusal to Wallace. Before hearing the news, he put the letter in his pocket and went down to his office with the intention of releasing it to the press. When he reached his desk, the first thing he saw was the morning paper with the story of the Landis dismissal. Taylor considered Landis a leading New Dealer. "When I saw that and started to think of all the other recent Truman dismissals and appointments, I got so disgusted I changed my mind, tore up the letter I had written, and decided to wait awhile."[30]

Taylor particularly wanted to see what kind of men would be

[26] *Oregonian*, January 11, 1948.
[27] Ibid.
[28] *Daily Worker*, December 15, 1947.
[29] *Salt Lake Tribune*, January 6, 1948.
[30] Ibid.

chosen to replace certain Roosevelt appointees. On January 28 Truman demoted Marriner S. Eccles from the chairmanship of the Federal Reserve Board, and two weeks later he dismissed Thomas J. Perran, Jr., the surgeon general. Their replacements were what Taylor considered "friends of the banking interests."

Taylor discussed his position with his "former neighbor SOB," Harry S. Truman. According to Taylor, Truman told him bluntly, "Glen, you don't want to go off and run with that crazy man and ruin your career. Just stick with me and we'll take care of you." Taylor and the president also discussed the world situation. When the Idaho senator expressed his concern that the current foreign policy was leading the United States and Russia toward an armed conflict, Truman answered, "Well those damn Russians. All they understand is force." By the end of the conversation, Taylor was convinced that the militarists and extremists had the president's ear. Yet the Idahoan still hung back from the Wallace crusade.[31] According to one source, Taylor's reluctance was attributed to the amount of pressure exerted upon him by the administration.[32]

It took a final shove by C. B. Baldwin, Wallace's new campaign manager, to settle the matter. Baldwin told Taylor either to join now or to forget it. Even though he realized that the chances of a third party were slim, Taylor asserts, he did have some hope. The victory of a Wallace peace candidate, Leo Issacson, in a special New York City congressional election on February 17, encouraged Taylor to believe that the new party might have an impact at the polls. The Idaho senator termed the Issacson triumph "a very heartening demonstration that the people of America are tired of war and war talk, and are trying to support candidates for office who lead in trying to get along with Russia."[33] The real question in the senator's mind, however, was one of ideals; Taylor believed that honor and decency were at stake. He eventually made the decision to run with Wallace so that "I could get up every morning and look at myself in the mirror and say, 'You did the best you could.' "[34]

By February 20 Taylor's mind was made up. He sent a copy of the statement announcing he would run with Wallace to August

[31] Interview with Glen H. Taylor, June 14, 1967. This meeting probably took place on December 12, 1947. PPF 1626, Truman Papers, shows that the two men met at Truman's office on that day.
[32] *Daily Worker*, January 7, 1948.
[33] Ibid., February 20, 1948.
[34] Interview with Glen H. Taylor, June 14, 1967.

Rosqvist of the Idaho Federation of Labor. Taylor wrote to Rosqvist that even though the labor leader might not agree with his decision, "I hope it will have no effect upon our personal friendship."[35] The next day, however, Taylor denied a newspaper article claiming that he had decided to run—typical political behavior. The Idaho liberal said, "I don't know where they got their information. They didn't get it from me." That same day he received telegrams from state Progressive organizations in Ohio, Missouri, and California urging him to enter the race.[36] A wire from the Progressive group in Maryland was typical: "We can look forward to you as a vice-presidential candidate on the Wallace ticket."[37] Following a phone talk with Wallace and another visit from C. B. Baldwin, Taylor finally made his decision public.

On the night of February 23, 1948, over CBS radio, with Henry Wallace at his side, Taylor told the nation why he had decided to place his future with the new third party. The speech, delivered at 6 P.M., Eastern time, was titled, "Is This the Time for a Third Party?" Glen Taylor's answer was yes.[38]

Attempting to identify with Franklin D. Roosevelt, Taylor quoted at length from a 1940 address in which Roosevelt had attacked conservative Democrats and Republicans, an alliance which Taylor had lamented many times in the past. Now, he added, conservatives were in control of the national Democratic party. Categorizing national Democratic leaders as "conservative lip-service candidates who only talked like they favor liberal democracy," he claimed that Roosevelt had saved the party from splitting into liberal and conservative factions in 1940 by consenting to run for a third term. Taylor exaggerated the New Deal president's criticism of the party in 1940, when he claimed: "I, no more than Roosevelt, could remain in the party which betrayed the principles in which I believe. Happily in 1948 we have a place to go where we can actively carry on the fight. I am not leaving the Democratic Party. It left me. Wall Street and the military have taken over."[39]

The Idaho senator continued with a familiar accusation against the administration for undermining and weakening the United Nations. Reaffirming his faith in the American people, Taylor said

---

[35] Taylor to Rosqvist, February 20, 1948, Political File, Rosqvist Papers.
[36] *Lewiston Tribune*, February 22, 1948.
[37] *Daily Worker*, February 23, 1948.
[38] Ibid., February 20, 1948.
[39] *Spokane Spokesman-Review*, February 24, 1948. This newspaper carried the entire text of Taylor's announcement.

he knew they could cope with "the most serious crisis of their time," the threat of a third world war. Taylor then addressed himself to his Idaho constituents who had elected him to carry out Roosevelt's policies and to work for peace. Taylor said he would be untrue to his promises if he did not take the action he had decided on. The road the country was traveling left him no choice. He told the radio audience, "We dare not falter because a few steps farther down the road we are presently traveling lurks oblivion. Not just another war . . . but atomic and bacteriological oblivion."[40]

The new vice-presidential candidate then reiterated his plan for keeping America out of Communist hands. Alluding to the Communist supporters of the third party, Taylor said, "I am happy to have the support of all those who go along with our program," but then he leveled a warning and a challenge at the Communists: "just let me say to the Communists so there will be no misunderstanding: my efforts in the future as in the past will be directed toward the goal of making our economy work so well and our way of life so attractive and our people so contented that Communism will never interest more than the infinitesimal fraction of our citizens who adhere to it now."[41]

Taylor concluded with praise for Henry Wallace as the man who had contributed more to the welfare of the farmer than any other American. According to Taylor, Wallace's image was that of a man who wanted to live in peace with all the world, and Wallace's name had become synonymous with human welfare. The Idaho liberal announced that he was going to cast his "lot with Henry Wallace in his brave and gallant fight for peace. . . . I am happy and proud, Mr. Wallace, to be associated with you in this great new undertaking."[42]

It became obvious in the press conference following Taylor's

[40] Ibid.

[41] Ibid. The Communist party paper, the *Daily Worker*, supported the Progressive party, but took exception to the quoted Taylor remark. In an editorial published on February 25, 1948, the Communist party organ chastised Taylor for joining the "Red-baiters." The editorial encouraged Taylor to keep up the fight for better living standards and applauded him for consistently striving for the betterment of the workingman.

[42] Ibid. The Progressive movement reached its high-water mark about this time. Polls published in March predicted that the Wallace-Taylor team would receive between eleven million and fifteen million votes. *Daily Worker*, March 9, 1948. These polls were probably inaccurate. Schmidt's, *Quixotic Crusade* is much more exact on the potential of the Progressives.

address that the overriding issue for the new party was going to be communism. Again Taylor was asked if he would repudiate Communist support, and he angrily replied: "Will the old party bosses renounce the support of . . . the National Association of Manufacturers? Will any politician renounce the support of the high moguls of steel trust?"[43] Reminding the reporters that the Communists had supported Roosevelt in 1940 and 1944, the new candidate added, "This new party believes that everybody should run things. Now you wouldn't expect the Communists to support the silk hat crowd, would you?"[44] Finally, in direct answer to the question regarding Communist support, Taylor said, "I'm glad to have their vote. I'm glad to have the votes of any people who support our program."[45] Taylor told the newsmen that he had no fear of being branded a Communist, that he was used to the label, "even though it doesn't apply." He said he had never even read Karl Marx until recently, and then only a couple of chapters. Taylor said he was happy that he was now free to fight the bipartisan conservative coalition and all its works—the Taft-Hartley law, universal military training, the drive toward war, high prices, racial discrimination, and suppressed civil rights.[46]

In Idaho and the Northwest, the reaction to Taylor's announcement of his candidacy ranged from political realism to hostility. A small minority who may have supported his decision were non-vocal. According to Warren Magnuson of Washington, Taylor was on "another horse-back ride to oblivion. This is a two party country. Wallace and Taylor are not going to change that."[47] Wayne Morse of Oregon added, "Senator Taylor has made an unwise decision and a serious political mistake. His program is not in the best interest of preserving our system of American political democracy."[48] Robert Coulter, Taylor's longtime political enemy in the Democratic party of Idaho, said, "Taylor . . . is an opportunist. He is a publicity seeker. . . . He will do anything to see his name blazoned on the front pages of the press of the country."[49] Charles Gossett, the former senator whom Taylor helped defeat in 1946, believed Taylor's departure from the party might "work out for the best—you know, separate the sheep from the goats and let

43 *Oregonian*, February 24, 1948.
44 *Daily Worker*, February 24, 1948.
45 Ibid.   46 Ibid.
47 *Seattle Post-Intelligencer*, February 24, 1948.
48 *Oregonian*, February 24, 1948.
49 *Idaho Statesman*, February 24, 1948.

them be counted."[50]   The Idaho State Democratic chairman, Dan Cavanagh, admitted that Taylor was doing a "good job representing Idaho, but when a man is bigger than his party, . . . he is getting into water way over his head."[51]   Another well-known Idaho Democrat, F. M. Bistline, said, "The Senator is sincere about his beliefs. Don't question that. But I think this is more a matter of taking advantage of an opportunity." Bistline rhetorically asked the press, "What would you do if you had a chance to run for vice-president on any ticket?"[52]

The *Lewiston Morning Tribune,* the only daily paper in the state that Taylor considered even neutral toward him, ran an editorial on February 24, entitled "He Should Resign." They reasoned that Taylor did not have "the moral right" to continue to represent Idaho as a Democratic United States Senator now that he had broken all ties with that party and declared uncompromising war upon it and its candidates. By that act, according to the editorial, he disqualified himself for the office to which he was elected by a majority of the people in Idaho in 1944; he was no longer a Democrat pledged to support the national Democratic administration.[53] The *Statesman,* Boise's daily, editorialized: "we rejoice with Idaho Democrats in general at Senator Taylor's withdrawal from his party. . . . They are well rid of an unscrupulous political blackguard."[54]

Anticipating the harsh response to his candidacy, Taylor wrote an open letter to the Democrats of Idaho telling them why he had made the decision. He explained how discouraging it was to combat "the dominant reactionary influences" on the Senate floor. He reemphasized his contention that "Wall Street and the militarists" were in power and that the alliance of the Truman administration with bankers and militarists had "betrayed the rank and file and those of us who believe in the principles for which Franklin Delano Roosevelt fought and died."[55]   Concluding with a plea for continued personal friendship, Taylor wrote, "I hope that those who disagree with me will give me credit for being sincere and that we may continue to be friends although we differ in our approach to this problem."[56]

[50] *Salt Lake Tribune,* February 24, 1948.
[51] Ibid.   [52] Ibid.
[53] *Lewiston Tribune,* February 24, 1948.
[54] *Idaho Statesman,* February 25, 1948.
[55] Ibid.   [56] Ibid.

Taylor did not have time to sit and ponder his fate in the "Gem State." Senate debates on the Marshall Plan and the Universal Military Training bill awaited him in Washington. Much of his preconvention activity was designed to prove to Idahoans that, "Simply because I have accepted this new responsibility does not mean I will in any way slight my work as an Idaho senator. It just means I'll have to work that much harder."[57] Taylor assumed the role of the new party's spokesman in the Senate chamber, but evenings and weekends found the vice-presidential candidate anywhere from Macon, Georgia, to Coeur d'Alene, Idaho.

One of Taylor's Senate duties, from the new party's standpoint, was to engage in a continuous attack on the Truman administration. On March 5 Taylor wrote a letter to the president suggesting that the latter should request the resignations of army Generals Douglas MacArthur and A. C. Wedemeyer on the grounds that they had criticized the Truman policy toward China in testimony delivered before the House Foreign Affairs Committee. MacArthur and Wedemeyer had strongly advocated continued military and economic support of Chiang Kai-shek in China, even though Truman and Secretary of State Marshall were convinced that Chiang's government was hopelessly corrupt.[58] Taylor contended that Truman had fired Wallace because the former secretary of commerce was critical of foreign policy, and "in order that you may be consistent with the policy which you laid down in the case of Mr. Wallace, I suggest that the resignations of General MacArthur and General Wedemeyer must also be requested."[59] Truman brushed this aside with a totally noncommittal, sarcastic note: "I am appreciative of your interest in my Administration and in the welfare of China."[60]

During a debate on whether or not the Senate should recommend that the veto in the United Nations Security Council be abolished, Taylor managed to change the topic to the Marshall Plan. He told his colleagues that the United States was not trying to give economic assistance to Europe, but instead was attempting to dominate all of Western Europe economically. According to Taylor, the Truman Doctrine and the Marshall Plan would make the United

[57] *Lewiston Tribune*, February 28, 1948.
[58] U. S., Department of State, Papers Relating to the Foreign Relations of the United States, *United States Relations with China*, 1950, pp. 766-75.
[59] Taylor to Truman, March 5, 1948, OF150, Truman Papers.
[60] Truman to Taylor, March 8, 1948, ibid.

Nations powerless and useless.[61] Using this opportunity to let loose a thrust at what he considered the true enemies of peace in America—the anti-Communist extremists, Taylor said, "The glory of spending money to fight Communism commands such attention in the press of America that even to bask in the reflection of the spot light, throws an aura upon all those who can even get close to the center of the stage."[62] Taylor blamed the "reactionary press, the generals and admirals, big figures in the finance and business world and, of course, those politicians who like to go with the tide" for creating a tidal wave of support for "giving away billions and billions to try and bribe people not to be Communists."[63]

Declaring that the United States had not even tried to achieve peace with the Russians, Taylor said that before the administration formed economic and military alliances, it should at least attempt to talk things over with the Soviets. Taylor said he assumed "that the Russians are not absolutely hopeless, and that it is possible to get along with them." He acknowledged that by taking this stand he was laying himself "open to the charge of being a Communist— a Communist sympathizer, at least." The liberal senator then warned his colleagues: "if they want to call me 'red,' . . . by insinuation or innuendo . . . I say, let them beware, because I shall come back in kind."[64] Now speaking to a nearly empty chamber, but to a packed gallery, Taylor concluded with attacks on American oil interests, the press, and American economic control over Latin America.[65] Before taking his seat, the Idaho senator made sure that when the Senate reconvened the next day, he would again have the floor.

The following day, March 10, Taylor introduced a substitute bill for the Marshall Plan. He began his lengthy remarks with an affirmation of his love for the United States: "this is by far the best country on earth. . . . If I did not love my country, if I were willing to see it destroyed, I would skip the whole thing."[66] But the true patriot, said Taylor, had to remain an objective critic of his country and himself. Speaking to only eleven colleagues, Taylor continued: "If I were easily terrified, I would turn my back on . . . [the] . . . struggle . . . and make my peace. . . . I cannot

[61] *Cong. Rec.*, 80th Cong., 2d sess., 1948, 93, pt. 2:2387.
[62] Ibid.
[63] Ibid.
[64] Ibid.
[65] *Oregonian*, March 8, 1948.
[66] *Cong. Rec.*, 80th Cong., 2d sess., 1948, 93, pt. 2:2453.

do that. For the sake of my wife and children, I almost wish I could." He then added, "We cannot save ourselves by hiding in the mob and joining in the clamor because in another war the mob will be destroyed—all of us."[67]

With this introduction, Taylor placed before the Senate his "Peace and Reconstruction Act of 1948." The act was designed to repudiate the military implications of the Truman Doctrine by turning all peacekeeping operations over to the United Nations. Economic rehabilitation, the aim of the Marshall Plan, was to be financed by contributions from the member nations of the UN, with top priority for aid going to those who had suffered the most during the war. Contrasting his bill with the Marshall Plan, Taylor claimed that his was for peace and reconstruction, whereas the Truman Doctrine prepared for war and put Europe on a permanent dole. Finally, he stated, "If the American people could choose freely, they would choose for peace, not war; for genuine reconstruction, not permanent poverty. I am convinced they will choose our way in November."[68] Taylor's substitute bill, which was not taken seriously, was defeated, 3–74 the same day. Only Claude Pepper and William Langer voted with Taylor for the proposal. The Marshall Plan easily won approval.[69]

Two days later, Taylor's old friend and colleague Wayne Morse, while admitting he knew the Idaho senator was not a Communist, said that there was nothing in Taylor's speech and proposal that could not have been written in the Kremlin. The Oregonian accused Taylor of presenting Russian propaganda and the Communist position. Taylor replied that the fact that he shared the Communist opinion of the Marshall Plan and the Truman Doctrine did not mean he was a Communist.[70]

Taylor continued to criticize the Truman foreign policy and administration officials throughout the spring of 1948. On March 21, at the same time that petitions were being circulated in Idaho demanding his own recall, Taylor sent Truman a letter demanding that Secretary of Defense James Forrestal be asked to resign so that "our national policy . . . will be free from the taint of oil imperialism."[71] Taylor had discovered that Forrestal's business

---

[67] Ibid., p. 2454.
[68] Ibid., p. 2458.
[69] Ibid., p. 2749.
[70] Ibid., p. 2684.
[71] *New York Times*, March 22, 1948, p. 15. According to the *Daily Worker*, March 22, 1948, Taylor accused Forrestal of hindering the formulation of an

address was the same as that of the investment banking firm, Dillon-Read, Inc. This firm, according to Taylor, handled the financing operations of Texaco and Standard Oil of California, the American owners of the Arabian-American Oil Company. Forrestal's relationship with the oil interests explained, Taylor believed, both the Truman Doctrine and United States reluctance to aid in the establishment of a Jewish state in Palestine. Taylor continued his attacks on Forrestal for the rest of the campaign.

Each weekend Taylor went to some area to help organize the new party and give its adherents an enthusiastic speech. His orations outside Washington were similar to those given in the Senate, except that they were even more cutting and bitter. On April 16, in St. Cloud, Minnesota, he said: "This country would be even more belligerent than Russia is now if Russia was furnishing armament to Mexico, for instance, in as great quantity as we are arming Turkey, a Russian neighbor. If war comes because America does things bigger and better than anyone, we shall have bigger concentration camps and better roasting ovens."[72] At Fairmont, West Virginia, Taylor told his audience that "fear is behind the Russian moves. . . . They are trying to build a bulwark of countries around Russia to protect themselves."[73] A month later in Macon, Georgia, the Idaho senator, keynoting the Georgia Progressive Convention, again assailed United States foreign policy. He warned the delegates that "we are fighting for our lives. I don't suppose our brass hats, . . . if they started a war, would stop after dropping 249 atom bombs."[74] Invariably Taylor concluded his speeches with a reiteration of his contention that America and the Soviet Union could exist peacefully together.

It is difficult to assess Taylor's success or failure during the campaign. Henry Wallace's uncle, Dan Wallace, wrote that he traveled to Brainerd, Minnesota, to hear Taylor and was quite impressed, especially when Taylor engaged in conversation. Dan Wallace wrote, "When off the record he clicks well with people and seems to have great possibilities as he develops with experience."[75]

effective and balanced foreign policy. Besides the Middle East and oil, Taylor pointed to the Palestine partition and circumvention of the United Nations as examples of Forrestal's influences. This letter was not located at the Truman Library.

[72] MacDougall, *Gideon's Army*, 2:452.
[73] *Lewiston Tribune*, April 4, 1948.
[74] *Daily Worker*, May 10, 1948.
[75] Dan Wallace to Henry Wallace, May 23, 1948, 66413M, Wallace Papers.

James Lecron, a Progressive supporter from Berkeley, California, wrote to Wallace after hearing Taylor speak at the University of California, "He handled himself extremely well and made an excellent speech which evidently pleased the students."[76]

By late spring the Progressive crusade was moving in high gear. Their vice-presidential candidate spent most of his time during May and June championing two causes which were an intrinsic part of the Progressive program. The liberal Idahoan attacked Jim Crow in Alabama and railed against universal military training and the draft on the Senate floor. On these two vital issues, Taylor found himself in the forefront of the battle to create an America where liberty and peace reigned supreme.

[76] James Lecron to Wallace, March 31, 1948, 66223M, ibid.

VIII. *Fighting Jim Crow & the Draft*

Glen Taylor's attempt to unseat Senator Theodore Bilbo in 1946–1947 made him a champion of the black American. Many Negroes, in the North and South, joined the Progressive party because of its vociferous denunciation of racial discrimination.

As the Progressive party's vice-presidential candidate in 1948, Taylor went into the southern states and confronted segregation directly. It was the policy of the Progressives not to speak at segregated meetings. Taylor became involved in one of the most dramatic episodes of the entire campaign when he refused to address the Southern Negro Youth Congress in Birmingham, Alabama, because of that city's ordinance requiring segregated public gatherings. Representatives of the Youth Congress which was on the attorney general's list of Communist-front organizations, persuaded Taylor to tell an audience of 150 blacks and twenty whites why he could not address them.[1] As the Progressive candidate approached the Alliance Gospel Tabernacle, a small Negro church, police officers surrounded the entrance.[2]

Patrolman W. W. Casey physically blocked the entrance and told Taylor, "Buddy, you can't go in there. The entrance for white people is on the side." Attempting to shove his way past the officer, Taylor answered, "I'm not particular about these things."[3] Casey grabbed the politician under the arms and swung him around to face two more armed policemen. In the ensuing melee, Taylor was knocked from the small three-step porch and landed on all fours.[4] Leaping up with his fists clenched and swinging at the officers, he shouted, "I'm a United States Senator. You can't arrest me!"[5] He was mistaken. After he had torn his trousers, cut his hand, and bruised his shin while he was pushed over a low wire fence, Taylor was literally thrown into a squad car. As the police car pulled away with sirens blaring, the youngsters inside the church began singing, "Taylor is our leader. . . . We shall not be moved."[6]

Taylor was taken to the police station and brought before Birmingham's noted segregationist police commissioner, Eugene "Bull" Connor. Convinced that Taylor was merely seeking notoriety and headlines, Connor put the senator in the "bullpen" with the common criminals, after a prolonged fingerprinting and frisking session.[7] Later Taylor told reporters, "They treated me very rough —anything but gentlemanly. God help the ordinary man."[8] He then remarked, "I was also shown in the jail . . . how Negroes are treated. An officer told a tall, slim Negro to 'turn around, n----r, before I knock your head off.' "[9]

There was considerable reaction to Taylor's arrest among Progressive leaders throughout the country. To many, a constitutional question was the key issue. As Taylor said, "My arrest and han-handling by the city police, who barred my entrance to a meeting in a local Negro church is a blatant violation of my constitutional rights."[10] Collins George, one of the editors of the *Pittsburgh Courier,* added, "Now is the time to test the constitutionality of the U. S. Supreme Court decisions against Jim Crow."[11] The following day the Civil Rights Congress offered legal aid to the Idaho senator.[12]

Support for Taylor poured in from other areas. Many labor

---

[1] "Subversive Organizations and Publications," Democratic National Committee Clipping File, Truman Papers. Taylor often attacked Attorney General Tom Clark and his list of subversive organizations. In one speech, he told an audience at the Manhatten Center, "The only purpose behind such prescribed lists is to browbeat people into silence. If we do not stand up and speak now on behalf of the right of others to speak and assemble peaceably, in a short time no one will be able to stand up and challenge the ruling oligarchy of militarists and monopolists whom a mischance of fate has placed in such dominant control of our foreign policies." *Daily Worker,* March 25, 1948.

[2] "Glen Taylor and Jim Crow," *Newsweek* (May 10, 1948), p. 24.

[3] *Cong. Rec.,* 80th Cong., 2d sess., 1948, 94, pt. 5:5186. Angry at the Senate for refusing even to mention the incident, Taylor gave the august body a blow-by-blow description when he returned to Washington.

[4] Ibid.

[5] Curtis D. MacDougall, *Gideon's Army,* 3 vols. (New York: Marzani and Munsell, 1965), 3:391.

[6] *Daily Worker,* May 3, 1948.

[7] *Cong. Rec.,* 80th Cong., 2d sess., 1948, 94, pt. 5:5186. Taylor also claimed that the officers who drove him from the church to the jail took a long "round-about" course in order to harass and intimidate him.

[8] "Anything But Gentlemanly," *Time* (May 10, 1948).

[9] *Daily Worker,* May 3, 1948.

[10] Ibid.

[11] Ibid.

[12] Ibid., May 4, 1948.

leaders openly assailed Birmingham for arresting Taylor, and a group of University of Michigan professors and students held a rally in response to the Birmingham incident.[13] Henry Wallace forecast the death of the Democratic party because of the Taylor case. Referring to the case of Matthew Lyon in 1799, Wallace pointed out that in spite of Lyon's imprisonment for violating the Alien and Sedition Acts, the Vermont congressman was reelected. According to Wallace, "No party . . . can claim to be liberal and still stand for Jim Crow. Glen was not violating any law. He was upholding the basic law of the land, the Constitution of the United States."[14]

At the subsequent trial, Judge Oliver B. Hall attacked those working for social equality and a breakdown of racial barriers as outside influences that were "bad for the colored people themselves."[15] When Hall ridiculed Taylor as a guitarist, the senator yelled something back at the judge. Immediately Paul McMahon, a policeman, quieted the senator by remarking, "Buddy, you are under arrest and you'll have to be quiet."[16] Later McMahon told reporters, "The feelings of the nigras was running high and I knew that we might start something that we couldn't stop."[17] Silenced, Taylor was forced to restrict himself to squirming as he listened to more of Judge Hall's pronouncements on racial equality.

The episode resulted in Taylor's conviction on charges of breach of the peace, assault and battery, and resisting arrest. Upon hearing of the conviction, Taylor announced, "The sentence is of no consequence. It was not unexpected, and I planned to appeal it anyway."[18] Fined fifty dollars and given a 180-day suspended jail sentence, Taylor, through his attorneys, appealed the decision to the Alabama Supreme Court, which upheld the Birmingham police court's decision. Taylor was angry because the state court refused to hear testimony on the legality of the Birmingham segregation ordinance, the constitutionality of which Taylor considered to be the important issue in the case.[19]

[13] Ibid., May 16, 1948.
[14] Ibid., May 6, 1948.
[15] Ibid., May 23, 1948.
[16] Ibid.
[17] Ibid. Most of the *Daily Worker's* reporting on the Taylor case was handled by Abner W. Berry, a black author. His most extensive article, entitled "Alabama Justice Was Defendant at Taylor Trial," appeared on May 23, 1948.
[18] Ibid., May 6, 1948.
[19] *New York Times,* March 10, 1950, p. 3.

In June 1950 Taylor's attorneys, in a petition to the United States Supreme Court, asserted that compulsory segregation abridged the civil rights of both whites and blacks because it denied white citizens "who desire freely to assemble and associate with Negroes, the right to do so."[20] The Supreme Court refused to hear the Taylor case, so the city of Birmingham began the preliminaries for extradition proceedings. "Bull" Connor, the police commissioner, announced, "We are going to get him, wherever he is, at once!" Taylor replied from Pocatello, Idaho, that he had "no intention of turning myself over to that chain gang."[21] The city of Birmingham sent the necessary papers to Alabama's governor, James E. Folsom, requesting that he demand extradition. Following an examination of the case, Folsom declared that he would not ask for extradition because of the suspended sentence and the pettiness of the litigation. The Birmingham incident thereupon passed into history.[22]

During these legal proceedings, Taylor continued to agitate for increased civil rights for American blacks. From his new position outside the major parties, he was able to blast both the Democrats and Republicans. In one speech, the Idaho senator exclaimed, "Both old parties stand condemned. . . . The Republicans are exposed because they have a majority in Congress and could take action. . . . The Democrats stand condemned because . . . Truman has the power by executive order to eliminate segregation in the armed service and in federal employment. Nothing has been done by either party."[23]

The Progressives counted heavily on the Negro vote if they were to make any kind of impact at the polls. As Taylor stated in his column, "Fighting Words," which was carried in the *Citizen,* a Progressive monthly: "It is significant to note how strong Negro participation has been in the organizational meetings of the New Party in the South. Some day all Americans, white and black, will pay tribute to these brave people, even as those of us who have seen this inspiring sight with our own eyes pay tribute to them now."[24] Taylor later was to discover a new platform from which

20 Ibid., June 6, 1950, p. 23.
21 Ibid., October 10, 1950, p. 28.
22 Ibid., November 16, 1950, p. 17.
23 *Daily Worker,* June 8, 1948.
24 Glen H. Taylor, "Fighting Words," *Citizen,* May 1948. This paper may be found in the New York Public Library. Taylor's column appeared only in May and June.

to fight discrimination when the Truman proposal for universal military training came to the Senate floor.

Peacetime conscription, like racial discrimination, was to become one of the major issues of the Progressive party's election campaign. The campaign was taking place during the hateful, suspicious days of the Cold War. The world was becoming bi-polarized ideologically—the so-called free world against the Communist bloc. The political and economic instability of many governments in Europe, the Middle East, and Asia, and the threat of the Communists taking advantage of the chaotic conditions, led to the philosophy of containment as epitomized by the Truman Doctrine and the Marshall Plan. Believing that force should be met with force, Truman, in March 1948, called for a larger army and requested conscription as a method to raise that army.[25]

The most vociferous individual opponent of Truman's proposal for the draft was Glen Taylor. Taylor's opposition to selective service in 1948 resulted in part from his dislike of the military establishment, a dislike he had expressed many times in the past. As a candidate for the Senate in 1940, he had announced his displeasure when Roosevelt called for the establishment of the draft. According to Taylor, a large standing army could not be trusted because "with a huge army just waiting, some General will want to use it."[26] As a freshman senator he attacked the army because of its treatment of conscientious objectors and because of archaic court-martial proceedings. On January 24, 1946, Taylor had written to Truman urging the President to "grant a full amnesty and pardon to all persons who have heretofore on grounds of conscientious principle refused to comply with any provision of the Selective-Service Act of 1940,"[27] and arguing that, "As a nation we have been disposed to temper justice with mercy. In this case it is a matter of replacing no longer needed expediency with simple justice."[28]

In a 1947 speech, Taylor had accused the army and its court-martial system of being "completely deficient in safeguarding the right to a fair and impartial trial which we have always believed to be the birthright of every American."[29] According to Taylor,

---

[25] Barton J. Bernstein and Allen J. Marusow, eds., *The Truman Administration: A Documentary History* (New York: Harper and Row, 1966), p. 270.

[26] Interview with Glen H. Taylor, June 14, 1967, Millbrae, California.

[27] Glen H. Taylor to Harry S. Truman, January 24, 1946, Official File 111, Truman Papers.

[28] Ibid.

many of the defendants were not "adequately represented by counsel and the judges at the trial seemed to be men whose background is utterly devoid of training."[30] He had concluded this 1947 speech with a request that the army review all cases of men still serving prison terms.

Taylor's dislike of the military establishment again became evident in 1948, when he concentrated his attack on the principle of the draft. The Truman proposal for peacetime conscription in March 1948 called for a bipartisan effort to institute universal military training in order to meet any emergency and to let "the world know of our determination to back the will to peace with the strength of peace."[31] From the first, Taylor was very critical of the president's proposal.

The day after Truman's message, Taylor warned his colleagues that he would fight any such proposal. "If the President meant that we must all unite for military training, if he meant that all political factions must unite to reimpose the draft upon the American people —if that is what the President meant,"—the senator paused, took a deep breath, and continued—"I can guarantee that there will be political opposition, that there will not be unanimity, and although we may not be permitted to carry on for a very long period of time, we shall certainly fight the drive toward war, this surrender to Wall Street and the military, to our last breath of Freedom."[32]

Taylor was speaking to a packed gallery and an inattentive Senate. His deep blue eyes flashed with emotion, his delivery was near perfect, and his physical gestures were timed excellently. But his words were what captivated the gallery audience: "If speaking out against military conscription and against the militarization of our country carries any blame with it, I am perfectly willing to accept it; but . . . I feel it will redound to my credit that I oppose this measure."[33] After a brief pause, Taylor resumed: "As a member of the new party that is appearing on the American scene, I am happy to accept responsibility for trying to delay or defeat this

---

[29] *Cong. Rec.*, 79th Cong., 1st sess., 1947, 93, pt. 2:2053.

[30] Ibid.

[31] Bernstein and Marusow, *The Truman Administration*, p. 271. In his memoirs, Truman makes a big issue of the need to get American boys in physical shape. He was upset that 34 percent flunked their induction physical. He believes that if universal military training had been enacted, it is doubtful there would have been a Berlin crisis or the Korean War. Truman, *Memoirs,* 2:71-73.

[32] *Cong. Rec.*, 80th Cong., 2d sess., 1948, 94, pt. 3:2993.

[33] *Cong. Rec.*, 80th Cong., 2d sess., 1948, 94, pt. 7:8778.

peacetime conscription measure. . . . If the two old parties want
the responsibility of instituting a peacetime military conscription,
they are perfectly welcome to it, so far as I am concerned and so
far as the new party is concerned."³⁴ The Idaho senator concluded
with a pointed denunciation of the entire diplomatic course being
followed by the administration and asserted that it reminded him
of Germany during the 1930s.

As soon as Taylor finished, many of his senatorial colleagues,
including Wayne Morse of Oregon, Homer Capehart of Indiana,
Alben Barkley of Kentucky, and William Knowland of California,
took turns viciously attacking Taylor's attitude and his statements.
The Idaho senator apologized for having to disagree with his dis-
tinguished associates, but he emphasized that he believed what
he had said.³⁵ From this point on, during the three months before
peacetime conscription actually came before the Senate for consideration, Taylor, as the Progressive spokesman, repeatedly attacked the administration on the issue of conscription.

Taylor's opposition to the draft reached a climax in June 1948,
when the issue was brought to the Senate floor. As soon as it
became evident from the debate that peacetime conscription was
gaining favor, Taylor joined William Langer of North Dakota in
a filibuster against Senate approval of reenacting selective service.

Taylor based his argument against the draft on five major
premises. In the first place, he contended, peacetime draft was a
clear break with American tradition. Second, Taylor feared that
conscription would create a huge military complex that would
keep the economy geared to military rather than consumer production. His third argument was, "With atomic bombs available
to threaten annihilation, why have a large army?" Fourth, the
Idaho senator maintained that before any more black citizens were
drafted into the army, the commander in chief should use his
executive power to integrate the existing armed forces. Finally,
he contended that the resumption of military training was an admission to the world that America was arming for war and that
her foreign policy had failed.

Regarding the first point, that a peacetime draft constituted a
fundamental change in American life, Taylor said, "Never have we
had peacetime conscription. The question is whether our Nation
is to be militarized or whether it is to remain a great, free nation,

³⁴ Ibid.
³⁵ Ibid., pt. 3:2994-95.

as it has been . . . since our country was founded."[36] The Idaho Progressive argued that in wartime the United States had always done better militarily than her enemies who had mandatory military service, but in peacetime it had not flaunted military strength. It would be foolish, Taylor said, to fall for the idea that "it is possible to have peace by getting ready for war. . . . The old admonition is that those who live by the sword shall perish by the sword."[37] As justification for his filibuster against the draft attempting to postpone Senate action, Taylor explained, "Since we are in the process of losing all our ancient liberties, if I can just postpone this matter a little while, this urge to emulate the countries of Europe, . . . I think the urge for the adoption of the proposed draft system will pass, and we shall regain our equilibrium and our sanity and will have no more of this business."[38] It was Taylor's belief that although preventing a peacetime draft was difficult, getting rid of it once it was adopted would be much harder.

Taylor's second argument against the draft stemmed from his abhorrence of the idea of a large standing army and the possibility of an economy based on armament production. In a Portland, Oregon, speech in 1947, the Idaho senator had charged that the State Department had been turned over to representatives of the military and Wall Street. He had asked his audience, "Do they want to get us into war, or do they want to keep us just short of war so that there will be billions spent on armaments?"[39]

During one of his 1948 speeches against the draft, Taylor warned his colleagues against a military industrial complex: "Once it is saddled on us it will be impossible to get rid of it, because when a large segment of our industry is making guns, tanks, and planes, jobs will depend upon making guns, tanks, and planes, and profits will depend upon making guns, tanks, and planes."[40] Paraphrasing a passage from the Bible, he said, "Where your purse is, there also is your heart." He grimly predicted that once an armament economy was accepted, war would be inevitable. "I fail to find in history any instance where a country built up a great arms establishment and did away with it without using it."[41] Reemphasizing the point,

[36] Ibid., pt. 7:8778. Taylor's statement was not accurate, since the Selective Service Act of 1940 was officially a peacetime measure.
[37] Ibid., pt. 6:7585.
[38] Ibid., pt. 7:8991.
[39] *Daily Worker*, October 10, 1947.
[40] *Cong. Rec.*, 80th Cong., 2d sess., 1948, 94, pt. 6:7586.
[41] Ibid.

he then added, "Every factory that is opened up to producing armaments makes it that much more difficult ever to get out of the armament business, ever to make a really sincere effort to try to attain peace in the world because it becomes a vested interest."[42] Taylor cynically concluded that he had no doubt that the economy could survive another war, but he feared what would happen "if peace broke out."

Taylor's third reason for opposing the draft was that the stock-piling of atomic bombs made the draft unnecessary. During the filibuster he declared, "Inasmuch as we have . . . enough bombs to kill everyone in the world, including ourselves, I fail to see the percentage in starting a war. No one is going to win. We are all going to die if a war were to come."[43] And since modern warfare would be universally destructive, Taylor further stated, "there is no need for this idiotic draft . . . I do not see that it makes any difference whether we draft them first or kill them first."[44] Sarcastically the Progressive vice-presidential candidate asked, "Why worry whether those who are destroyed have on a uniform or whether they are in civilian garb?"[45] The threat of annihilation by an atomic explosion was real in 1948, and therefore Taylor believed that the best thing to do was to try to keep the peace. A policy aiming toward peace, rather than preparing for war, he asserted, was what the Progressive party offered.[46]

Taylor's fourth reason for opposing the draft involved the problem of segregation. An outspoken advocate of full equality for Negroes, Taylor told his colleagues that the draft not only forced military service on the Negroes, "but once they are inducted, then we segregate them, and discriminate against them."[47] In opposing the conscription bill, he proclaimed, "I am . . . speaking to prevent further insults, further hurt being done to certain of our American citizens whose skins are off-color. . . . I at least will not inflict upon them the compulsion of serving in the armed establishment where they have to submit to flagrant discrimination, where they are made flunkies and bus boys." It was difficult enough for blacks to avoid segregation in American society, but if they were drafted, there was no way for them to avoid it. "We will at least have

42 Ibid., pt. 7:8780.
43 Ibid., p. 8781.
44 Ibid., p. 8802.
45 Ibid., pt. 6:7586.
46 Ibid.
47 Ibid., pt. 7:8791.

them out in the open, where they do not have to go and be discriminated against if they want to keep away from it."[48] The Idaho liberal cautioned his colleagues that if the draft act was passed and discrimination was not outlawed, many young men in America, like those of Nazi Germany, would be brought in contact with the idea "of a super-race . . . for the first time when they go to the military camps and see some other Americans segregated because God made their skins a different color."[49]

Taylor was extremely critical of Truman for not providing the vigorous leadership necessary to wipe out discrimination in the armed forces and throughout the executive branch of government. "The President has had the power to abolish segregation and discrimination in the armed services. He has failed to do so. He has had power to abolish discrimination and segregation in Federal employment simply by issuing an Executive order. He has failed to do . . . even that simple thing."[50] Taylor, the Progressives, and Hubert H. Humphrey share some of the credit for prodding Truman into using his executive powers to initiate measures designed to stamp out segregation in the executive branch later in 1948. The real impetus for executive action, however, came from the civil rights leadership. A. Philip Randolph, the National Association for the Advancement of Colored People, and others met with Truman and prodded the president toward positive action.[51]

Taylor's final argument rested upon the premise that the resumption of the draft admitted to the world that the United States' foreign policy was not working, that the United Nations was only a "paper lion," and that America was embarking on an arms race. During the two-day filibuster against the draft, Taylor contended that the Truman policy was losing America friends around the world, especially among the new emerging nations of Africa and Asia, as well as in South America. Arguing that the United States was supporting reactionary "cardboard governments" throughout the world, Taylor claimed those governments would "not amount to a hill of beans if any trouble starts."[52] The Idaho senator indicted American diplomacy for "helping bad people everywhere." For example, he said, "In China we are helping Chiang Kai-shek,

48 Ibid.
49 Ibid., pt. 6:7256.
50 Ibid., p. 7254.
51 Richard M. Dalfiume, *Desegregation of the U.S. Armed Forces, 1939-1953* (Columbia: University of Missouri Press, 1969), pp. 163-66.
52 *Cong. Rec.*, 80th Cong., 2d sess., 1948, 94, pt. 6:7588.

whose government is so corrupt that it takes a part of the guns we send them to fight the Communists and sells them to the Communists. . . . That keeps the Communists in business, which scares us so badly that we send China more guns, which are sold to the Communists, and we are scared some more, so we send China more guns."[53] Taylor branded as ridiculous the contention that all world discontent was Communist-inspired. He believed the "Red Scare" was artificial and had been whipped up out of all proportion. Although he was condemned by his associates as being heretical, he told the Senate that he believed the Russians wanted peace: "the Russians have figured out some crazy fool idea whereby they can live better in peacetime than in wartime."[54]

When Taylor's colleagues finally wrested control of the floor from him on June 19, 1948, thus ending the filibuster, he was reading one of the many telegrams he had received congratulating him on his "noble effort." The final telegram he read was from a young New York housewife who thanked Taylor for representing "the desires and interests of the people instead of the special interests of the enemies of peace. God give you strength."[55] At this point, Owen Brewster of Maine called Taylor to order for using "language unworthy of the conduct of a Senator." Irving Ives of New York, who was presiding, upheld Brewster's contention that Taylor had accused those who supported the draft of being "enemies of peace." Reluctantly Taylor sat down, and the Senate passed peacetime conscription shortly afterward.[56] Determined to the end, Taylor one month later introduced a bill to repeal the law.[57] Naturally, his repeal legislation never got out of committee, so in 1949, he reintroduced a repeal act, but it suffered the same fate.[58]

Taylor's attempt to defeat peacetime conscription did not mean that he was turning his back on the military completely. His philosophy was that in peacetime, "service in the Army should be considered as an occupation, as a job. . . . We pay enough money to get men to work in the State Department and in other departments of Government, and I feel that in peacetime we should pay enough money to get the necessary men to serve in our armed forces."[59] Taylor contended that the United States was not at war

[53] Ibid.
[54] Ibid., p. 7587.
[55] Ibid., pt. 8:8995.
[56] Ibid.
[57] Ibid., p. 9449.
[58] Ibid., 81st Cong., 1st sess., 1949, 95, pt. 1:550.

in 1948, and there was no need to draft an army. According to him, a decision to draft was an admission of aggression.

The Progressives were partly successful in their drive to defeat universal military training and the draft. Although the Selective Service bill was enacted, universal military training remained a wishful thought on the part of Truman and the Department of Defense.

Taylor's role in the new party's campaign continued to be that of a rabble-rouser, recruiter, and newsmaker. The ex-trouper, familiar with showmanship, used the same techniques he had employed in Idaho elections since 1938. One of the conditions under which Taylor had finally consented to join Wallace was that Dora and the children could travel with him on his campaign trips.[60] He took his family, which now included a third son, Gregory, born in 1946, everywhere during the campaign. The last week of July 1948 Taylor took the entire family to the new party's convention in Philadelphia.

---

[59] Ibid., 79th Cong., 1st sess., 1945, 91, pt. 7:9020.
[60] MacDougall, *Gideon's Army*, 2:307.

IX. *The Fall of Gideon's Army*

Henry Wallace's decision to launch a new party was a direct result of a number of divergent forces. The party's convention in July 1948 was the outgrowth of a series of events beginning with Roosevelt's death and Truman's ascension to the presidency. By the summer of 1946 there were two main currents of political unrest plaguing Truman. One was criticism of foreign policy, led by Henry A. Wallace, then secretary of commerce. The second, criticism of domestic policy, was led by labor leaders who were disturbed over Truman's handling of labor problems and were thinking in terms of a new and powerful labor party. Wallace originally wanted to work within the Democratic party, but after his dismissal from the Truman cabinet, the dedicated New Dealer began to work with the third-party advocates.[1]

Support for Wallace's criticism of the Truman foreign policy came mainly from six groups: the old line New Dealers, the Political Action Committee of the CIO, leaders of other labor organizations, the Negro civil rights groups, a sprinkling of professional politicians (such as Taylor, Kilgore, and Pepper), and the Communist fringe. Originally the Communists were critical of the Wallace speech at Madison Square Garden in September 1946, but after Wallace was fired, they changed their tack. Two quotations from the *Daily Worker* illustrate this reversal. The day following the address, the *Worker* reported that Wallace had "implied the U. S. was innocent in this struggle between Britain and Soviet Russia." The paper also accused Wallace of "expounding the peace ideals of the late President Roosevelt . . . but defending the policies which are undermining those ideals."[2] Only four days later, the paper declared "that the main features of Mr. Wallace's speech represented a criticism which we have long been making in our own modest way."[3]

After Wallace announced that he would form a third party, only one group, the Communist Party of America, lined up behind him. Wallace, who hoped to "usher in the century of the common man" with his "Gideon's Army," declared his opposition to all forms of Red-baiting and proclaimed his willingness to accept the support of any and every group working in the interests of peace.[4] The Communists greeted Wallace's announcement with enthusiasm, and a *Daily Worker* editorial called his decision to run for the presidency "an historic challenge to a vast and sinister conspiracy against the true interests of the United States."[5]

Old New Dealers, labor leaders, the CIO Political Action Committee, professional politicians, and the Negro groups split into factions because of Wallace's candidacy. The most important such split, from Wallace's viewpoint, was that among the New Dealers. Wallace had counted heavily on carrying most of the liberals and former Roosevelt backers into his fold, but Harold Ickes, Chester Bowles, Eleanor Roosevelt, and Leon Henderson turned instead to the Americans for Democratic Action. They eventually returned to the Truman camp after an unsuccessful attempt to persuade General Dwight D. Eisenhower to seek the Democratic party's nomination. The two most prominent New Dealers to stay with Wallace were his former aid in the Agriculture Department, Rexford Tugwell, and Elmer Benson, the ex-Farmer-Labor party governor of Minnesota, but even Tugwell was "an uneasy member of the Progressive Party" by fall.[6] After Taylor had accepted Wallace's offer of the second spot on the ticket, he too had the support of the Communists, which he did not repudiate. During

---

[1] David Shannon, *The Decline of American Communism* (New York: Harcourt Brace and World, 1959), pp. 145-46. See also MacDougall, *Gideon's Army*, 3 vols. (New York: Marzani and Munsell, 1965), pp. 188-223.

[2] *Daily Worker*, September 13, 1946.

[3] Ibid., September 17, 1946. The Communist party stand on Wallace was described by Simon Gerson, the party designee for a New York City Council slot. Gerson stated, "The New Party is anti-monopoly, anti-Facist, anti-war. It is not by its nature a socialist or communist party and we are not seeking to make it one." Ibid., July 19, 1948.

[4] *New York Times*, December 30, 1947, p. 1.

[5] *Daily Worker*, December 30, 1947.

[6] MacDougall, *Gideon's Army*, 3:633. See also Schmidt, *Henry A. Wallace: Quixotic Crusade* (Syracuse, N.Y.: Syracuse University Press, 1960), pp. 37-39. Naturally many liberals shied away from the Progressives because they believed a split would elect a Republican. Taylor attempted to answer this argument when he made his decision to join Wallace. He simply said, "If I were convinced that all we could do was elect a reactionary Republican, I would not run. I think we'll win." *Daily Worker*, February 26, 1948. Two excellent studies of liberal attitudes during this period are Alonzo Hamby, "Truman and the Liberal Movement" (Ph.D. diss., University of Missouri, 1964), and Clifton Brock, *Americans for Democratic Action* (Washington: Public Affairs Press, 1962), pp. 68-152.

his campaign, however, Taylor remained independent of either the Communists or even Wallace, for that matter.

Taylor campaigned extensively prior to the July convention; however, he was virtually on his own. Although both Wallace and Taylor were engaged in what they considered "a united crusade for peace," they rarely met for strategy discussions or to compare the reactions they received. In fact, Taylor claims that from February until the November election, "we may have spent half an hour together in conversation. That's all."[7]

The July convention was held in Philadelphia. One of its first acts was to adopt the name Progressive for the new party.[8] Of the delegates gathered in Philadelphia, it was estimated that over 60 percent were under forty years of age. There were very few professional politicians. Nearly 40 percent held membership cards in labor unions.[9] For many observers, the convention had the aura of an evangelistic revival meeting, not that of a political convention. One reporter spoke of a "soda parlor atmosphere, not a smoke-filled room."[10]

For one thing, the candidates were already chosen—there was no opposition. Wallace was the self-appointed general of this "Gideon's Army," and he had chosen Taylor as his running mate. Although there was considerable debate over the platform, Wallace and Taylor had picked their main issue—peace—and had already campaigned on that issue for six months.

Wallace and Taylor remained at the convention from start to finish. They did not dictate policy, especially not to the platform committee, and it was in that body that the harmony of the convention broke down. Rexford G. Tugwell, a professor at the University of Chicago, acted as the committee's chairman. Lee Pressman, who had been a Communist party member during the 1930s, was its secretary. The press was not allowed to cover the platform committee's meetings, but it soon became evident that there were some serious conflicts. The Communist issue divided it from the

[7] Interview with Glen H. Taylor, June 14, 1967.

[8] It was a foregone conclusion that the name of the party would be the Progressives. Taylor and Wallace had used the name interchangeably with the "New Party." The day after he announced his candidacy Taylor remarked, "It won't hurt us to fall heir to the tradition of Theodore Roosevelt and Bob LaFollette; of course, they didn't win, but this is the third try and this time we'll win." *Daily Worker*, February 24, 1948.

[9] *New York Times*, July 23, 1948, p. 10.

[10] Ibid.

beginning. Tugwell repeatedly had denied charges of Communist infiltration in the Progressive movement, but he began to change his mind when he saw the proceedings at the convention.[11]

While the platform committee was organizing its work, Cedric Thomas, a delegate from Maine, opened a hornet's nest when he urged the group to declare that the Progressive party was not Communistic. Most of the members reacted adversely to this proposal, so the Maine realtor retreated and formally moved to include in the platform Taylor's statement that the objective of the Progressive party was to make "our economy work so well and our way of life so attractive and our people so contented that communism will never interest more than the infinitesimal fraction of our citizens who adhere to it now." Mrs. Paul Robeson and Martin Popper, executive secretary of the National Lawyers Guild, claimed this was no less than Red-baiting, and the committee defeated the motion.[12]

The proposed platform included a statement that the Progressive party would "fight for the constitutional rights of Communists and all other political groups." Thomas moved that the language be simply "the constitutional rights of all political groups," eliminating the direct reference to the Communists. But this motion was also voted down.[13]

The concluding platform committee battle was fought over the language used to describe American foreign policy. Frederick L. Schuman of Williams College believed the proposed platform was disappointing because it bitterly condemned the Truman administration's foreign policy yet was silent about the policy of the Soviet Union. Schuman presented an amendment saying that the threat to world peace was "the joint responsibility of the Soviet Union and the United States." He took his proposal directly to Wallace, who agreed with him, and the amendment was inserted in the platform.[14]

The evidence is conclusive that there were a number of Com-

---

[11] Shannon, *The Decline of American Communism*, pp. 166-67, records that Tugwell brought one of his graduate students, John C. Brown, into the meetings as his assistant; actually Brown took notes for his dissertation, "The 1948 Progressive Campaign: A Scientific Approach" (Ph.D. diss., University of Chicago, 1949). Brown's dissertation contains the best account available of the proceedings of the platform committee.
[12] Brown, "The 1948 Progressive Campaign," pp. 161-68.
[13] Ibid., pp. 169-75.
[14] Ibid., pp. 187-90.

munists and Communist supporters among the delegates to the convention and on the platform committee; however, an overwhelming majority of the delegates were liberals. According to David Shannon, in his book *The Decline of the Communist Party,* Tugwell tried to get Wallace to repudiate the Communists at the convention, but the idealistic Wallace refused to do so. Both Wallace and Taylor were well aware of the dangers the Communists presented to their candidacy. Wallace told a New Hampshire audience before the convention that "if the Communists would run a ticket of their own this year, we might lose 10,000 votes, but we would gain 3,000,000."[15] Apparently Wallace was willing to sacrifice political practicality for ideals. Since the Progressive leaders declined to reject Communist support, and there was no Progressive of any stature who was willing to speak out against Communists, the new party was labeled as pink from the time of the convention to its eventual demise.[16]

The final platform was constructed around a central plank which promised that the Progressives would cooperate with the Soviet Union in order to end the Cold War. The Progressives also advocated repudiation of the Truman Doctrine, repeal of the draft act, negotiation of a peace treaty with a unified Germany, and substitution of a United Nations recovery program for the Marshall Plan. Most of these issues had already been part of the Wallace-Taylor campaign. Domestically the Progressives proposed public ownership of railroads, large banks, the merchant marine, electric power, and the gas industry. They also advocated government financing of certain industries to create more competition and came out strongly for old-age benefits, civil rights, a one-dollar-per-hour minimum wage, federally owned housing, price controls, and repeal of the Taft-Hartley Act.[17] Many of the ideas represented by these domestic planks antedated not only the political careers of Wallace and Taylor but also the existence of the Communist party in the United States. The foreign-policy planks represented the beliefs not only of the Communists but also of those liberals who had "found it necessary to form a new party for their expression."

---

[15] *New York Times,* July 3, 1948, p. 16.

[16] Brown and Shannon agree that the influence of the Communists was significant and devastating. MacDougall, *Gideon's Army,* 2:534-63, believes that the role of the Communists has been overemphasized. Schmidt, *Quixotic Crusade,* pp. 186-205, is inclined toward the MacDougall position.

[17] Kirk H. Porter and D. B. Johnson, eds., *National Party Platforms, 1840-1960* (Urbana: University of Illinois Press, 1961), pp. 436-47.

Peace was the prevailing concern of the Progressives, and the party drew strength from pacifists, isolationists, and some theologians.[18]

The party's candidates appeared before the convention twice, once at the time of their nomination, and again when they delivered their acceptance speeches. Larkin Marshall, a Macon, Georgia, Negro lawyer and a Progressive party candidate for the United States Senate, nominated Glen H. Taylor for vice president. Marshall concluded his nominating speech with the following statement: "He passes the hardest test to which I can put him. He believes that all men are created equal, and when men malign him because of that belief and their torrent of wrath in fierce imprecation over him breaks, he keeps his counsel as he keeps his path. It is for the nation, not for himself that he speaks."[19] A spontaneous demonstration, with singing and cheering, followed the nomination. Taylor had risen from radio entertainer to candidate for the vice-presidency in ten years.

The next evening, July 24, Taylor and Wallace accepted their nominations at Shibe Park, a baseball stadium, where delegates and supporters gathered for a concluding rally. There were over 30,000 in attendance. Paul Robeson and Pete Seeger sang to create a festive mood; then, according to Progressive custom, William S. Gailmor asked the crowd for its dollar bills and loose change.[20] Finally, late in the evening, Taylor and Wallace were presented to the roaring crowd.

The Idaho senator, speaking from a rostrum constructed near second base, prefaced his prepared speech with a genuine display of emotion when he said, "Thank you for that wonderful reception. This is the most wonderful moment of my life."[21] Then Taylor launched into his speech conveying his typical political optimism but issuing a sincere, idealistic warning concerning the future of the nation and the world. "Today the forces of greed have embarked America on a policy of preparing for a war of extinction . . . that is the only issue; whether we shall live out our lives and

[18] Schmidt, *Quixotic Crusade*, p. 196.
[19] MacDougall, *Gideon's Army*, 2:527.
[20] Pete Seeger, Woody Guthrie, Lee Hays, and others connected with *People's Songs* published a booklet titled "Songs for Wallace." These ballads were written specifically for the Wallace-Taylor movement and included "I've Got a Ballot," "Great Day," "Friendly Henry Wallace," "We'll All Join Gideon's Army," and "The Same Merry-Go-Round." No Progressive gathering was complete without a sing-along. *People's Songs* and "Songs for Wallace" can be located in the New York Public Library.
[21] MacDougall, *Gideon's Army*, 2:531.

the lives of our children in peace or whether we shall perish. . . .
It is as simple and straightforward as that. It is life or death. It
is peace or war. . . . We are going to win this election. I know
we will win it because I do not believe that God in his mercy
will inflict this terrible atomic ordeal on mankind."[22]

Taylor concluded with a sarcastic jab at Birmingham, Alabama,
and Police Commissioner "Bull" Conner. Alluding to his rough
treatment in Birmingham two months earlier, Taylor told the
cheering throng that he was going back and that "their Jim Crow
police chief," who was a delegate to the Democratic national convention, would "have to put up or shut up." The vice-presidential
candidate challenged the Alabama city to "throw me in jail for
180 days as they threatened they would if I came back to Birmingham or they will have to eat crow—Jim Crow."[23]

The crowd applauded enthusiastically at the conclusion of Taylor's speech. Then there occurred what one scholar has described
as the "most controversial incident of the evening."[24] Interrupting
the screaming crowd, Taylor lifted his arms high above his head
and called for silence. He introduced Dora, his brother Paul, and
his three sons, Arod, Paul, and Gregory. The family then joined
him in singing "I Love You as I Never Loved Before." This musical
offering was treated with derision in the nation's press, evoking
familiar controversy about Taylor's undignified campaign techniques. For this reason, among others, Taylor considered newspaper
coverage of the convention "disgustingly rotten."[25]

Norman Thomas, the Socialist candidate for president, called
Taylor's speech "amazingly cheap," referred to the song as an
"excruciating barber-shop family quartet," and added that these
were "only two of the disgusting features of Saturday night's demonstration."[26] The editorial staff of the *Christian Century* also was
disgusted with the Taylor performance and thought Wallace would
not get much help from his running mate. According to this
editorial, disillusionment with the two old parties, "which might
make thousands of independents consider voting for Wallace, will

[22] *Cong. Rec.*, 80th Cong., 2d sess., 1948, 94, pt. 12:A5098-99. The Wallace-
Taylor acceptance speeches were printed in their entirety in the *Congressional
Record.*
[23] Ibid., p. A5099.
[24] MacDougall, *Gideon's Army*, 2:531.
[25] Ibid.
[26] *Oregonian*, July 25, 1948. Norman Thomas was a consistent critic of the
entire Progressive movement.

hardly make them ready to chance occupancy of the White House by the man who tried to woo the nation with a tenth-rate rendition of a barber shop classic."[27] H. L. Mencken, on one of his last on-the-spot assignments before the stroke which ended his career, referred to Taylor as "a third-rate mounteback from the great open spaces" and categorized his speech of acceptance as "an effort worthy of a corn doctor at a county fair."[28] Kinder press representatives viewed the Shibe Park gathering as a football game with cheerleaders, a carnival, or an evangelistic revival. However, there was unanimity on the fact that it produced a "display of almost fanatical enthusiasm by both delegates and spectators."[29]

The one point that Wallace and Taylor repeatedly belabored in their acceptance speeches was that Truman had betrayed the New Deal—in regard to domestic reforms as well as foreign relations. The Progressives' aim, therefore, was to wrest power from the president in order to reinstitute Roosevelt's policies. In fact, the 1948 contest between the Progressives and the Democrats can be described as a power struggle between two sons of a dead king. Truman and Wallace each believed he was the legitimate successor to the architect of the New Deal. Truman had the power of office. Wallace and his running mate, Glen Taylor, embarked on a "quixotic crusade" to convince the American people that they were the true descendants of Franklin D. Roosevelt.

The evening after the close of the convention, Taylor journeyed across town and spoke to 1,800 Young Progressives of America. Mrs. Lawrence Steefil of Minnesota introduced Taylor to the crowd of cheering youth. "We have learned in America how big a mistake can be made in choosing a vice-president. . . . One night in Alabama we discovered that in choosing Glen Taylor we would not be making a mistake."[30] After singing a parody of the "Isle of Capri," Taylor spoke to the delegates. Most of his remarks were geared to an attack upon the draft, which he called "the culminating act of the joint Republican-Democratic drive towards a new world war."[31] The Idaho senator then announced dramatically that he

27 "Wallace Party Launched," *Christian Century*, August 4, 1948, p. 771.
28 H. L. Mencken, *The Vintage Mencken* (New York: Random House, 1955), pp. 224-25.
29 *New York Times*, July 25, 1946, p. 36.
30 *Daily Worker*, July 26, 1948.
31 Ibid. The *Worker* was so upset because of the arrest of twelve leaders of the American Communist Party that they did not give the convention the attention it might otherwise have received.

had to catch a train for Washington—he expected to rise early the next day and prepare a bill to repeal the draft. This proposal was received by the Young Progressives with wild enthusiasm. "The kids howled like maniacs—waved their pennants, and clapped their hands."[32]

Truman's chances for reelection, diminished to some extent by the defection of liberals, were dealt a second severe blow when the southern Democrats bolted from the Democratic party's right side. Gleefully confronting the now trifurcated Democratic party was the Republican party, with its candidate, New York Governor Thomas E. Dewey. Truman was convinced that the defections of the Progressives and the States' Righters would hurt his voting strength, but he considered it his "duty to carry forward the program that had taken the nation from the depths of the depression to prosperity and world leadership."[33]

On Monday, July 26, a grumbling Congress, including Glen Taylor, returned to Washington for a special session. Truman has referred to his decision to bring Congress back to Washington as his "trump card."[34] He asked Congress to pass laws which would halt rising prices, meet housing needs, aid education, extend and protect civil rights, increase the minimum wage, extend Social Security coverage, and provide cheaper electricity.[35] In short, the president requested the immediate implementation of his "Fair Deal" programs. The result was a standoff. The special session lasted twelve days, during six of which a southern filibuster blocked Senate consideration of an anti-poll tax bill. Truman used the failures of the Eightieth Congress as ammunition for his 1948 campaign.

Taylor was frustrated during the special session mainly because of the close alliance between Republicans and Southern Democrats. After one week, he told a national radio audience that "neither the Democrats nor the Republicans dare enact the legislation to carry out their campaign promises." The established political parties, he said, were only paying lip service to reform and social welfare legislation.[36] On August 3 he called the parties the "tools of monopoly, reaction, and war."[37]

[32] MacDougall, *Gideon's Army,* 3:591.
[33] Truman, *Memoirs,* 2:219.
[34] Ibid., p. 241.
[35] Ibid., pp. 242-44.
[36] *Cong. Rec.,* 80th Cong., 2d sess., 1948, 94, pt. 12:A5100-5102.
[37] *New York Times,* August 4, 1948, p. 1.

On the final day of the special session, Taylor again leveled an attack on both major parties. He said that Truman had requested the special session to "needle the Republicans about high prices, housing, civil rights, and a number of other pressing issues," but apparently the president himself was not seriously interested in seeing these measures enacted since he had relapsed into semiactivity and failed to press his party or the Congress into action. The entire session, Taylor said, was a farce. "The score for the special session, for both parties, is virtually a goose egg."[38] Because, in his opinion, the two major parties offered similar programs, Taylor predicted that the Progressive party would meet with enthusiasm and support from "millions of Americans who formerly found in Franklin Roosevelt's New Deal a government sincerely interested in bettering their lot."[39]

The Progressives' fall campaign during the next three months was, in a way, anticlimactic. With poor newspaper coverage and the continual charge of communism, Progressive popularity sagged lower and lower. Following the special session, when Taylor was able to devote his time to campaigning, the press either ignored him or portrayed him—in word and pictures—as little more than a hillbilly jester, a buffoon in high public office."[40] According to one observer, Taylor was virtually boycotted by the nation's larger papers after the convention. Although vice-presidential candidates normally receive little attention compared to the ticket leader, the blackout of news on what Taylor was saying was excessive.[41] Furthermore, only three major daily papers, the *New York Times*, the *New York Post*, and the *Baltimore Sun* assigned reporters to travel with the Progressive presidential candidate.[42]

Taylor began his campaign in Idaho immediately after the conclusion of the special session. For nearly two weeks he crisscrossed the Gem State, appealing for its four electoral votes and attempting to ensure his political future. Starting in northern Idaho, Taylor attempted to capitalize on local issues to better his

[38] *Cong. Rec.*, 80th Cong., 2d sess., 1948, 94, pt. 8:10172. An excellent, concise examination of this special session, called the Turnip Session, is R. Alton Lee, "The Turnip Session of the Do-Nothing Congress: Presidential Campaign Strategy," *Southern Social Science Quarterly* 43 (December 1963): 256-67. Lee suggests that a good deal of the legislation Truman requested was intended only as political ammunition against Congress.

[39] Ibid., p. 10174.

[40] Schmidt, *Quixotic Crusade*, p. 231.

[41] MacDougall, *Gideon's Army*, 3:693-94.

[42] Ibid., p. 694.

position, but before he proceeded very far south, he was again haranguing about foreign policy and the drift toward war. In Moscow he told an audience at the University of Idaho, "I don't think we can expect much help from the old parties in the way of aid to education. They have turned down the road toward fascism."[43] He then attacked the Truman foreign policy for creating tensions with the Soviet Union. At Rexburg, when two men threw peaches and eggs at him while he spoke, Taylor blamed the incident on Truman's "Red-baiting" tactics. Taylor spent two weeks in Idaho, a rather lengthy stay for a candidate seeking national office, but Idaho's senior senator believed it was necessary. As late as August 25, a Gallup poll indicated that only 30 percent of the nation's voters knew Taylor was running."[44]

Everywhere the Progressive candidate went he was accused of consorting with the Communists. Idaho editorials severely criticized him for joining the Progressives and playing into the hands of the "Reds." One Idaho weekly editorialized that "The Communists have pressed down on the brow of these men [Wallace and Taylor] the Red Crown of Communism. Neither has seen fit . . . to put it off and throw it into the dust."[45] When the Lewiston school board refused to allow the Progressives use of the high school auditorium because of the Communist controversy, Taylor accused them of betraying the confidence inspired in them by the people.

Although Taylor was painted pink by political and newspaper opponents, he retained his ability to move a crowd. After a rally in Coeur d'Alene, E. T. Taylor, a Republican, reported: "Why, Glen Taylor had these people singing together, donating together to his campaign, and finally praying together—for Taylor's success. It was one of the greatest and best staged shows I've seen in years."[46]

Eventually Taylor resorted to some of the same extremist tactics which were being used against the Progressives. He repeatedly spoke of Germany's Third Reich as a prototype for 1948 America. Over and over he insisted that the militarists and Wall Street were

[43] *Lewiston Tribune,* August 24, 1948.

[44] *Seattle Times,* August 25, 1948. Taylor held forty-four meetings during his stay in Idaho. Most of them were well attended.

[45] *Idaho Statewide* (Boise), August 26, 1948. See also *Salt Lake Tribune,* August 18 and October 4, 1948. The *Idaho Statesman* attacked Taylor and the Progressives throughout the campaign.

[46] *Idaho Statewide,* September 16, 1948.

guiding Truman toward the Third World War. In a Portland, Oregon, speech he attacked Secretary of Defense James Forrestal; Under Secretary of the Army William Draper, a former associate of Forrestal's at Dillon-Read, Inc.; and John Foster Dulles, a corporation lawyer and foreign policy adviser. Taylor listed these three as the "most powerful fascists" in the nation. Forrestal and Draper were in office at the time, and Taylor predicted that should Dewey win, Dulles would be his secretary of state.[47]

Taylor often asked his audiences to empathize with their counterparts in the Soviet Union. At San Francisco, he told a meeting of the International Union of Mine, Mill, and Smelter Workers that if he were a Russian, it would frighten him to look across the water at the "greatest nation in the world arming against me. Truman is not a vicious man, but neither was General Hindenburg. He was a front for Hitler and that's all Truman is—a front man."[48] Less than a week later, at the University of Wisconsin in Madison, Taylor went further. He simply stated that fascists were in control of the United States government. "If I were a Russian at the Moscow conference," he went on, "I would not agree to anything. Vishinsky's statement that we are aggressively preparing for war is truthful on the very face of it."[49] Addressing about five hundred persons who came in the rain to Kiel Auditorium in St. Louis, Taylor called Forrestal "a potential American Hitler" and Truman "a well-meaning Hindenburg behind whose back a military-cartel crowd is planning the dirty work of war."[50]

Thus Taylor, who was accused of participating in a Communist conspiracy designed to take over the government, enunciated his belief that the genuine conspiracy came from the right, not the left. The following excerpt from a Newark, New Jersey, speech describes the full-blown plot as Taylor saw it: "This country is being run by the same evil men who were instrumental in financing Hitler. They are carrying out his program in this country; using Goebbels's technique of the Red smear to silence opposition, giving monopoly a free hand and are bent on destroying organized labor." Concluding, Taylor postulated, "I believe their intentions are the same as Hitler's—to establish a dictatorship here in America,

---

[47] *Oregonian*, September 3, 1948.
[48] *New York Times*, September 14, 1948, p. 20.
[49] Ibid., September 20, 1948, p. 16. The Council of Foreign Ministers of the nations comprising the permanent members of the United Nations Security Council was in session in Moscow.
[50] *St. Louis Post-Dispatch*, October 11, 1948.

dominate the world militarily and exploit it economically."[51] Taylor used this analysis of the conspiracy for the rest of the campaign.

Progressive rallies were, on the whole, well attended and, although there was usually some heckling, well behaved. Taylor took his wife and three sons with him on the campaign trail until school started in the fall. One of the Progressive balladeers, usually either Pete Seeger or Paul Robeson, accompanied Taylor and often led the audience in a sing-along featuring many of the "Songs for Wallace." Dora Taylor and Arod, now thirteen, joined the senator for a few musical numbers as well, the critics notwithstanding.[52] The fact that Taylor included his family in the act was upsetting to at least one Progressive adherent. Mabel Cooney, Wallace's secretary, thought it would have been better "if the Taylor children had been put to bed, instead of falling off stools in taverns every night."[53]

In many appearances Taylor went through a ritual of raising his right hand to a ninety-degree angle and swearing that he was not a Communist. Quickly he would add, "I tell you this here, but if that committee in Washington [House Un-American Activities Committee] called me down there and asked if I am a Communist, I'd tell them it was none of their damn business."[54] Boos and eggs greeted Taylor when he made this pledge in Jacksonville, Florida, late in October. Although he was hit by some of the two dozen eggs thrown in the barrage, the Idaho senator remained unruffled.[55] After a short trip through California, Taylor returned to Pocatello, Idaho, on November 1 for one last rally and to await the voice of the people.

In all, Taylor spent nearly three weeks during his campaign for the vice-presidency in his home state. Whatever his motives for doing so, it was a pointless effort. Idaho had little to offer in the way of a liberal voting bloc, and it had only four electoral votes. It was not a state with heavy labor influence, but a state with a traditionally conservative rural area. Taylor's candidacy as a Progressive created considerably animosity among some Idaho natives. Two Boise war veterans, E. L. Fuller and Donald Smith, circulated

[51] Ibid., September 29, 1948.
[52] *St. Louis Post-Dispatch*, October 11, 1948, describes a typical Taylor-Seeger rally, which included more singing than speaking and ended with the customary solicitation of funds.
[53] MacDougall, *Gideon's Army*, 3:603.
[54] Ibid., p. 829.
[55] *Salt Lake Tribune*, October 21, 1948.

petitions in March of 1948 demanding Taylor's recall. Some newspapers also encouraged the recall move or else demanded Taylor's resignation.[56] The extent to which Taylor's time in Idaho was wasted may be judged from the fact that the Progressives polled less than 5,000 votes in the Gem State when election time came.[57]

Nationally the Progressives suffered a devastating defeat at the polls. When the returns were counted, the Wallace-Taylor ticket had received only 1,157,140 votes, or 2.7 percent of the total vote. The main source of support for the Progressives was New York, where they obtained over half a million votes. But by cutting into the Democratic total in this electorally potent state, the Progressives helped give the state to its governor, the Republican candidate Thomas Dewey.[58] However, New York and Michigan were the only states where the Progressives had such an effect on the outcome of the election.

Some analysts, however, give Wallace supporters some credit for having aided Truman's victory. Apparently when many Progressive backers got into the voting booth, they realized that a vote for Wallace might be a vote for the Republican candidate, and they could not bear the thought of Thomas Dewey in the White House. The Progressives are also given credit for having forced the Democratic party to adopt a more liberal platform than it might otherwise have adopted in order to appeal to its traditional New Deal supporters.[59]

Glen Taylor has found some solace in the political setback he

[56] *New York Times*, March 27, 1948, p. 15. The *Burley Herald Tribune* supported the recall attempt, and the *Lewiston Morning Tribune* called for Taylor's resignation.

[57] Schmidt, *Quixotic Crusade*, pp. 327-35. Full statistics on the Progressive vote are cited here. Some polls forecast that the Progressives would get between 7 and 10 percent of the vote. Ibid., p. 258. The Progressives' low vote in Idaho is in contrast to 107,000 votes for Taylor when he was elected to the Senate in 1944.

[58] Ibid., pp. 327-35.

[59] Schmidt, *Quixotic Crusade*, pp. 245-47, and MacDougall, *Gideon's Army*, 3:859-61, both explain Wallace's small vote on the basis of this factor. Eric F. Goldman, *The Crucial Decade* (New York: Random House, 1960), pp. 88-89, and Jules Abels, *Out of the Jaws of Victory* (New York: Henry Holt, 1959), pp. 291-93, agree, but also suggest other reasons for Truman's amazing victory. Many midwestern farmers voted for Truman simply because they feared that prosperity would end if Dewey was elected. The Progressives had no appeal to the agrarians. For an excellent account of the Progressive effect on the Democratic party see Allen Yarnell, "The Impact of the Progressive Party on the Democratic Party in the 1948 Presidential Election" (Ph.D. diss., University of Washington, 1969).

suffered. It is his opinion that time and history will show that the Progressives, basically he and Wallace, were much closer to the truth than their contemporaries suspected. The son of Pleasant John Taylor, itinerant preacher, relies on the Bible: "A prophet is without honor in his own household."[60]

[60] Interview with Glen Taylor, June 14, 1967.

X. Some Historical Questions

One obvious reason why the 1948 Progressives failed to reach their expectations at the polls was the political agility of Harry Truman. Although the president denied that during his first two years in office he had drifted away from the liberal policies of Roosevelt, many ex-New Dealers and especially labor leaders believed that he had. Truman may not have altered his position during 1948, but certain actions on his part made him more palatable to liberals. His veto of the Case bill and the Taft-Hartley Act, both despised by organized labor, vindicated him in the eyes of the labor unions.[1] His strong position on civil rights, as set forth in the 1948 Democratic platform, brought many liberals back into the fold simultaneously with the conservative departure. Truman shrewdly conducted a campaign which emphasized liberal social reforms and the failure of the Eightieth Congress to institute those changes. In short, the Democrats succeeded in capturing much of the Progressives' program: "For the first time in American history, the thunder of a party of discontent had been stolen, neither four nor forty years later, but in the very midst of the campaign."[2]

Undoubtedly the Red smear injured the Progressives severely. In an era when the nation was ripe for a Joseph McCarthy and already convinced that communism was the ultimate evil, in a time when the United States and the Soviet Union appeared to be on the brink of atomic war, American Communist support was bound to be detrimental to the Progressive party. The Communist takeover in Czechoslovakia, the Berlin blockade, and the beginning of the Communist Chinese victory, all during 1948, made Wallace-Taylor peace speeches sound like appeasement. The year 1948 was also the year of the Alger Hiss-Whittaker Chambers affair and the arrest of the American Communist leaders. Anything remotely connected with communism in 1948 spelled doom.

The Democratic party's ploy of pointing an accusing finger at the Progressives and calling them "Reds" proved to be successful. As early as January 2, 1948, Frank McNaughton, a White House correspondent, prophesied that Wallace would not "cut as much third party ice as first glances would indicate. . . . It is doubtful that he can long survive a campaign slogan that 'A vote for Wallace is a vote for Stalin'—and that's what the Democrats intend to pin on him."[3] In New York City Truman told a Saint Patrick's Day audience: "I do not want and I will not accept the political support of Henry Wallace and his Communists. If joining them or permitting them to join me is the price of victory, I recommend defeat. These are days of high prices for everything, but any price for Wallace and his Communists is too much for me to pay. I'm not buying."[4] Just two days after the speech, Democrats close to the president were convinced that Truman had taken the proper course. Sam Rayburn, the House minority leader, believed that Truman's stock had "gone up to beat hell" on the strength of his stand against internal communism.[5] Both Rayburn and Howard McGrath, the Democratic national party chairman, wanted Truman to continue to haul "Communist vs. Freedom out into the open field of debate where Wallace can't preach appeasement without appearing as a fellow traveler." Truman's advisers believed that if he kept hammering away at the issue of communism, more and more people would begin to see the "Red network" around Wallace and would take their moderate, sincere liberalism back to the Democratic ticket.[6] For many voters this is apparently what happened.

Truman maintained the "Red" ploy until after the Progressives' convention. In April Walter Reuther suggested that the president condemn extremism in the Middle West which had resulted in a mob raid on a Communist labor leader in Ohio and a riot at

[1] Truman, *Memoirs*, 1:553. The Case bill was passed in 1946 and was designed to safeguard the nation against crippling strikes. The bill was in part a reaction to the United Coal Miners' strike during that same year. Truman vetoed the bill because he believed it would not stop strikes at all. He also disliked the bill because it took away from the secretary of labor all responsibility for the operation of the mediation board.

[2] Schmidt, *Henry A. Wallace: Quixotic Crusade* (Syracuse, N.Y.: Syracuse University Press, 1960), p. 91. Schmidt's conclusions are overstated. Truman had incorporated all these suggested reforms in his Fair Deal program. His decision to capitalize on them during the campaign stole some of the Progressive ammunition.

[3] McNaughton to Don Bermingham, January 2, 1948, McNaughton Papers, Truman Library.

[4] *Truman Public Papers*, 4:189.

[5] McNaughton to Bermingham, March 19, 1948, McNaughton Papers, Truman Library.

[6] Ibid.

a Progressive rally in Evansville, Indiana. Instead Truman replied that it was a local matter for the local officials to handle.[7] When the participation of known Communists at the Progressive convention turned the press against the new party, Truman's opposition abated. He returned to his heated verbal assaults on the Eightieth Congress.

Wallace and Taylor refused to sacrifice their idealism for votes. On numerous occasions both denied personal Communist affiliation, but neither would refuse Communist support. Taylor's statement to a Salt Lake City audience was typical: "I hold no suit for Communism, but if Communism can be outlawed, we can be outlawed—then you have a dictatorship."[8] Continually reiterating his position that neither he nor Wallace were Communists, Taylor bitterly scored against such forces as the House Un-American Activities Committee. The Idaho senator referred to the rash of spy scares and investigations as "Hitler's tactics" and a "violation of the American concepts of justice,"[9] and pointed out that "One of the main goals of the new party is to keep America from going fascist."[10] This goal, added to their comprehensive domestic program and critical view of American foreign policy, threw the Progressives into the same bed with the Communists.

Taylor's younger brother, Paul, ran for a congressional seat on the Progressive ticket in northern California. According to the Idaho senator, his younger brother was investigated by the FBI even before he became a candidate. Speaking in San Jose, Taylor told an audience of nine hundred, "My own brother, right here in San Jose, who is not a government worker, has been investigated—simply because he is my brother."[11] Paul Taylor contended that Wallace and Taylor were both aware of the Communst forces at work within the new party, but that they both thought liberals should remain with the Progressives and fight the Communist element from within the organization.[12]

The Communist scare kept the Progressives from becoming a

[7] *Truman Public Papers*, 4:210.

[8] *Salt Lake Tribune*, May 24, 1948.

[9] *Daily Worker*, October 7, 1948.

[10] Ibid., April 12, 1948.

[11] Merrill Raymond Moreman, "The Independent Progressive Party in California, 1948" (Master's thesis, Stanford University, 1950), p. 148.

[12] Ibid., p. 132. Paul Taylor ran against a candidate supported by both major parties, yet he obtained nearly 40 percent of the vote. This was his first and last venture into politics.

viable political force. Commentators agree that it was the charge of communism which splintered the coalition that had formed the Progressive party. One active Progressive, Elmer Benson, made the exaggerated statement that Wallace and Taylor could be elected in August if it were not for the "Red Scare."[13] Another observer declared, "More than any other influence, that [Red] label served to stifle the growth of the new party and carry it to its early demise."[14]

One of the most detrimental effects of the Communist issue was that it inhibited party growth and caused internal dissension, including the platform fight at the convention. Wallace and Taylor received advice from many quarters, and inevitably their advisers, professional or otherwise, had something to say about Communists in the party. Many believed that if Wallace would repudiate the Communist party, the Americans for Democratic Action and other liberals would flock to his camp.[15] Wallace and Taylor refused and they suffered politically because of their devotion to principle.

According to David Shannon, there would have been a third party even without the Communists. He contends that the non-Communist left gave the new party its start, but that by the end of the campaign Communists or fellow travelers had replaced the liberal left in some key positions throughout the Progressive organization. Undoubtedly, it was this close association with the Communists that caused the party to do so poorly at the polls.[16] However, according to Karl Schmidt, it was "the Communist bogey, rather than the Communist party itself, that had the greater influence on the destiny of the Wallace Progressive party."[17]

Publicly Taylor attempted to play down the Red taint. A month before the election he told a press conference, "The red smear is beginning to lose some of its effect because people are beginning to recognize it as a disservice to the country."[18] Questioned

---

[13] Ibid., pp. 141-42.

[14] Albert Bilik, "A New Party: Success and Failure" (Master's thesis, Columbia University, 1949), p. 112.

[15] Lee Fryer to Louis Adamic, July 10, 1948, 68397N, Wallace Papers. Fryer, an executive of the National Farmers Union, suggested a number of things Wallace needed to do to win greater support. Among them was more reliance on Glen Taylor for policy meetings and planning. Adamic agreed with Fryer concerning Taylor, but said a decision to rid the new party of the Communists was unnecessary and undesirable. Adamic's notes on Fryer's letter, ibid.

[16] David Shannon, *The Decline of American Communism* (New York: Harcourt Brace and World, 1959), pp. 150-51.

[17] Schmidt, *Quixotic Crusade*, p. 279.

[18] *Daily Worker*, October 3, 1948.

further, the vice-presidential candidate stated, "They started their red scare too soon and its worn out on them. It is starting to backfire."[19] Obviously, Taylor's fingers were not on the nation's pulse; his evaluation of the importance of the Red smear was in error.

Although the Progressives and Communists worked together for a victory in 1948, they were not without their serious differences. Early in the campaign, Taylor was chastised twice by the *Daily Worker* for so-called red-baiting. The *Worker* also did not appreciate Taylor's remark that his goal was to make the system work so well that communism would lose its appeal.[20] When Taylor said the Communist takeover in Czechoslovakia was unfortunate and probably the result of "pressure by the Russians,"[21] two *Daily Worker* columnists, Joseph Starobin and Milton Howard, criticized Taylor for his comments. They concluded that obviously the Progressive candidate had "not thought it through."[22]

Taylor believes that the Progressive party was launched with the intent of preserving peace and should be remembered as an attempt to prevent World War III, not as an attempt by the Communists to assume power.[23] Although disappointed in the outcome of the campaign, Taylor accepted defeat pragmatically. In his words, "The President stole our thunder"; now he would wait to see if Truman fulfilled his promises.[24]

After the defeat Taylor planned to work with the Progressive party and prepare for the 1950 campaign as a Progressive. A week following the 1948 election, Wallace, Taylor, Tugwell, and others met in Chicago and outlined plans for a permanent party, but enthusiasm was generally lacking.[25] By the summer of 1949, after some mild Democratic pressure against the rebel senator, Taylor announced that he was returning to the Democratic party.[26]

[19] Ibid.
[20] Ibid., February 25, 1948.
[21] Ibid., March 1, 1948.
[22] Ibid., March 7, 1948.
[23] Interview with Taylor, June 14, 1967.
[24] *Lewiston Tribune*, November 11, 1948.
[25] *Daily Worker*, November 11, 1948.
[26] The pressure (or retaliation) consisted mostly of accepting postmaster nominations made by Idaho's junior senator, Bert H. Miller, over Taylor's. After Taylor returned to the party, his patronage rights were restored and he was appointed to the important Interior and Insular Affairs Committee in 1949. When Taylor left the party, he was put on the bottom of every priority list for committees, but this did not last long. *New York Times*, November 4, 1948, p. 6.

Actually, he was never out of the party so far as his activities in the Senate were concerned. He attended Democratic party caucuses, cosponsored some of the administration's domestic legislation, and attended Democratic social functions.[27]

The Idaho senator made his decision public on July 29, 1949, on the weekly Mutual Broadcasting System radio show "Meet the Press." Taylor said that he was "pretty thoroughly convinced that our political destiny rests with the two major political parties. The American people do not want any splinter party." He told his interviewers that he was now back in the Democratic party, and "I intend to run for office as a Democrat if I run." From the questions the panel asked Taylor, it was apparent that the overriding issue in any future Taylor campaign would be communism and Taylor's participation in the Progressive movement. Lawrence Spivak immediately asked Taylor, "Senator, how is it that a person like you would run on a party ticket that was widely accepted as Communist-run and Communist-dominated, which the Progressive party was?" Quickly denying the allegation, the Idaho senator retorted that the Progressive party was the "most democratic organization" he had ever been connected with.[28] Nevertheless, Taylor concluded, the American system was welded to a two-party political composite, and since there was no room for a third party, he was returning to the Democrats.

In September 1949 Taylor attempted to reestablish a working relationship with the victorious Truman by paying a belated visit to the White House. He thought it was about time to congratulate Harry Truman on his victory the previous November and to remind the president that he would be running for reelection as a Democrat in 1950. Following an exchange of pleasantries, Taylor told Truman that he was very happy to see Truman defeat Dewey. However, when the subject of recent politics was discussed, the fundamental difference between the two men was apparent. Taylor observed: "I have voted with you on every domestic issue, but I

[27] *Minneapolis Morning Tribune,* January 10, 1949. Taylor cosponsored a national health bill and a minimum wage bill. Apparently, Taylor's only complaint was that he had not been asked to escort his new Senate colleague from Idaho, Bert Miller, down the aisle when Miller was sworn in.

[28] The transcripts of the "Meet the Press" show, July 29, 1949, can be found in the Arthur Kriendler Collection, Glen H. Taylor item, the Library Archives of Rutgers University, New Brunswick, N.J. Taylor was interviewed by Lawrence E. Spivak of the *American Mercury,* Warren Frances of the *Los Angeles Times,* Mae Craig of the *Portland* (Maine) *Press Herald,* and I. F. Stone of the *New York Compass.*

still cannot agree with your get-tough foreign policy." Harry Truman's answer was characteristic: "That is the only way to handle the Russians."[29] Taylor told reporters after the visit, "I didn't want to look like I was jumping on somebody's bandwagon. . . . He's a good sport—he didn't rub it in."[30] Truman may not have made the rebel senator beg, but Taylor was to learn that the chief executive was not totally forgiving.

Glen Taylor joined the Wallace crusade because of foreign policy and the alleged defection from the New Deal on the part of Truman. By so doing, he fulfilled the needs of himself as well as Henry Wallace. Wallace had sought someone who held public office to run with him and Taylor complied. The fact that the two men ever got together for the Progressive crusade is amazing. This is in part explained by the complex character of Henry Wallace. Wallace had very few close friends and even some of those referred to him as a distant person.[31] The former secretary of agriculture felt at home talking about philosophical idealism, hybrid corn, and farming, not practical politics. Wallace was for the common man, but was not a common man. He was well-to-do, reserved, and a firm believer in peace. In contrast, Taylor was for the common man and of the common man. Taylor had always been relatively poor and had known hunger pains. He was outgoing and determined to plead the cause of all humanity. If defeated, Wallace could return to his farm and his accumulated wealth. Taylor realized that he had probably committed political suicide and might be jobless and in debt after the 1950 election.

Wallace and Taylor seem to have spent very little time together in consultation during the entire campaign. The qualifications which made Taylor politically acceptable to Wallace were that Taylor held public office and the two men were in basic political agreement. The Wallace-Taylor relationship, formed to save the world, did not lay the foundation for a lasting friendship. A few years later, when asked about Glen Taylor, who had sacrificed his political career by joining him, Wallace mused, "He was a nice fellow. I wonder whatever became of him."[32]

[29] Drew Pearson, "Washington Merry-Go-Round," *Washington Post*, September 24, 1949.
[30] "Fall Planting," *Time* (October 3, 1949), p. 10. This was definitely not the behavior of an apolitical man.
[31] MacDougall, *Gideon's Army*, 3 vols. (New York: Marzani and Munsell, 1965), 1:85.
[32] Ibid., p. 86. Wallace knew fully what had happened to Glen Taylor;

In spite of the differences between Wallace and Taylor, the real significance of the Progressive party is its stand on foreign policy. The Progressives' dissent in matters of foreign policy traditionally has been viewed as appeasement of the Russians, but recent historical scholarship throws new light on the Progressive position. In fact, these new studies basically agree with Taylor's assessment of the origins of the Cold War.

Instead of blaming the Cold War entirely on the Russians, many recent monographs show that the responsibility for the Cold War must be shared.[33] Generally, these historians view the Cold War as a series of tragic misunderstandings on the part of the Soviets, the Americans, the British, and the French. They trace the anxieties of each nation back to earlier grievances. Allied intervention in the Russian Civil War, American refusal to recognize the Communist regime, the Nazi-Soviet non-aggression pact, and the delayed second front in Europe during World War II contributed to fear and distrust. With the benefit of historical hindsight, revisionist historians argue that the frigid postwar conditions were the results of attempts by both the United States and the Soviet Union, together with their respective allies, to establish political and/or economic dominance over either neighboring or friendly governments in order to prevent the other power from doing so. The emergence of a power struggle between the Soviet Union and the United States coincided with the surge of nationalism throughout the colonial empires of the Netherlands, Great Britain,

---

Taylor could never divorce himself from the Progressive crusade and Henry Wallace. They corresponded and defended each other throughout the 1950s.

[33] Some of the most prominent revisionist works include Gar Alperovitz, *Atomic Diplomacy: Potsdam and Hiroshima* (New York: Simon and Schuster, 1965); Walter LaFeber, *America, Russia, and the Cold War, 1945-70* (New York: John Wiley and Sons, 1971); William A. Williams, *The Tragedy of American Diplomacy* (New York: Dell Publishing, 1962); Martin F. Herz, *Beginnings of the Cold War* (Bloomington: Indiana University Press, 1966); Ronald Steel, *Pax Americana* (New York: Viking Press, 1967); David Horowitz, *The Free World Colossus* (New York: Hill and Wang, 1965); Neal D. Houghton, ed., *Struggle Against History* (New York: Simon and Schuster, 1968); Gabriel Kolko, *The Politics of War* (New York: Random House, 1968); and *The Roots of American Foreign Policy* (Boston: Beacon Press, 1969); and Fred J. Cook, *The Warfare State* (New York: Macmillan, 1962). Barton Bernstein and Thomas C. Paterson have also written numerous articles that question the traditional view of the Cold War. Historiographically, most of these authors give credit to D. F. Fleming's two-volume classic, *The Cold War and Its Origins* (Garden City, N.Y.: Doubleday, 1961), and to Walter Lippmann's collection of essays, *The Cold War: A Study in U. S. Foreign Policy* (New York: Harper and Brothers, 1947).

and France. The ideological and military tension almost demanded that the new nations make a choice. In the bipolarized world, neutrals were suspect.

All these factors contributed to the very complex postwar world of 1948 and the Cold War. Glen Taylor believes that the Progressive approach to world affairs might have provided new alternatives to the Cold War and these, if accepted, could have prevented some hot wars.[34] Although Taylor's assertions have been expanded and given historical credence, Taylor himself has been almost totally ignored by current critics of Truman's foreign policy. The showman senator too often has been dismissed without even a footnote.[35]

Historians reassessing the Cold War are now taking a position similar to that of the Progressives in 1948. They are asking questions such as: Was there any kind of conspiracy on the right? Was the decision to rearm after the war based on false assumptions? Did the United States make every possible effort to cooperate with the Soviet Union? Did the United States project an image of power and might that frightened the peoples of other nations? The answers some historians are now giving are, at times, very close to the Taylor positions.[36]

Although this revisionist scholarship has created a tremendous amount of historiographical excitement, most students of the postwar period still lean toward a standard approach to the Cold War. Admitting that certain American actions were misunderstood and feared, these scholars trace the origins of the Cold War to Communist ideology designed to foment revolution and to the personality of Joseph Stalin. They ask the question: "Could there be any meaningful negotiation with the Soviet Union as long as Stalin lived?"[37] For the traditionalists the question is rhetorical

[34] Interview with Glen H. Taylor, June 14, 1967.

[35] For the most part, these monographs mention Wallace and sometimes refer to Claude Pepper of Florida. It is possible that because of Taylor's frequent publicity antics, revisionist historians have chosen others to represent contemporary criticism of American foreign policy during the early days of the Cold War.

[36] The above-named scholars agree the decision to rearm was based on false assumptions, that the United States did not explore every possible avenue for peace, and that America's mass production of A-bombs scared the people of other nations.

[37] See Robert Ferrell, *George C. Marshall* (New York: Norton, 1969); John Spanier, *American Foreign Policy since World War II* (New York: Praeger, 1968); and Dexter Perkins, *The Diplomacy of a New Age* (Bloomington:

and the answer is obvious. However, much of what the Progressives opposed and proposed is worth further discussion.

Perhaps the most relevant cause espoused by Taylor, Wallace, and the new party was their distaste of the growing political-industrial-military alliance. Long before President Eisenhower's warning concerning a military-industrial complex, Taylor recognized America was undergoing a basic change. An isolated example of this alteration was the new Department of Defense and one of their activities. James Forrestal, speaking to the first graduating class of the Armed Forces Information school in August 1948 discussed that basic transformation in American life. The secretary of defense told the new publicity experts that it was their duty to reverse the traditional American antipathy toward the military. He stated: "It is difficult . . . because our democracy and our country are founded upon an underlying suspicion of armies and of the force that they reflect and represent." Forrestal then told the graduates of their new duty. "Part of your task is to make people realize that the Army, Navy, and Air Force are not external creations but come from and are part of the people. It is your responsibility to make citizens aware of their responsibility to the services."[38] For the first time in history, citizens had to be aware of their responsibility to the military during peacetime. If universal military training, which Taylor opposed so bitterly, had passed it would have contributed to the reversal of the roles of master and servant.

It can still be argued, as Taylor did in 1948, that the military, aided by big business, have acquired unprecedented influence in foreign and domestic affairs. Their control of the national economy

---

Indiana University Press, 1967). Nearly all standard United States diplomatic history textbooks follow the so-called traditionalist point of view. Samuel F. Bemis, *A Diplomatic History of the United States* (New York: Holt, Rinehart, and Winston, 1964); Robert A. Ferrell, *American Diplomacy* (New York: Norton, 1969); and Thomas A. Bailey, *A Diplomatic History of the American People* (New York: Appleton-Century-Crofts, 1969), are three obvious examples. There are many others of note. Perhaps the most concise accounts are Arthur M. Schlesinger, Jr., "Origins of the Cold War," *Foreign Affairs* 46 (October 1967):22-52, and Norman A. Graebner, "Global Containment: The Truman Years," *Current History* 57 (August 1969):77-83, 115-16. Although influenced by revisionist scholarship, both Graebner and Schlesinger are critical of the revisionist conclusions.

[38] *Army and Navy Journal*, August 14, 1948. Both Fred Cook and William A. Williams are severe critics of the Truman policies. Both authors are guilty of letting their assumptions become facts. However, they contribute significantly to Cold War historiography and their works cannot and should not be dismissed.

since World War II is graphically illustrated by examining the federal budget. Naturally, during the 1946–1948 period there was a decline in defense spending. This is attributed to the process of reconversion following the war. A more serious charge has been made, as Taylor did earlier, that the military-industrial alliance encouraged the Cold War in order to maintain a permanent war economy and avoid business recessions. The contention is that through a powerful propaganda web, the military-industrial complex with the willing assistance of politicians, perpetuates national emergencies in order to promote the arms race and justify unnecessary defense spending.[39]

Proponents of and apologists for the development of a warfare state agree that it was absolutely necessary to contain communism. Glen Taylor disagreed and vehemently opposed the instrumentalities of containment; the Truman Doctrine and the Marshall Plan. As a Progressive spokesman, Taylor believed that containment was a mere smokescreen behind which American business could economically dominate the rehabilitation of war-torn Europe and Asia. Just as the ghost of Peter the Great was responsible for Soviet behavior in Eastern Europe, so was the ghost of John Hay and the Open Door accountable for American actions. As Truman pointed out prior to enunciating the Truman Doctrine, "The pattern of international trade which is most conducive to freedom of enterprise is one in which major decisions are made not by governments but by private buyers and sellers."[40] In other words, the American president was advocating an Open Door for American private enterprise. There was no doubt that America emerged from the war as the leader of the economic world and the Truman administration believed that the choice was theirs to sustain and expand private enterprise. Simultaneously, it was necessary to avoid a domestic depression and the political consequence thereof.

The Truman Doctrine indirectly blamed the Soviet Union for all the world's ills and was a unilateral action. The American government made no attempt to achieve their stated objective, containing communism, through either negotiations with the Rus-

[39] Cook, *The Warfare State*, pp. 95-99, 110-125.
[40] Williams, *Tragedy of American Diplomacy*, p. 270. Unfortunately, Williams's volume is not footnoted. A good, concise source is Thomas G. Paterson, "The Quest for Peace and Prosperity: International Trade, Communism, and the Marshall Plan," in *Politics and Policies of the Truman Administration*, ed. Barton J. Bernstein (Chicago: Quadrangle Books, 1970), pp. 78-112.

sians or within the framework of the United Nations. A free Greece, at least free from communism, was a worthy goal, but America's concern stretched clear into the oil rich Middle East. In order to keep the oil trade in the "proper hands," the United States was found collaborating with the reactionary Arab leaders, the American oil interests, and the British imperialists.[41]

The Marshall Plan was billed as a great expression of America's inherent humanitarianism and it did represent a generous urge to assist the battle-weary masses of Europe. It is interesting to note that China and Latin America were excluded from massive assistance, though their needs were great from both a humanitarian and a policy point of view.[42] Disposing of America's "great surplus" offered a new economic frontier to the American capitalists, as well as a way to avoid losing democracy at home. Marshall believed that unless his plan was adopted, "the cumulative loss of foreign markets and sources of supply would unquestionably have a depressing influence on our domestic economy and would drive us to increased measures of governmental control."[43]

This is not meant to imply that the economic interpretation for the origins of the Cold War has been established. The political and ideological considerations cannot be dismissed. It is important to stress humanitarian considerations, but national self-interest was also a factor.

A general conclusion that can be reached concerning the origins and causes of the Cold War is that neither power bloc was blameless. Not only do the Americans and the Russians share the responsibility for what happened, but the citizenry and governments

---

[41] The United States' Middle East policy received new criticism from the Progressives during the 1948 campaign. The newly created nation of Israel was recognized by the United States, very likely for political reasons; however, war broke out between the Israelis and the Arabs. American policy was between a rock and a hard place according to Taylor: "We cannot achieve peace as long as the conspiracy of oil imperialism dominates our policies. We cannot tender recognition with one hand to the people of Israel, and arm the sons of Israel with the other. Recognition must be made to the gateway to peace, not the burial ground of the hope for freedom." *Daily Worker*, March 17, 1948. The speech this quotation is taken from was delivered at the Polo Grounds to a crowd estimated at 40,000.

[42] Williams, *Tragedy of American Diplomacy*, p. 271.

[43] Ibid.; see also LaFeber, *America, Russia, and the Cold War*, pp. 47-51. The Truman administration was in a quandary about such things as balanced budget, potential recession, and foreign assistance. Not all of them viewed the Marshall Plan as a guarantee of a flourishing economy. See Bernstein, "Economic Policies," in *The Truman Period as a Research Field*, ed. Richard S. Kirkendall (Columbia: University of Missouri Press, 1967), p. 109.

of both nations must realize that although coins have two sides, humans have only one life. The Soviet Union viewed the Marshall Plan, originally designed for all of Europe, not just the West, as an attempt by the Americans to dominate not only the reconstruction of Europe, but her economic future as well. They refused to join the Marshall Plan and embarked upon a renewed series of repressive actions throughout Eastern Europe.

In many respects the Truman foreign policy was based on an attempt to blame all world problems on the Russians. This was exactly what Taylor warned against—an extremist witch hunt. The American people were bombarded with a "hate the enemy" campaign, while the nations of the world were officially at peace. Fear is the basest of all human emotions and in 1957 General Douglas MacArthur offered a caustic commentary on the previous decade. "Our government has kept us in a perpetual state of fear —kept us in a continuous stampede of patriotic fevor—with the cry of a grave national emergency. . . . Yet, in retrospect, these disasters seem never to have happened, seem never to have been quite real."[44] The sad indictment of America's policies, right or wrong, is that many political critics were emphatically discarded as either Communist-sympathizers or idealistic dreamers. Taking into consideration what the American people believed to be true in 1948 (an international conspiracy was attempting to take over the world), it is no small wonder that the Progressives were trounced by the masses they attempted to reach.

In summary, the Progressive party should not be categorized as a party of appeasement. Discussing real issues, they attempted to offer solutions designed to create peace and stability. Their timing was bad, and they were condemned because of their bedfellows. Over the years, it has become apparent that Henry Wallace and Glen Taylor had plenty to tell America. Their rejection at the polls was understandable, yet perhaps unfortunate. Both men were political corpses after 1948.[45]

44 Williams, *Tragedy of American Diplomacy,* p. 272.
45 Schmidt, *Quixotic Crusade,* pp. 313-20.

XI. *Struggle for Reelection*

Glen Taylor did not regard the 1948 election as a total loss. Far from it. He still believes that Harry Truman and the Democrats were forced to steal the Progressives' liberal domestic platform.[1] The success of Truman, who ran on what Taylor considered a replica of the Progressive domestic program, made it easy for the Idaho senator to transfer his allegiance back to the Democrats. The former actor summed up his position in 1949 by saying, "I never left the Democratic party; I was just like a player that MGM loaned to another company. . . . I just ran and now I'm back with the Democrats."[2] The Democrats accepted his return with little enthusiasm, but Taylor began to work for the domestic reforms that Truman had advocated during his 1948 campaign.

When Harry Truman had called Congress into the special "Turnip Day" session following the 1948 conventions, he asked the legislators to pass laws to halt rising prices, meet the housing shortage crisis, and to provide aid for education. He also had asked for a national health program, civil rights legislation, an increase in the minimum wage, extension of Social Security coverage, and funds to provide cheap public power and reclamation projects.[3] Although Taylor vigorously supported these Truman proposals, he still fought against the administration's foreign policy as exemplified by the North Atlantic Treaty Organization and the continuation of mammoth foreign aid to Western Europe, Greece, and Turkey. He also bitterly opposed loyalty oaths and McCarthyism. These were the issues, along with charges of communism and his association with the 1948 Progressives, that would eventually destroy Taylor politically.

The unsuccessful attempt to obtain a Columbia Valley Authority in the Pacific Northwest has already been discussed at length, as has Taylor's civil rights record. The CVA issue was Taylor's primary concern in 1949 and 1950, but he did work for other Fair Deal measures. Although he was nominally still a Progressive until the summer of 1949, Taylor joined Democrats Pepper, Murray, and Wagner in sponsoring administration-approved bills designed to increase Social Security benefits by establishing a national health insurance and public health program.[4]

In July, Taylor introduced the "Full Social Security Act of 1949," which was intended to create virtual full employment. A statement issued by the Idaho senator described the provisions of the bill briefly and simply. Every person willing to work, but unable to secure employment because of disability or lack of job openings, was to be paid 85 percent of his previous earnings until he secured employment. There was an enforcement clause which stated that the unemployed must accept suitable employment if offered and that they must actively seek work. Taylor's bill would also have provided for elderly citizens by giving them retirement benefits ranging from 40 to 70 percent of their average previous earnings, according to the number of their dependents. Taylor hoped that as a result, "high purchasing power in the hands of all people would guarantee a steady demand for . . . products."[5]

Another area in which Taylor strongly supported Truman was that of attempting to meet the demand for more low-rent and low-cost housing. In February 1949 Taylor was one of the sponsors of the Housing Act of 1949 that authorized federal aid to assist local agencies in slum clearance projects and in the construction of low-rent public housing.[6] He continually advocated increased federal support for construction of cheaper housing as well as for educational facilities for the newly developed areas in the United States.

Since his involvement with the Progressives had been an outgrowth of his views on foreign policy, it was only natural that Taylor remained concerned about foreign policy and its effect on domestic America. For example, Taylor believed that the initiation of loyalty oaths was a direct result of a foreign policy based on fear of communism. Taylor claimed that any loyalty oath infringed the civil rights of individuals as guaranteed by the Constitution. As an indication of his distaste for loyalty oaths and loyalty investigations, throughout 1947 and 1948 Taylor had con-

---

[1] Interview with Glen H. Taylor, June 14, 1967. See also Karl M. Schmidt, *Henry A. Wallace: Quixotic Crusade* (Syracuse, N.Y.: Syracuse University Press, 1960), p. 91, who arrives at the same conclusion.

[2] Quoted in Frank McNaughton to Bob Hagy, April 16, 1949, McNaughton Papers, Truman Library.

[3] *Truman's Public Papers*, 4:406-11.

[4] *Cong. Rec.*, 81st Cong., 1st sess., 1949, 95, pt. 1:38; pt. 4:4956; pt. 7:8719.

[5] Ibid., pt. 8:10259.   [6] Ibid., pt. 2:1538.

tinually inserted articles, letters, and editorials in the *Congressional Record* which opposed Truman's Executive Order 9835, issued on March 22, 1947.[7] In this Executive Order, Truman had set up a permanent program to ferret out all disloyal and subversive elements in the government. Truman hoped to provide the maximum protection for the United States against infiltration of the government by disloyal persons, while at the same time protecting loyal government employees from unfounded accusations. He recommended that each department and agency should set up its own loyalty procedures within minimum standards established by the president. All persons entering the employ of any department or agency would be investigated for loyalty by the Civil Service Commission. The records of persons already employed would be checked against FBI files for information that might adversely reflect on their loyalty.[8]

After the arrest of the leading Communists in America in 1948, Taylor feared that government loyalty oaths and investigations, the activities of the House Un-American Activities Committee, and the McCarran Internal Security Act were creating a national hysteria. The McCarran Act, which was passed in 1950, required all Communist organizations to publish their records, barred Communists from working in defense plants or obtaining passports, and established a Subversive Activities Control Board to aid in the work of exposing Communists.

During a Senate debate on whether or not loyalty oaths should be required for all scientists working for the Atomic Energy Commission, Taylor and Claude Pepper of Florida tried to stem the prevailing tide. The Idaho senator agreed with Pepper that opposition to this trend would no doubt draw slander and unfair accusations. Nevertheless, quoting Harold Urey, one of the scientists who had helped create the atomic bomb, Taylor pointed out that scientists believed the current wave of investigations and

[7] Ibid., 80th Cong., 1st sess., 1947, 93, pt. 10:A1329; pt. 13:A4855; 2d sess., 1948, 94, pt. 9:A244. The loyalty oaths and internal security measures began under Roosevelt in 1940. His program restricted the scope of the FBI and demanded positive documentation for all charges.

[8] Truman, *Memoirs*, 2:319-24. For a detailed discussion of the loyalty program see Earl Latham, *The Communist Controversy in Washington* (New York: Atheneum, 1966), and Athan Theoharis, "The Escalation of the Loyalty Program," in *Politics and Policies of the Truman Administration*, ed. Barton J. Bernstein (Chicago: Quadrangle Books, 1970), pp. 242-68. Both of these authors contend that the Cold War was responsible for a suppression of individual rights.

character assassinations was hurting the atomic energy program.[9]

It was Taylor's opinion that if America had enemies, the "hysteria which has seized the country" was playing into the hands of those enemies. "I feel that we are really letting the Russians run the show for us. We are adopting their methods. I think our greatest weapon against totalitarianism is the freedom we have. We are sacrificing that freedom in the name of fighting totalitarianism, and I cannot go along with such a policy."[10] His worst fears began to be realized the next year when one of his senatorial colleagues, Joseph R. McCarthy of Wisconsin, began issuing fabricated statistics on the number of Communists in the executive branch of the government.[11]

When it was proposed that all recipients of federal scholarships for the study of atomic energy should receive a thorough FBI loyalty investigation, Taylor privately tried to persuade his colleagues that this was a foolish course of action. Appealing to their common sense, he told them that it cost approximately $25,000 to conduct a full-scale FBI investigation of an individual, and nothing would be proved by such investigations. According to the Idaho senator, the Communists could pay some student to go to college, and the Communist student would take the same classes and receive the same information as the scholarship recipient. His counsel fell on deaf ears, and such investigations were authorized and carried out.[12]

Taylor took the opportunity provided by the Senate's discussion of the nomination of Dean Acheson as secretary of state to voice once more his opposition to Truman's foreign policy. He repeated his contention that America's current policy would lead to disaster and that the current hysteria about loyalty oaths was a blight on the society. It was a sad thing, said Taylor, that Acheson was "forced to undergo what amounted to a third degree" in front of the Senate Foreign Relations Committee. The Idaho senator claimed that Acheson was deemed loyal enough to serve his

---

[9] *Cong. Rec.*, 81st Cong., 1st sess., 1949, 95, pt. 8:10563.
[10] Ibid., p. 19564.
[11] Robert Griffith, *The Politics of Fear: Joseph R. McCarthy and the Senate* (Lexington: University Press of Kentucky, 1970), pp. 52-114. See also Richard Rovere, *Senator Joe McCarthy* (Cleveland, Ohio: World Publishing, 1959), pp. 124-34.
[12] Interview with Taylor, June 14, 1967. A special congressional hearing was held in May 1949 on the fellowship program. See U. S., Congress, Joint Committee on Atomic Energy, *Hearings, Fellowship Program*, 81st Cong., 1st sess., 1949.

country only after the prospective secretary of state made statements in which he "took some rather severe blows at the Soviet Union."[13]

Admitting that he did not expect any fundamental change in foreign policy, Taylor said that he was happy to vote for Acheson's confirmation because the new secretary was a civilian rather than a military officer like his predecessor, George C. Marshall. The Idaho liberal reiterated his conviction that the United States was "spending fabulous sums of money only to buy enemies." Amid applause from the galleries, Taylor concluded with a verbal assault on American aid to Chiang Kai-shek, Greece, and Turkey. He was especially caustic in his denunciation of Europe's imperialistic powers. Claiming that the American people were moving toward isolationism, Taylor said the reasons for this trend were apparent. "They are tired of spending billions of dollars and having their taxes increased in order to send money around the world—to Great Britain, for her imperialist ventures against the Jews in Palestine; to the Dutch, for their imperialist ventures against the Indonesians; and for all the sad things that are occurring throughout the world, and for which we are getting the blame, indirectly at least."[14]

Taylor continued to speak out against the Truman foreign policy and refused to support the administration's proposals for foreign aid. He based his opposition on the same points he had used in 1947 and 1948: that the United States aid program undercut the United Nations, supported imperialism, bolstered reactionary regimes, and prolonged the Cold War. In an April speech in which he opposed the continuation of the Marshall Plan, Taylor conceded that possibly some good had been accomplished by the European Recovery Act. "Hungry people have been fed. Economies have been rehabilitated. But I do not feel that the good which has been accomplished can anywhere near off-set the harm which has been done the United Nations and the cause of world peace by our taking the ball unilaterally and running with it."[15] He concluded with a grim prophecy: "I believe that our whole foreign policy is ill-conceived and eventually will be proved to have been a very poor course of action for us to follow."[16]

[13] *Cong. Rec.*, 81st Cong., 1st sess., 1949, 95, pt. 1:461.
[14] Ibid., 461-62.
[15] Ibid., pt. 3:4141.
[16] Ibid.

In the same speech, Taylor told his colleagues that he expected to vote against the recently concluded North Atlantic Pact, because he did not "recall any incident in history in which armed alliances have prevented war or even assured victory for those who allied themselves together in such an alliance."[17] True to his word, Taylor spoke against the NATO treaty when it was debated in the Senate. He appealed to an emotion which "is generally not thought of as being a most worthy emotion, jealousy." He pleaded with the Senate to be jealous of its constitutional role and not to serve as merely a rubber stamp. Taylor accused the administration of "presenting grave and important matters to the Senate in the nature of a fait accompli" and the Senate of ratifying administration proposals because of the fear that "we might embarrass our policy makers and the Nation."[18]

His main arguments against NATO were that the United Nations was being bypassed again and that a military alliance in Western Europe would only be the prologue to another war. He also expressed a fear that the additional drain on the American treasury would "further increase the national debt at the risk of facing national bankruptcy." As an alternative to NATO, Taylor proposed: "I believe we should first of all make an all-out effort to build up the United Nations. We should continue and increase our efforts to reach an agreement for worldwide disarmament." Again Taylor appealed for direct talks with the Russians. "Certainly we should quit this business of even entertaining the thought that we should not negotiate with the Russians on the theory that it might thaw out the cold war and thereby cause the American people to embrace a feeling of false security."[19]

According to the Idaho senator, one of the most distasteful aspects of NATO was that the United States was making it possible for the European imperialists to impose their will upon colonial peoples. Portugal, the Netherlands, France, and Britain would be using American arms to keep struggling colonies in Africa, the

17 Ibid., p. 4142. Taylor was incorrect in his pre-NATO judgments. Although the organization is currently under fire, it has not led to war.
18 Ibid., pt. 7:9779. At another time Taylor accused John Foster Dulles, then a New York senator, of attempting to keep the American people artificially alarmed, so that the NATO treaty would pass. *Daily Worker*, July 21, 1949.
19 *Cong. Rec.*, 81st Cong., 1st sess., 1949, 95, pt. 7:9785. Article 51 of the United Nations Charter permitted the establishment of regional suborganizations. Although NATO was legal, Taylor feared it would cause the Soviet Union to retaliate, as they did with the Warsaw Pact.

Middle East, and Asia under control. He recalled that in a 1947 speech against the Truman Doctrine he had said, "our foreign policy was losing us friends all around the world." The Idaho liberal declared that the statement was even more true now because of continual arms assistance to reactionary regimes.[20]

The speech concluded on an unexpected humorous note. Taylor launched a verbal atack on Winston Churchill for coming to America and making his "iron curtain" speech that had aimed to destroy the alliance which had successfully prosecuted the Second World War. After proposing that Churchill initiate steps to remove the iron curtain, Taylor said of the former prime minister, "He caused the whole miserable business. I wish he had stayed home and minded his own business." The presiding officer, Senator Edward J. Thye of Minnesota, absentmindely replied, "Without objection, it is so ordered." As laughter echoed through the chamber, Taylor cheerfully replied, "Good. I hope that it will appear in the Record."[21] Senator Thye, who was reading when his Idaho colleague made this remark, looked up with surprise and waited until someone told him what he had done.[22]

As usual, Taylor voted with the minority and NATO was passed quite easily. Bipartisan foreign policy disturbed Taylor, particularly because so few of his colleagues in the Senate even attempted to offer solutions to the Cold War. Only Claude Pepper and William Langer usually agreed with Taylor on foreign policy issues. During the tense days of early 1950, prior to the outbreak of the Korean War, Taylor was finally encouraged by the actions of some other senators.

On February 2 Brien McMahon of Connecticut called for international control of superweapons and cooperation in the peaceful use of atomic energy. Taylor joined Democrats Herbert H. Lehman of New York and Paul Douglas of Illinois in praising the McMahon suggestion. The Idaho senator said, "if we had had more of this type of thinking beginning with the end of the war, and even before the end of the war, we might not be faced with the terrible dilemma which confronts us today."[23]

Four days later Millard Tydings of Maryland submitted a

20 Ibid., p. 9786. NATO power has not been used to keep colonial peoples subjected to the imperialistic nations. In fact, most of the European nations lost their colonies.

21 Ibid., p. 9787.

22 *New York Times*, July 21, 1949, p. 1.

23 *Cong. Rec.*, 81st Cong., 2d sess., 1950, 96, pt. 1:1341.

resolution asking the Senate to approve world disarmament. The Tydings resolution, placing responsibility for disarmament in the hands of the United Nations, requested that the UN accomplish the job by 1954. Admitting his pessimistic attitude toward the world situation, Taylor said that McMahon and Tydings showed "more statesmanship than I have found in all the other talk which has occurred in the Senate of the United States during the five years that I have been a member of the Senate." He said he would "do everything I can to back them up."[24] Unfortunately the Korean War postponed the possibility of meaningful dialogue between the United States and the Soviet Union.

Taylor believed that he had consistently voted his convictions throughout his term in the Senate, and he wanted to campaign on his record when he ran for reelection in 1950. Although he was discouraged about his lack of influence on foreign policies, Taylor was proud of his record as a champion of liberal reforms and of civil liberties. When the Council Against Intolerance in America nominated Taylor in 1948 for its Thomas Jefferson Prize for the Advancement of Democracy, he was immensely pleased.[25] Even though, in the end, he was not the recipient of the award, he believed that his record had been vindicated. He returned to Idaho early in the summer of 1950 to place his future in the hands of the voters.

Taylor's "maverick" record as a Democrat obviously made him politically vulnerable in 1950. As early as September 1949, Taylor had announced that he would run for reelection as a Democrat. He also said that he would campaign for Truman's domestic program, but regretfully admitted that he could not agree with the president's foreign policy. In an interview, Taylor told a reporter, "I wish I could go along with the President. . . . It would be much more pleasant. I can't get it out of my head that we can't get along with the Russians."[26] Taylor's attitude on Truman's foreign policy, as well as his involvement with Wallace, which according to his

24 Ibid., pt. 2:1478-79.
25 Henry A. Atkinson to Glen H. Taylor, January 19, 1949, reprinted in "Man of the People," a pamphlet Taylor's staff prepared for distribution during the 1950 primary. According to Taylor, the pamphlets were left in local Democratic party headquarters throughout the state, but were never widely distributed. A copy is in the writer's possession. Some of the people on the Council were Thomas E. Dewey, John Dewey, Reinhold Niebuhr, Richard Neuberger, and Senators Robert Milliken, Herbert H. Lehman, Theodore Green, and Leverett Saltonstall. It was by no means a radical group.
26 *New York Times*, September 21, 1949, p. 25.

critics marked him as a Communist, became the principal ammunition used against him during his 1950 attempt at reelection.

With the announced support of Idaho's AFL and CIO and the small Farmer's Union locals, and with his patronage rights restored, Taylor set out to deal with the two challengers in the Democratic primary, former Senator D. Worth Clark and Compton I. White, a congressman. The Democratic National Committee allegedly promised that if Taylor won the primary, he would have the full support of the national party in November.[27] Richard Neuberger, in an article in the *Nation*, accurately forecast Taylor's difficulties in obtaining renomination. The Oregon journalist predicted that Taylor would lose because he had the support of only the minute liberal elements in Idaho and because thousands of Republicans, taking advantage of Idaho's open primary, would cross party lines and vote for the conservative Clark. Neuberger also said that there would be a vicious smear campaign against Taylor.[28] He was right on both counts.

Neuberger did not forecast another form of opposition that was facing Taylor. Many people who had supported the Progressives in 1948 were very upset with Taylor's reassimilation into the Democratic party. Fred Marchant of Kellogg, Idaho, the executive secretary of the Idaho Progressive party, was worried about some of Taylor's recent actions on foreign policy.[29] Taylor's support of the Truman administration in Korea and his vote to continue some Marshall Plan aid caused this concern on the part of Idaho Progressives. However, as John G. Rideout, another Idaho Progressive, pointed out, Taylor was much better than Clark or White.[30]

Both Wallace and Taylor had been criticized by old-line Progressives for their attitude on Korea. One man who wrote to Wallace asking him to explain his position, expressed sympathy toward Taylor and his motives: "I can understand Senator Taylor's present position . . . because Glen Taylor had economic pressures bearing on him which endangered the immediate security of his family."[31] It is not known how the few Idaho Progressives voted

[27] "Back in the Fold," *New Republic* (March 13, 1950), p. 7.
[28] Richard Neuberger, "Glen Taylor Rides Again," *Nation* (May 20, 1950), pp. 469-70. See also "The Senate's Most Expendable," *Time* (March 20, 1940), p. 18.
[29] Fred Marchant to John G. Rideout, quoted in John G. Rideout to Henry A. Wallace, July 10, 1950; 250231M, Wallace Papers.
[30] Ibid.
[31] Robert Drake to Wallace, July 16, 1950; 250257M, ibid. See also

in 1950, but their failure to cast their ballots for Taylor may have been significant since the final vote was close.

For obvious political reasons, Taylor attempted to ally himself with the administration and obtain Truman's support prior to the primary, but Truman proved to be unforgiving. As president, he refused to endorse any of the candidates in the Idaho primary and treated them all as equals.[32] Undaunted, Taylor asked the administration to send speakers into Idaho who would campaign for CVA. He telegraphed presidential assistant Donald S. Dawson: "I am going right down the line for CVA in my campaign and hitting it hard. . . . Any help on this issue now in way of high-level statements or speakers badly needed and appreciated."[33] Dawson gave Taylor's telegram to David E. Bell, a close adviser of Truman, who bluntly told Dawson, "It does not seem to me that Taylor's telegram required an answer." Bell then informed Dawson that Interior Secretary Oscar Chapman agreed that "any administration statements about the CVA at this time will have to be made with due recognition of the fact that the primary in Idaho does not come until August 8."[34]

Although upset by Truman's lack of support, Taylor continued to use CVA as his major campaign issue. Many of Taylor's supporters felt that dropping the CVA issue would brighten his chances for reelection. Idealistically Taylor replied: "Well, if that's the way it is, that's the way it will have to be. . . . I am for CVA because I believe in my heart that that is the only way we can ever get reasonably quick development of the resources of this great State of ours."[35] The Columbia Valley Authority, however, was not an issue that excited Idaho's voters in 1950, and it partially contributed to Taylor's political demise.

Truman's refusal to endorse Taylor disturbed the Idaho senator particularly because his chief primary rival, D. Worth Clark, was so conservative that he had actually debated whether to run as a Democrat or as a Republican.[36] Any lingering hopes for pres-

---

Lawrence H. Hammer to Wallace, July 17, 1950; 25032M, ibid.; Albert Muldavin to Wallace, August 28, 1950; 250885M, ibid.; France Lynsolm to Wallace, December 6, 1950, 251153M, ibid.

[32] *Truman Public Papers*, 6:287.

[33] Telegram, Glen Taylor to Donald S. Dawson, June 19, 1950, OF 360-A, Truman Papers.

[34] David E. Bell to Dawson, June 28, 1950, ibid.

[35] *Cong. Rec.*, 81st Cong., 2d sess., 1950, pt. 16:A5433.

[36] Neuberger, "Glen Taylor Rides Again," p. 470.

idential approval suffered a severe blow in early May, when Truman made a railroad trip through the Gem State. On May 3 Taylor's office announced that he had been invited to accompany Truman on his special train while it was in Idaho.[37] This announcement immediately created political repercussions among Idaho Democrats. Daniel Cavanagh, the state chairman, wired Truman's press secretary, Charles G. Ross, saying: "This alleged invitation to Senator Taylor, on which he had capitalized in releases to the press, is being construed in Idaho as giving presidential support to Senator Taylor in the coming direct primary and has raised a storm of protest." With tongue in cheek, Cavanagh added, "Unfortunately, this resentment is being directed against the President and I am more concerned about this phase than the help to Taylor."[38]

Cavanagh sent his telegram on May 4, the same morning that Taylor's announcement appeared in the Idaho papers. That afternoon, when Truman held a press conference in Washington, he was asked if Taylor had been invited. He answered briskly, "He has not. . . . When we go through Idaho, I will be glad to see the Senator from Idaho and shake hands with him, as I will with every other public official."[39]

After Truman's press conference, Taylor released to the press the text of the invitation. It stated: "The President will be pleased to have you join the party at any point convenient to you and to accompany him through your state." But the Idaho senator added, "If the President says I'm not invited, then that settles it. I'm not going to comment further."[40] Ross, in a telegram to Cavanagh, attempted to cover the apparent slip: "The president stated flatly at his press conference yesterday that he has not invited Senator Taylor to ride with him on his train through Idaho."[41]

Truman's natural reluctance to support or assist Taylor meant that Taylor would have to campaign as he always had in the primaries—alone or with his family. Taylor hired a Western band

---

[37] *Lewiston Tribune*, May 4, 1950.

[38] Telegram, Dan J. Cavanagh to Charles G. Ross, May 4, 1950, OF 200-3-I, Truman Papers.

[39] *Truman's Public Papers*, 6:287.

[40] *Lewiston Tribune*, May 5, 1950.

[41] Telegram, Ross to Cavanagh, May 5, 1950, OF 200-3-I, Truman Papers. The invitation to Taylor was probably sent by a Truman aide who did not realize the situation in Idaho.

which also traveled around the state with him. After a few of Taylor's songs, the band played briefly for dancing, and then Taylor would launch into a defense of his record. He proudly emphasized the fact that during his five years in the Senate, Idaho had received more federal assistance for reclamation, flood control, and public welfare than in any other five-year period in the state's history.[42] He correctly assessed his opposition when he predicted that his record would not be attacked directly, but that his foes would brand him a "Red" because of his involvement with the Progressives. In a Pocatello speech, Taylor said that if he "made a mistake in running with Wallace . . . it was a mistake of the heart and not of the head."[43]

Taylor tried to make his voting record, the CVA, and anti-extremism the main themes of his 1950 campaign. Denouncing the extremist techniques used to defeat Millard Tydings of Maryland and Claude Pepper of Florida in Democratic primaries during June 1950, Taylor said that he hoped the "rumors that my opposition intends to operate from the lowest levels by shouting accusations and insinuations up through manholes turn out to be erroneous." He would refuse to be put on the defensive, he said, or to spend his time answering "false accusations and half-truths."[44] He also said there might be whispering campaigns questioning his integrity as a father and husband because of his ex-wife's 1945 suit for child support. Furthermore, he denied rumors started by a former Senate aid who accused him of obtaining kickbacks from his employees.

John Corlett of the *Idaho Daily Statesman* observed that Taylor must suffer from a guilty conscience because the senator was raising these issues before anyone else did.[45] But Taylor said he was only trying to destroy rumors before they got started. Taylor may

[42] Lewiston Tribune, June 21, 1950.
[43] *Idaho State Journal* (Pocatello), June 15, 1950. In retrospect, Taylor's mistake was probably more of the head than the heart, at least partially.
[44] *Idaho Statewide*, June 15, 1950. A pamphlet entitled "The Red Record of Claude Pepper" was prepared and used against the Florida Democrat. It featured pictures of Pepper with Henry Wallace, Paul Robeson, and other leftists. The pictures, for the most part, had been taken during the 1944 campaign at Democratic rallies. The case against Pepper was built on the concept of guilt by association, but it was successful. The Tydings defeat is a well-known episode that involved Senator McCarthy's attacking Tydings as "soft on communism." Tydings had chaired the committee which investigated McCarthy's charges about Communists in high office. Rovere, *Senator Joe McCarthy*, p. 36.
[45] *Idaho Statesman*, June 18, 1950.

have headed off some embarrassing rumor-mongering about his personal life, but he was unable to curb the Communist accusations hurled against him, in part because the national hysteria called McCarthyism was now sweeping the country.

Taylor had spoken out against Senator Joseph McCarthy's "Red Scare" from the beginning. Just eighteen days after McCarthy's notorious Wheeling, West Virginia, speech Taylor criticized Mc-Carthy on the Senate floor and inserted in the *Congressional Record* an ediorial which attacked the Wisconsin senator's first assertion that the federal government was filled with Communists.[46] In a Boise radio speech during the 1950 campaign, Taylor referred to Truman's offer to open State Department files to the Senate committee investigating McCarthy's charges. He said: "McCarthy is not satisfied with that—he wants the FBI files too. I am convinced, however, that if he got the FBI files, he wouldn't be satisfied but would probably insist on seeing the books of St. Peter in a last desperate effort to prevent final collapse of this whole fantastic business."[47] It was Taylor's expressed hope that the public would "rise up and demand an end to it all." He declared, "It is difficult to decide whether free institutions are more in danger from the activities of the secret police or from the activities of subversive characters."[48]

Try as he would, Taylor was unable to make political headway by pointing to the dangers of extremist actions. Both Democrats and Republicans viciously attacked the Idaho senator for his alleged Communist leanings. The invasion of South Korea by the North Koreans in June 1950 gave considerable aid to the anti-Taylor forces despite the fact that Taylor supported the attempt to halt North Korea because it was a United Nations action. In a radio broadcast, he stated: "Under these circumstances I can only hope that the United Nations will emerge triumphant and strengthened from the Korean ordeal, that the fighting can be confined to that area and will not spread, and that gradually through the years, like a man walking a tightrope over Niagara, we can precariously inch along and skirt the brink of chaos until some time in the future the United Nations will be strong enough to say to any would-be aggressor, 'lay down your arms.'"[49]

[46] *Cong. Rec.*, 81st Cong., 2d sess., 1950, 96, pt. 13:A1405-6.
[47] *Lewiston Tribune*, May 15, 1950. Griffith, *The Politics of Fear*, is an excellent account of the fear demonstrated by the Senate regarding McCarthy.
[48] Ibid.

D. Worth Clark, Taylor's principal primary opponent, said that the Korean situation emphasized the need for "elimination of our Henry Wallaces from positions of power in public life. A public official doesn't have to be a card-carrying communist to be a communist stooge or dupe."[50] Repeatedly Clark accused Taylor of being "duped by communists into playing their game at the expense of Americanism."[51] Clark, who had served in the China lobby after his term in the Senate, criticized Taylor for refusing to vote for aid in China prior to the Communist takeover in 1949. He claimed that American boys were not being killed in Korea because of "Taylor and his Communist associates."[52]

Compared to the Republican attacks on Taylor, however, Clark's charges were mild. The Idaho GOP picked up Senator McCarthy's theme and applied it to the Democratic incumbent. Former Idaho Congressman John Sanborn defended McCarthy after Taylor's attacks on the Wisconsin demagogue.[53] The most vociferous Republican, however, was a Payette attorney, Herman Welker, who was seeking the Republican senatorial nomination. Although Welker faced two other Republicans in the contest for the Senate nomination, he ignored his GOP opposition and concentrated his entire fire on Taylor. In a speech on July 4, Welker announced that there were "87 communists in Idaho," plus many more "radicals and stooges and crackpots who consistently follow the party line and play right into the hands of the communist cause. I include the Henry Wallaces and Glen Taylors."[54]

Welker repeatedly challenged Taylor to a debate, but the incumbent steadfastly refused to discuss anything with Welker. Taylor took the position that he was running against Clark and White in the primary, and therefore, he tried to ignore Welker and his barrage of charges. John McMurray, Welker's campaign manager, claimed that Taylor was dodging Welker because the Payette lawyer "would rip Taylor and his communist-line activities into

---

[49] Glen H. Taylor's Record on Foreign Affairs, Glen H. Taylor File, CIO-PAC Research Department, Washington, D.C.

[50] *Idaho State Journal*, June 26, 1950.

[51] Ibid., July 7, 1950. See also *Lewiston Tribune*, July 9, 1950; *Idaho Statesman*, July 9, 1950.

[52] *Lewiston Tribune*, August 1, 1950. The China lobby was a group supporting Chiang Kai-shek who attempted to persuade the United States to give Chiang massive financial and military assistance.

[53] Ibid., August 3, 1950.

[54] *Idaho State Journal*, July 5, 1950.

shreds and Taylor knows it."[55] In a Lewiston speech, Welker
attacked Taylor because the senator refused to "debate his Americanism with me," and added that Taylor's friendship "with the
communists" was a great source of embarrassment for Idaho.[56]
Calling Taylor "the weakest link in the history of the U. S. Senate,"
Welker persistently hammered at Taylor's refusal to debate him,
even though they were not actually opponents in the primary. A
master of demagoguery, Welker categorized Taylor as a "political
coward who hasn't the courage to debate me. He knows I would
hang his hide on the fence . . . and expose his communist-line
activities."[57]

One of Taylor's supporters, John Carver, did agree to debate
Welker concerning Taylor's record. After listening to Welker's
familiar spiel, Carver calmly told a Caldwell audience that if the
public "analyzed the charges, they have no substance." Carver, a
dedicated New Dealer, said it was stupid to say Taylor lacked
courage or that he was a Communist. According to Carver, it
took "courage to run for the vice-presidency on the third party
ticket, and then courage to come back in the Democratic party."
Carver logically asserted that "if communists supported the third
party, that doesn't mean the third party is Communist. . . . This
campaign of smear is achieving a new low."[58]

Clark, Welker, and the other senatorial candidates of both parties
were indebted to the *Idaho Daily Statesman* for much of the
material used in their attacks on Taylor. The Boise daily, long one
of Taylor's severest critics, launched an unparalleled assault on
Taylor and his record. According to John Corlett, the political
editor, it was the only time that he ever set out, "under the
direction of my publisher and editor, to destroy a person and that
person's philosophy."[59]

In the July 2 editorial entitled "A Man Is Judged by the Company
He Keeps . . . and by What He Does," the *Statesman* declared war
on Taylor. The paper stated that it intended to run a series
patterned after the pamphlet used against Claude Pepper in

[55] Ibid., July 27, 1950.
[56] *Lewiston Tribune*, August 2, 1950.
[57] *Idaho State Journal*, August 4, 1950.
[58] *Idaho Statesman*, July 25, 1950. Carver was later appointed to the Bonneville Power Administration by the Kennedy administration.
[59] Interview with John Corlett, September 14, 1967. The owners of the
Statesman, Margaret Cobb Ailshie and James Brown, were convinced that
Taylor and his office were being used by the Communists.

Florida, "The Red Record of Claude Pepper." It also set the tone for its subsequent attacks on Taylor by quoting Paul Robeson, the Negro singer and Russian sympathizer, who had said, "The Soviet Union is the only country I've been in where I felt completely at ease."[60] The paper then asserted that Robeson was an "acquaintance" of Taylor's and claimed that Robeson had been identified with the Communist party since 1936. In conclusion the *Statesman* used a quotation from the *Daily Worker,* which called Taylor and Pepper "the heroes of the 80th Congress."[61]

Day after day throughout early July, the Boise daily published sections of "The Red Record of Claude Pepper," which had been prepared by a former FBI agent, Lloyd C. Leemis. At the same time, the paper devoted a considerable amount of editorial space to scathing assaults on Taylor for "consorting with known Communists." After establishing what the paper considered a direct correlation between Taylor, Pepper, and the Communists, the *Statesman* abruptly shifted its attack to Taylor alone, with the publication of a series called "The Red Record of Glen Taylor—As He Made It."[62]

In the initial editorial of this series, Taylor was accused of participating in so-called Communist-front groups such as the Congress of Civil Rights, the Win-the-Peace Conference, and the National Council of American-Soviet Friendship, all included in the attorney general's catalog of subversive organizations. Quoting from Taylor's speeches in opposition to the Truman Doctrine, the Marshall Plan, NATO, and the Universal Military Training Act, the paper compared the positions he had taken with those of the *Daily Worker* or some official of the Soviet Union. Contending that Taylor did not represent Idaho or America, the paper accused the senator of "representing the Russians on the floor of the United States Senate with more words than all the other senators in history."[63]

It is difficult to assess the effect of the Boise newspaper's campaign, but on July 28 three prominent Idaho Democrats called Taylor a Communist or placed him squarely in the Communist

[60] *Idaho Statesman,* July 2, 1950.
[61] Ibid.
[62] Ibid., July 24, 1950. The Pepper and Taylor series were carried throughout July and the first week of August. The editorials against Taylor appeared almost daily.
[63] Ibid., July 6, 1950.

camp.[64] When Taylor repeatedly accused his opponents of trying to smear him and his record, the *Statesman* replied with a quotation from J. Edgar Hoover, director of the FBI, who had warned that "crying smear" was part of the Communist line. The newspaper maintained that "the 'smear' accusation is a smokescreen which more and more Idahoans are understanding every day."[65] When Taylor criticized the paper's drive to unseat him, the Boise daily retorted, "It's the Communist line because the Communists fear the free press." All Taylor's words opposing American foreign policy were labeled as "imbedded in Communist favor."[66] There was no mention of Taylor's genuine concern over the possibility of a Third World War. His liberal stand for the civil rights of all Americans, whether they were blacks, laborers, or Communists, was not mentioned; nor were respected Americans who agreed with Taylor. The paper ignored the fact that many Idahoans, including Corlett, the paper's political editor, had expressed the belief that Taylor was doing a good job of representing Idaho's specific interests in the Senate.[67] In short, the *Statesman*'s attack on Taylor was a sad example of the rampant extremism and hysteria that was becoming a national trend.[68]

After attempting to emphasize what he considered to be the issues, Taylor finally accepted the Boise daily's offer of a full page in which to reply to the paper's charges. He added the condition that his material must be printed exactly as submitted. Margaret Cobb Ailshie, the publisher, wanted Taylor to confine himself to communism, but doubted that "a single newspaper page will be sufficient." Following a few days of bickering about censorship, Taylor bought a full-page ad in the *Statesman* instead of accepting Mrs. Ailshie's offer so that he could put in it what he wanted.[69]

Taylor's attempt to retaliate by discrediting the Boise paper was too little and too late. Among the items he placed on the page he had purchased was a photograph that had appeared previously in the *Statesman* and the *Idaho Falls Post Register*. It was a

[64] Ibid., July 29, 1950. The three were Carl E. Brown of McCall, P. C. O'Malley of Pocatello, and Frank McCall of Salmon.

[65] Ibid., July 27, 1950.

[66] Ibid., July 30, 1950.

[67] Ibid., April 24, 1949.

[68] The attacks on Pepper and Taylor were not isolated cases. McCarthy was in the process of attacking and causing the defeat of Millard Tydings in Maryland.

[69] Ibid., August 6, 1950.

picture taken in Washington, showing the Idaho congressional delegation greeting Wilson Chandler, president of Idaho's Junior Chamber of Commerce. In the *Stateman's* version, Taylor had been cut out of the picture entirely, leaving the impression that the Democratic senator was not present, which, according to Taylor, was "a deliberate lie." On the same page, Taylor also reproduced an article from the *Statesman* which carried the subheading "Favors Socialized Medicine." The first sentence of the article, however, was a quotation from a speech in which Taylor denied that he was a proponent of "socialized medicine."[70] The headline, Taylor claimed, was obviously a manipulation of the truth.

The third item on the purchased page was an open letter to Mrs. Ailshie, in which Taylor wrote, "Communism is not the issue. . . . I am no Communist, and you know it. Otherwise, you would not have been so careful to avoid making the direct charge." The Idaho senator told Mrs. Ailshie, "Doubtless you would relish the spectacle if I would get down and wallow in the mire with your paid character assassins, but I long ago learned a lesson." Referring to the pictures reproduced on the page, he asserted: "If a newspaper will indulge in the deliberate misrepresentation and deceit in its day-to-day reporting of the news so graphically demonstrated on this page, it would hardly seem necessary to rehash a series of charges so obviously designed to distort and misrepresent."[71] Taylor's rebuttal had some logic, but lacked the impact of a month of "The Red Record." The fact is that it was too feeble to counteract the vicious attacks of the *Statesman*. Instead of denying the substance of the paper's charges, he had attacked the techniques employed by the newspaper.

He concluded the campaign with a typical Taylor rally in Pocatello featuring family singing, a speech, and a dance. Tired, discouraged, and with a feeling of helplessness, the Taylors retired to their campaign headquarters to await the verdict of the electorate.

Glen Taylor was defeated by less than 1,000 votes in the 1950 primary. The most important factor in bringing about his defeat was his alleged communism.[72] Another was that the Republican party encouraged its members to cross over and vote for Clark in

[70] Ibid.
[71] Ibid.
[72] Clark received 26,897 to Taylor's 25,949. Compton White obtained 14,599 votes. It was a very heavy turnout, but not enough for Taylor.

the open Democratic primary. John Corlett estimated that between 3,000 and 5,000 did just that.[73] As early as May 28, the *Statesman* had openly advised Idaho Republicans to "organize, support Clark and defeat both Taylor and White in the primaries."[74] Shortly before the election, Ray McKaig, Taylor's longtime enemy, had similarly advised his fellow Republicans, adding that "America will not survive with men like Alger Hiss and Glen Taylor leading America into Communism."[75]

Refusing to concede until after an official canvass, Taylor went to Pocatello and waited for the results. Under Idaho law, Taylor had to prove in court that a recount could change the voting result before one could be ordered. After returning to Washington, D.C., in late November, Taylor persuaded Guy Gillette of Iowa, chairman of the Elections subcommittee of the Senate Rules and Administration Committee, to conduct an investigation of Idaho's primary. The Idaho Farmer-Labor Legislative Council had produced a statement reporting that "In many instances ballots were indiscriminately destroyed, . . . election officials were advising people at the polls to enter the Democratic primary to aid in defeating . . . Taylor, and in some cases official ballots were not provided."[76] After sending two investigators to Idaho, one of whom stayed only about two days, the subcommittee decided to drop the idea of a recount, even though the brief investigation stated that "There was clear evidence of diverse irregularities in the balloting and also evidence that there was confusion in the counting of some of the ballots."[77] An official recount was never ordered.

Summing up his defeat, Taylor said, "it is mighty tough running against both parties in the primary. The combination of big money and big organizations is too much."[78] On the day following the election, Taylor's former neighbor in the Senate Office Building, Harry Truman, was asked if he had a comment on Taylor's apparent defeat. The president answered, "No, I have no comment. . . . I don't know anything about it."[79] Although it was

[73] *Idaho Statesman*, August 13, 1954. See also August 11, 1950.
[74] Ibid., May 28, 1950.
[75] Ibid., August 6, 1950.
[76] Ibid., August 31, 1950.
[77] Ibid., September 16, 1950. A mystery surrounds this recount investigation. One investigator left for Alaska only two days after arriving. Taylor did not have the economic means to fight, and he believed it was in the best interest to let the decision stand.
[78] *Idaho State Journal*, August 11, 1950.
[79] *Truman's Public Papers*, 6:581.

rumored that Taylor would tour the Pacific Coast the following summer in *The Desert Song,* he apparently wanted to stay in politics.[80]   According to Taylor, Truman sent word that he wanted to see the defeated Idaho senator. Taylor visited the president's office twice, once in December 1950, and again in February 1951.[81] The president chastised Taylor for running with Wallace against his advice, but gave Taylor credit for doing what he thought was right. Taylor claimed the chief executive offered him any kind of job that he wanted. Taylor surprised Truman by declining the offer despite the fact that he did not have any other job offers and did not have the faintest idea of how he was going to support his family.[82]

The evidence has not been found showing that Henry Wallace sent a message of consolation to the defeated Taylor. When Verda Barnes, Taylor's Idaho secretary, explained the defeat to Wallace by letter, Wallace responded simply by writing, "If you see Senator Taylor and Mrs. Taylor, please give them my very warmest regards."[83]

Taylor returned to Idaho and worked as a carpenter even though his ailing back forced him to wear a brace. Taylor recalled that while working on a roof in 102° heat, with the heavy, hot brace reaching from his rib cage to his hips, he reflected on the rewards of political virtue and was overcome by mental depression.[84]

Although an editorial in the *Lewiston Morning Tribune* of August 11, 1950, predicted that Taylor was not finished politically, for all intents and purposes he was.[85] Taylor's opposition to the measures designed to curb Communist aggression abroad and to ferret out disloyal subjects in the United States meant that he was once again out of step with the crowd. Persistent as ever, Taylor sought a Senate seat in 1954 and 1956, but as in 1950, he found that the "Red Scare" was still very much in evidence.

[80] *Oregonian,* December 11, 1950.

[81] The memoranda written by the White House secretary staff regarding Taylor's requests for a meeting are to be found in PPF 1626, Truman Papers.

[82] Glen Taylor to writer, June 27, 1968. It is doubtful that Truman offered Taylor any job, yet it is very likely that Truman did propose some form of federal employment.

[83] Verda Barnes to Wallace, September 5, 1950; 250919M, Wallace Papers. Wallace to Barnes, September 11, 1950, 250973M, ibid.

[84] Ibid.

[85] *Lewiston Tribune,* August 11, 1950.

XII. *The Last Two Campaigns*

On Glen Taylor's final day in the Senate, his colleague William Langer eulogized the outgoing Idaho senator as a man of the people and added, "As he leaves here, he can hold his head high and throw out his chest, knowing that he has kept the faith."[1] Taylor himself was more to the point in his last Senate speech. He described his political career by saying: "I am afraid there is too much in this country of wanting to . . . go along with the popular idea of the moment. I have not done that. I have known, when I did certain things, that I was not doing what was politically expedient, so I have no excuses to offer for my defeat."[2] If Taylor had extremism in mind as a "popular idea," especially that type epitomized by Senator Joseph McCarthy, he was not finished with it. This would become obvious when he again ran for the Senate in 1954.

Between 1951 and 1954 Taylor busied himself trying to make a living. As usual, he survived. After a few months as a carpenter in Pocatello, he returned to California and joined three of his brothers in the construction business. They found a wealthy Californian to finance their endeavor and then began to bid for jobs, splitting fifty-fifty with their benefactor. After they had successfully completed a project in Alaska, the backer told them that the sky was the limit, so the Taylor brothers bid on a ten-million-dollar job at Fairbanks. Years later Taylor described the outcome: "A few days before the bids were to be opened our financier's cupidity got the better of him and he wanted 80%, and having more pride than brains, we told him there was a warmer climate than Alaska, and as far as we were concerned he could take his money and go there; and that ended the construction company."[3]

Taylor maintained his permanent residence in Idaho, but stayed in California, either at Redding or Fresno. Because he had a broken disk in his back, the family decided to remain in California while Taylor recuperated.[4] This protracted stay in California provided ammunition for his opponents, both Democrats and Republicans, when he returned to Idaho in February 1954 and announced that he would seek the United States Senate seat then held by Republican Henry Dworshak.

The 1954 primary was mild compared to that of 1950. Taylor's opponents, Claude Burtenshaw and Alvin McCormack, apparently considered him politically dead and refused even to recognize his presence. Wearing a gray toupee and a back brace, Taylor, accompanied by nineteen-year-old Arod, went from house to house; later they took an automobile equipped with loudspeaker into every hamlet of the state. Although his campaign was mild, it was typical Taylor, and he used familiar issues—big corporations, bad foreign policy, pensions for the aged, and parity for the farmers.[5] The veteran campaigner also explained his brace to rapt audiences: Six years of sitting in the Senate had caused partial collapse of his backbone. "I gave my all for you people, sitting there in Washington. . . . And in the Senate the man who works the hardest is the one who does the most sitting. With this brace, I can outsit them all."[6] Though the state Democratic leaders avoided Taylor, the voters did not. He received 26,591 votes and the Democratic nomination.[7]

The 1954 Idaho election campaign following the nomination was typical of the rampant extremism sweeping the country. An example of the tactics the Republicans intended to use was a letter sent to Sherman Adams, President Eisenhower's domestic adviser, the week after Taylor secured the nomination. An insurance executive from Maryland, Roy C. Jacobson, wrote: "I ran across a story in a book the other day which can be devastantingly used against Glen Taylor in the Fall Election if the Administration is desirous of helping Dworak [*sic*]. . . . The book is RED MASQUERADE: *Undercover for the FBI* by Angela Calemairis. . . . It concerns

---

[1] *Cong. Rec.*, 81st Cong., 2d sess., 1951, 96, pt. 12:17116.

[2] Ibid.

[3] Speech by Glen Taylor, Payette, Idaho, September 30, 1954, p. 45. The text is located in the Glen Taylor file, John Corlett Papers, Boise, Idaho. Hereafter cited as Taylor speech, Payette.

[4] Ibid.

[5] *Lewiston Tribune*, August 15, 1954.

[6] "Home on the Range," *Time* (August 23, 1954), p. 11.

[7] Burtenshaw obtained 24,094 and McCormack 13,673. Burtenshaw was a college professor and is presently dean of students at Utah State University. He refused to discuss Taylor or politics in Idaho. It seems that Taylor could count on nearly 25,000 votes in a primary and if there were three or more candidates he could win the nomination. This happened in 1940, 1942, 1944, and 1954. He failed in 1950 and 1956.

Glen Taylor's atendence [*sic*] at a dinner of the National Council of American Soviet Friendship."⁸ Taylor indeed had attended the meeting, but the press had covered the event, so there was nothing secret about it. However, this letter was only the beginning of another devastating "Red smear" campaign.

Intending to make foreign policy and unfulfilled Republican promises the chief issues, Taylor embarked on his fifth attempt to become a United States Senator. At his best as a critic, the fifty-year-old candidate openly attacked the Republican foreign policy, especially as propounded by John Foster Dulles, Eisenhower's secretary of state, who preached liberation of oppressed people and massive retaliation against aggression. To Taylor, who had opposed Truman's foreign policy, the Republican extensions of this policy seemed even more repugnant. In one speech he said: "In between charges and hearings into Republican activities, between saber rattling debates over the Dulles foreign policy, the Eisenhower foreign policy, the Nixon foreign policy, the McCarthy foreign policy, and Knowland foreign policy, the Republicans have managed to find time to extend and elaborate upon some of the Democratic policies they so recently abhored."⁹

Taylor's main contention was that the United States had become a counterrevolutionary force because of its economically motivated diplomacy. He told a Payette, Idaho, audience: "We supported French colonialism, Dutch colonialism, British colonialism, any colonialism, and where there was no colonialism policy in the saddle, we found a cheap dictator to support instead of helping the aspirations of the common people; and we have reaped the harvest."¹⁰ As an example, he mentioned Indochina, where the Americans, through military and economic assistance, had attempted to restore French control after they had been driven from the colony, instead of supporting Indochinese independence.

Foreign policy, especially Taylor's view of it, was never a key vote-getter in Idaho, so Taylor turned to what he called the corruption of the Eisenhower administration. The Idaho Democrat scored the administration for broken promises to the farmer and for tax relief for the wealthy, but aimed his heaviest ammunition at the tidelands-oil distribution. Early in the Eisenhower admin-

⁸ Roy C. Jacobson to Sherman Adams, August 22, 1954, GF 109-A-2, Eisenhower Papers.
⁹ *Lewiston Tribune*, October 4, 1954.
¹⁰ Taylor speech, Payette, p. 32.

istration, the states had been given the rights to dispose of the offshore oil reserves, which for years had been part of the public domain; now the states were free to sell the oil to the highest bidder.

The conservationist Taylor branded this move simply as a give-away. He claimed that the Republicans, in one fell swoop, had given the tidelands oil to the states whose governments were controlled by the oil companies: "They might as well have deeded it over to Texaco and Standard Oil," he said.[11] According to Taylor, the people had to unite against further giveaways. He asked his Idaho audiences: "Do you also want to let the Republicans give away the oil in Alaska and anywhere it can be found on the public domain?"[12]

Much to his chagrin, Taylor found that foreign policy, tax reform, tidelands oils, and parity for farmers were not going to be the key issues during the campaign of 1954. Anticipating an extremist attack, Taylor signed a pledge to observe a code of fair campaign practices and challenged Dworshak to do likewise.[13] A victim of Red-baiting in 1950, Taylor now took the offensive against the Republicans and accused them of "making political hay out of communism." As he told a Montpelier crowd, "This weird strategy of subordinating the vital issues and exalting Communist hunters brought forth the most grotesque collection of office-seekers in America."[14]

As mid-October approached, it appeared to some that Taylor's chances of being elected were excellent. In fact, two weeks prior to the election, *Newsweek* gave him fifty-fifty odds on defeating the incumbent Dworshak; and according to the magazine, many Idaho political experts agreed.[15] Jack Bell, an Associated Press political writer, called the race "a toss-up" and claimed the last two weeks of the campaign were going to tell the story.[16] The *New York Times* survey cautiously observed that Taylor was leading Dworshak as the campaign entered its last month.[17]

11 Ibid., p. 22. The states were probably Texas and California.
12 *Lewiston Tribune*, October 10, 1954. This question might still be asked.
13 *Idaho Statesman*, September 22, 1954.
14 *Lewiston Tribune*, October 20, 1954.
15 "Let 'Em Wait," *Newsweek* (October 25, 1954), p. 31. The Democratic Senatorial Campaign Committee contributed $3,000 to Taylor's campaign in 1954, so it appears the National Committee had forgiven the renegade Democrat.
16 *Idaho Statesman*, October 22, 1954.
17 *New York Times*, October 4, 1954, p. 1.

The last two weeks of the campaign, however, changed the situation drasticall.y Taylor was subjected to an extremist attack from the right which surpassed that of 1950. Joe McCarthy's power was waning in the fall of 1954, but Idaho's junior Republican senator, Herman Welker, was doing his best to keep the communism issue hot in Idaho. When Taylor heard the rumor that Welker, his long-time personal enemy, might return to Idaho to assist the Dworshak effort, he told reporters: "I am particularly pleased to have Senator McCarthy's Charlie McCarthy, namely the Hon. Herman Welker, on the scene and ready to share responsibility for Henry Dworshak's forthcoming defeat."[18] Dworshak then took a seat on the sidelines as Welker went to work in his behalf.

In early October, Welker called into session a special subcommittee of the Senate Internal Security Committee. Since the Idaho Republican was the only senator who attended the subsequent hearings, Taylor referred to them as a "secret, one man hearing in a phone booth."[19] Herbert Philbrick, Matthew Cvetic, John Lautner, and other former FBI agents who had posed as Communists testified that Wallace and Taylor knew that the Communists were aiding the Progressive party in 1948.[20] Cvetic recalled vividly being in meetings where Taylor and Wallace had made remarks to the effect that they welcomed the vote of anyone.[21] Of course Taylor had made perfectly clear, when he first announced his decision to join Wallace, that he would not repudiate Communist support. In the paranoid hysteria of the 1950s, however, Welker's alleged findings were treated as new revelations. Lautner and Cvetic also claimed that Wallace and Taylor had been chosen by the Communists because they were known to be willing to work with the Communist party in the coalition Progressive party.[22]

Taylor's immediate response to the Welker hearings was to challenge Idaho's junior senator to subpoena him, prior to the election. Taylor demanded that the hearing be held in Idaho, with both parties represented, and that Taylor's counsel be permitted to cross-examine the previous witnesses. He also suggested that Welker owed it to the people of Idaho to take the stand and submit

[18] *Lewiston Tribune*, August 30, 1954.
[19] Ibid., October 21, 1954.
[20] U. S., Congress, Senate, Subcommittee to Investigate the Administration of the Internal Security and Other Internal Security Laws, *Hearings, Communist Propaganda*, 83d Cong., 2d sess., 1954, pts. 1-3.
[21] Ibid.
[22] Ibid. See also the *New York Times*, October 20, 1954, p. 18.

to examination.[23] Henry Wallace offered to testify that the Progressive Party was not controlled by any one political ideology or faction.[24] In fact, Wallace wrote to Attorney General Herbert Brownell demanding to know what the Herbert Philbrick file said about Wallace. He told Brownell, "No one seems to have known who the Communists were save the Communists themselves and the FBI agents."[25]

Welker promised to call Taylor before the Committee at the earliest possible time, but further committee hearings were never held. Welker, however, who left Washington to return to Idaho, persuaded Cvetic to join him and scheduled a speaking tour for the former FBI agent. While Cvetic toured traditionally Democratic northern Idaho speaking on the threat of Communist takeover, Welker was joined by Vice President Richard M. Nixon, Senator Barry Goldwater of Arizona, Secretary of Agriculture Ezra T. Benson, and Speaker of the House Joseph Martin. Senator Everett Dirksen of Illinois had made an earlier appearance.[26]

The activity of Vice President Nixon was a typical anti-Taylor smoke screen intended to confuse the Idaho voters. Nixon told a Pocatello audience that Taylor's record "is so well known in Idaho that I don't think any comment from me is necessary." Then he added, "Taylor is dedicated to a political philosophy opposite from that of the people of Idaho who voted two-to-one for Ike in 1952."[27] At Boise, Nixon dramatically confided to the political throng that "Glen Taylor is a sincere dedicated member of ADA."[28] The vice president assured another audience that the Communist party was fighting desperately to elect Democratic candidates because they "belong to a 'left-wing clique' in their party which has tolerated the Red conspiracy."[29]

In still another speech, he cited a secret memorandum he had discovered on January 23, 1953, showing that the Communists

23 *Lewiston Tribune*, October 22, 1954.
24 *New York Times*, October 21, 1954, p. 17.
25 Henry Wallace to Herbert Brownell, October 23, 1954; 450,169M, Wallace Papers.
26 *Lewiston Tribune*, August 30, 1954. Benson, a Mormon apostle, would appeal to the heavy Mormon sections of southern Idaho. See also the *Christian Science Monitor*, November 6, 1954.
27 *Idaho Statesman*, October 26, 1954.
28 *Washington Post-Times Herald*, October 28, 1954. The Americans for Democratic Action immediately denied any past or present association with Taylor; ibid.
29 Ibid., October 24, 1954.

planned to conduct their program within the Democratic party. The outgoing Democrats inadvertently had left behind in the files a blueprint for socializing America. Why he had waited until the off-year elections of 1954 to reveal such startling evidence, Nixon did not say.[30]

As Taylor attempted to emerge from the rhetorical whirlwind engulfing him, he began to realize that the opposition was aiming to destroy him completely. Perhaps the most startling development of the final week of the 1954 campaign was the sudden accusation, four years after he had left office, that Taylor had hired Communists to work for him while he was Idaho's senator. One of his former employees, Ross Haworth, made the charges while he was in Idaho, four days before the election.[31] Many of Taylor's former employees leaped to the candidate's assistance; they published one-quarter page advertisements in the Idaho dailies denying the Haworth allegations. George Curtis, Foy A. Blackburn, Verda Barnes, Everett Evans, J. Albert Keefer, and Irene Burton all attested to Taylor's loyalty and to Haworth's opportunism.[32]

Taylor filed a suit against his former employee. After the election, when Haworth was asked for a specific example of a Communist hired by Taylor, he named Jerome Spingarn, who still resided in Washington. Spingarn, in turn, accused Haworth of being a Communist.[33] These charges were ridiculous, but the facts were not made public until after Idaho voters had cast their ballots.

Taylor was to be subjected to one more final vicious attack. Two days prior to the election, Herman Welker returned to the state. He "now had Taylor cold," he said, and revealed that Taylor had affiliated himself with three organizations that were on the attorney general's list of subversive groups. Citing the American Committee for Yugoslav Relief, the Congress on Civil Rights, and the Independent Committee of the Arts, Sciences, and Professions, Welker

[30] "On the Last Lap, the G.O.P. Runs Wild," *New Republic* (November 1, 1954), pp. 3-4.

[31] *Lewiston Tribune*, October 30, 1954.

[32] Ibid., November 1, 1954. Irene Burton was then serving as Senator Wayne Morse's secretary. Verda Barnes was soon to return to Washington, D.C., as an assistant to Frank Church in 1956. J. A. Keefer served as liaison between the Department of Commerce and Congress after Taylor's defeat. Everett Evans was a member of the United States Bureau of Prisons, who had known Haworth after Taylor had dismissed his former aide. Evans claimed that Haworth had said nothing about subversives in Taylor's office until 1954. Haworth had been dismissed because, without Taylor's permission, he had processed an increased salary for his wife, who also worked in Taylor's office.

[33] Interview with Taylor, June 14, 1967.

concluded that Taylor's "collaboration with Communists and Communist-fronts was by no means limited to his vice-presidential candidacy on the Progressive ticket in 1948."[34] At one time or another in his career, Taylor had addressed all the above liberal organizations, and his speeches had been reported in the press. The groups, however, were virtually unknown to Idahoans.

Dworshak was reelected overwhelmingly as Taylor attempted to dig out of the mud thrown by his Republican opponents.[35] Defeated by nearly 60,000 votes, Taylor was literally stunned into silence. It had all happened so fast that Taylor was left with only a bitter memory and a desire to set the record straight.

Similar blitzkrieg tactics were employed in an attempt to defeat other western Democratic senatorial candidates, including former senator Joseph C. O'Mahoney of Wyoming, Senators James E. Murray of Montana, Richard Neuberger of Oregon, and John A. Carroll of Colorado. Full-page newspaper ads in Wyoming referred to O'Mahoney as "FOREIGN AGENT 783" and called him the hired attorney of Owen Lattimore. Murray was the subject of a twenty-four-page pamphlet entitled "Sen. Murray and the Red Web over Congress—The Story of Communist Infiltration of Your US Congress." Neuberger was accused of cheating on law school exams and Carroll was forced to view Colorado billboards plastered with the question "How Red Is Carroll?"[36] Adlai Stevenson called the Republican success in the West "McCarthyism in a white collar."[37]

After his defeat Taylor remained in Pocatello, where his sons were attending school. Temporarily, he returned to carpentry, building a house, then selling it. At this time, he and Dora began to experiment with the manufacture and distribution of toupees. Their greatest problem was the lack of consumer demand in the Pocatello area. They therefore worked out a plan: They would go to Salt Lake City, rent a motel room, advertise on television and in the newspapers, fit their prospective customers, and then return to Pocatello to make the toupees.[38]

One reason for remaining in Pocatello was that the persistent Taylor wanted to combat Welker in 1956. Revenge is a strong motivation, and Glen Taylor wanted to skin the vulnerable Welker.

[34] *Lewiston Tribune*, October 31, 1954.
[35] Dworshak received 142,269 votes to Taylor's 84,139 or a margin of 58,130.
[36] "On the Last Lap, the G.O.P. Runs Wild," pp. 3-4.
[37] Ibid.
[38] Interview with Taylor, June 15, 1967.

The Republicans knew that Welker was in trouble. A memorandum to Eisenhower, written in April 1955, indicates that Welker was ignoring the farmers, reclamation, and other local issues. The same memorandum discussed the attitude of Idaho's Democratic party leaders regarding another Taylor candidacy: "A determined effort is being made to get rid of Glen Taylor whom they regard as their Jonah. . . . The Democrat leaders feel they must get rid of him in the primary and will make a determined effort to do so."[39]

Embattled and scarred, Taylor outlined his plans for the 1956 campaign in a speech delivered at Berea College in March. He told his audience: "I have noticed that the official seal of Berea College bears the words, 'He who suffers, conquers,' because I have suffered two defeats hard running out there in Idaho."[40]

There was one force that neither Taylor nor Welker counted on as they prepared to do battle. Frank Church, a young Boise lawyer and the son-in-law of former governor Chase Clark, entered the Democratic primary against Taylor. A polished orator and a handsome young man, Church hoped to capitalize on the Taylor-Welker feud and emerge as the hope of the future.

Glen Taylor had carefully attempted to obtain strong support for his 1956 Senate bid. He went to Detroit in March and attended an informal meeting designed to raise money for his candidacy.[41] The meeting was held at the home of Lewis Frank who had been Wallace's chief speech writer as well as an editorial aide when Wallace was working for the *New Republic*. A long-time proponent of liberal causes, Frank had also taught at the CIO Political Action School. When the National Committee for an Effective Congress came out against Taylor, calling him a tool of the Mine, Mill, and Smelter Workers, Taylor wrote to Frank and to Henry Wallace asking them to persuade the Committee to change its recommendations.[42] Taylor also visited Wallace and asked him to write a

39 "The Situation in Idaho," April 4, 1955, Howard Pyle File, Eisenhower Papers. One Idaho historian has suggested that Herman Welker's only positive accomplishment as a senator was to persuade the Griffith family to sign Harmon Killebrew to a baseball bonus contract.

40 Speech by Glen Taylor, Berea, Kentucky, March 23, 1956, pp. 1-2. The text is located in the Glen Taylor File, John Corlett Papers, Boise, Idaho. Hereafter cited at Taylor speech, Berea.

41 Lewis C. Frank to Wallace, March 13, 1956; Wallace Papers. Frank told Wallace that Taylor had been underrated back in 1948 and that Taylor was more than deserving of all liberal support. Frank's letter also alluded to the communication he had received from Taylor.

42 Taylor to Wallace, April 11, 1956; 550,123M, ibid. Taylor had belonged

repudiation of the Cvetic and Philbrick charges.[43] Wallace responded by rebutting the charges, but he asked Taylor not to use his name in the campaign. Wallace then added, "I wish you well because I have always had the highest regard for your integrity. I know you have never been a communist nor consciously solicited their support."[44]

Beginning his campaign with a belated answer to the charges made by Welker and Cvetic in 1954, Taylor noted in a small pamphlet that since the 1954 election Senator Joseph McCarthy had been censured by his colleagues and Matthew Cvetic had been committed to a mental institution.[45] However, Taylor's hopes for returning to the Senate were derailed when Church defeated him in the primary by less than 200 votes.[46] As in 1950, Taylor tried to get the Senate Committee on Elections to investigate the primary and order a recount. Again he failed, so he conducted his own recount in Mountain Home, a city of 10,000 in southwestern Idaho. He concentrated his efforts on one precinct which had given him strong support over the years, but in 1956 had given him very few votes. After a few days of door-to-door polling, Taylor was convinced the city's official returns did not correspond with the results he was getting. He asked a notary public to go with him in order to validate each voter's signature, but Taylor was arrested for violating an anti-soliciting ordinance. Frustrated in his attempts at gaining a recount, he decided that he could win as an independent candidate, even though many Democrats told him that he would only split the party and enable Welker to be reelected. Taylor was convinced, however, that the state organization had stolen the election from him, and he allowed his more enthusiastic and dedicated supporters to encourage a write-in campaign in the general election. Taylor's independent candidacy never got off the ground, and Church defeated the incumbent, Welker, by a landslide.

---

to the Mine, Mill, and Smelter Workers while in California. It is probable that they contributed to his campaign, but so did many other unions.

[43] Ibid.

[44] Wallace to Taylor, April 18, 1950; 550,125M, ibid. Taylor also sought and obtained the support of a former Senate colleague, Governor Ed Johnson of Colorado, 550,287n, ibid.

[45] "The Democrat," undated pamphlet printed in Pocatello, Idaho, during the 1956 campaign. The pamphlet is in the writer's possession.

[46] Church received 27,942; Taylor, 27,742. Two other candidates, Burtenshaw and McCormack split 18,000 votes.

The 1956 campaign is significant not only because it was Taylor's last, but because he suffered a personal frustration. Taylor wanted to defeat Welker, but Church's narrow victory in the primary robbed him of this opportunity. Taylor received 13,415 votes as a write-in candidate. Church defeated Welker, 149,096 to 102,781.

With the following statement, Glen Taylor offically retired from politics after his 1956 defeat: "I am going to have to searchingly examine the ideas of political morality that have guided me during the 18 years I have been actively engaged in politics."[47] He retired firmly convinced that he had remained true to the ideals and concepts in which he believed.

[47] *Idaho Statesman,* November 7, 1956.

Conclusion: A Man of Heart

In many ways Taylor's idealism made him almost apolitical. Believing that the common man should receive help from the federal government, he used any available means to obtain such federal assistance, regardless of the political consequences. For example, Taylor continued to agitate for a Columbia Valley Authority long after the Truman administration decided to encourage cooperation between the governmental agencies and private power. The CVA issue was dead in both Idaho and Washington, D.C., yet Taylor, idealistically committed, refused to give up. Civil rights was another issue to which Taylor devoted much political time and energy during a period when the cause of the Negro was not as popular as it would later become. He had nothing to gain politically in Idaho by championing civil rights, but his ideals drove him beyond political considerations. On the other hand, his battles with the Idaho State Democratic party organization can largely be explained in terms of lack of political astuteness on Taylor's part. Because he consistently alienated this source of support, he was never able to construct a firm political foundation.

One of his most inflexible political characteristics was his penchant for Populist and depression-oriented themes even during periods of relative prosperity. Although Idaho has a strong Populist tradition, it was much easier to hate Wall Street, bankers, and monopoly when there was a high rate of mortgage foreclosure, when it was difficult to obtain credit, and when it was difficult to market crops. These conditions did not exist on a large scale in the period of comparative prosperity which accompanied and followed the Second World War. Taylor's devils seemed much less villainous in postwar America than they had during and immediately following the depression.

On the other hand, Taylor was close to the common people and he had the ability to put difficult and complex ideas across to the average citizen. Often quite willing to admit that he just did not know which way to vote on a complicated issue, Taylor would ask his constituents for their advice. Indeed this may have been a deliberate device to capitalize on his self-professed ignorance, but he based his theory of representative government on an advocacy of the people's wishes rather than on his own views.

However, by voicing his opposition to the country's postwar foreign policy, Taylor blantantly refused to go along with "the popular idea." In fact, by opposing the Truman Doctrine, the Marshall Plan, NATO, and the continuance of the selective service, Taylor not only ignored his constituents but left himself open to the charge of being a Communist-sympathizer. It was his disagreement with the Truman foreign policy that caused Taylor to commit his most serious political error.

There is no better example of Taylor's sacrificing politics for ideals than his desertion of the Democratic party for Henry Wallace in 1948, an action which led inexorably to the end of his political career. Why would a liberal freshman senator from a sparsely populated conservative state take a chance on sacrificing his future for a crusade? Taylor's sincere idealism led him to the conclusion that to do so was basically and morally correct. Apparently he realized that he might be signing his own political death warrant when he aligned himself with Wallace. In a Senate speech made during the 1948 campaign, Taylor discussed the dilemma he had faced in making the crucial decision. "It took some pretty serious thinking on my part to make up my mind to go with Henry Wallace. . . . It is fine to be a Senator. It is the best job I ever had, anyway I look at it—from the standpoint of salary, prestige, or anything else. It is wonderful. . . . But I have three boys. They must be educated. When I am out of the Senate I do not know what I shall do. I spent my earlier life in the theatrical profession. I cannot go back to it. One cannot drag three small boys around the country. They must go to school. So I do not know what will happen to me when I am out of the Senate."[1] Because of the personal and political risks, Taylor explained: "it was pretty serious when Mr. Wallace asked me to join in this great effort to save the world from extinction. That is what it amounts to. If I had not thought so, I might not have gone with him. But I felt that that was the issue that was involved, that we were being taken toward a war which could mean only, in all possibility, the end of life on this planet. So I joined Henry

[1] *Cong. Rec.,* 80th Cong., 2d sess., 1948, 94, pt. 7:8782.

Wallace. There are more important things than my political security, my political future, or my economic security."[2]

But idealism alone cannot totally explain the actions or motivations of Glen Taylor. Throughout his political career, Taylor, like many other public figures, only more so, remained an actor and a crowd-pleaser. Glen Taylor never lost his love of the limelight and the roar of the crowd. It was Taylor's second nature to fight for headlines or to crowd into center stage. This explains his using Paul Revere rides to dramatize his positions on key national issues. He admitted, regretfully, "If I play the guitar and croon sitting on a flight of granite steps, that's big news. If I work in the Senate to protect Idaho's rivers and pine forests, that's barely worth a one-deck headline."[3]

The fact that Taylor was a showman explains in part his lack of political astuteness. In Richard Neuberger's estimation, Taylor simply succumbed to the desire for headlines. Neuberger believed that Taylor provided Idaho with a potentially great liberal senator, but that Taylor lacked the humility and patience to construct his career on a broad political base. In a sense, Henry Wallace and his third party offered a shortcut to prominence, and although Taylor knew the odds were against him, he could not resist the temptation of partaking of "farmer" Wallace's enticing "apple."[4]

Although his idealism and showmanship caused him to violate political rules on major issues, especially in the decision to run with Wallace in 1948, Taylor is still remembered by many Idahoans as one of the most effective "errand boy" senators Idaho has ever had. Apparently Taylor and his staff were very successful in handling routine intercessions with the various executive departments. In 1949 newspaper columnist John Corlett, who was to be an instrument in the *Idaho Daily Statesman*'s 1950 attack on Taylor, wrote that Taylor was in a strange political predicament. According to Corlett, Taylor was assisting many Idahoans who opposed him politically. Corlett reported that Taylor's office had a reputation for getting things accomplished and, he added, "Republicans who bitterly fight Taylor in a campaign have no qualms about asking his office to reserve them hotel rooms or to help arrange interviews

[2] Ibid.
[3] Quoted in Richard Neuberger, "Glen Taylor: Crooner on the Left," *American Mercury* (September 1948), p. 265.
[4] Ibid., pp. 263-72.

with someone in government."[5] A. J. Keefer, Taylor's administrative assistant declared, "The senator has always worked on the principle that if we can do anything to help Idaho or an Idahoan we go all out for it regardless of politics."[6]

In spite of his ability to accomplish things for Idaho, Taylor was never favored for reelection. During the time of McCarthyism, Taylor was politically vulnerable because of his stand against anti-Communist extremism, his involvement with Wallace, and his opposition to the foreign policy formulated to contain the spread of international communism. His pronouncements regarding civil rights for both American Negroes and American Communists, regarding the breakup of colonial empires, and the causes of the Cold War provided ample ammunition for the perpetrators of the "Red Scare." Ironically some historians, writing with the perspective of hindsight, have contended that Taylor's position was closer to the truth than previously believed. Taylor's opposition to the foreign policy and the domestic "witch-hunt" of his day and his repeated pleas for tolerance and understanding have gained historical importance.

While many politicians and scholars silently watched the terror tactics of Joseph McCarthy and the resultant destruction of the careers of some government employees, Taylor openly voiced his opposition to these developments.[7] Throughout his public career Taylor critically scrutinized loyalty oaths, the "witch-hunting" House Un-American Activities Committee, and the Senate Internal Security Committee, as well as the tactics of McCarthy. As early as December 1945, Taylor recognized the danger posed by the extremists who specialized in hatred when he declared: "The hate merchants . . . make money out of marketing hate. Hate is the commodity they sell, the thing they live by, a purely destructive emotion which makes no jobs, builds no houses, raises no crops, and settles almost no problems of any kind."[8]

Glen Taylor's often repeated philosophy was that government

[5] *Idaho Statesman*, April 24, 1949.
[6] Ibid.
[7] Robert Griffith, *The Politics of Fear: Joseph R. McCarthy and the Senate* (Lexington: University Press of Kentucky, 1970), is already a classic on this topic. Richard Rovere, *Senator Joe McCarthy* (Cleveland, Ohio: World Publishing, 1959), pp. 255-72, also discusses the silence McCarthy created among his colleagues. Eric F. Goldman, *The Crucial Decade* (New York: Random House, 1960), pp. 211-15, contains a discussion of the effect McCarthyism had on universities and the arts.
[8] *Cong. Rec.*, 79th Cong., 1st sess., 1945, 91, pt. 9:11390.

should be aimed directly at solving social ills: "If we eliminate the suffering and hardship of periodic depressions we need never fear communism or Communists."[9] It was this philosophy, which he reenunciated when he ran with Wallace and which certain Progressives unsuccessfully tried to put in their platform, that Taylor used as a guide for his senatorial service. According to Taylor, a nation could destroy communism only by social action, not by witch-hunts. When the Democrats took office in 1932, he said, they inherited 102,000 Communists from the Republicans; they whittled the number to 24,000 by means of political reform.[10]

Guilty of pursuing his convictions so zealously that he almost became a demagogue of the left, Taylor preached a hatred of Wall Street, bankers, monopoly, and newspapers. By the end of his career, he was as much convinced that there was a conspiracy on the right as McCarthy and some of his cohorts were that a Communist conspiracy existed. After his years in public service, Taylor still maintained that a threat from the right was more ominous than one from the left. "Hitler used the technique of having the folks look for Communists. It is all right to look for Communists. . . . I have no sympathy for them. I would suffer most under a Communist system. They always take the most liberal people, and cut their heads off first." But, Taylor warned, "while you are watching for Communists—look what happened over in Germany. The Nazis sneaked in the door while everyone had his head under the bed looking for a Communist; you better rig yourself up a little rear vision mirror to look over the shoulder and see what's coming in that door."[11]

Taylor's abhorrence of extremism, at a time when few public figures dared speak out, implies that being a member of a dissenting minority does not necessarily connote treachery or traitorous activities. His opposition to the philosophy of containment, as manifested in the Truman Doctrine, the Marshall Plan, NATO, and massive foreign aid, did not make Taylor either a traitor or unpatriotic. His criticism of the administration's foreign policy was that the United States was supporting reactionary governments just because they professed to be anti-Communist. Contemporary foreign policy decisions designed to curb the spread of Asian communism, and the dissent aroused by these decisions, have given

[9] *New York Times*, April 11, 1947, p. 3.
[10] Taylor speech, Berea, p. 10.
[11] Taylor speech, Payette, p. 35.

Taylor's disagreement with the Truman foreign policy new significance. Many recent scholars assert that the idea of containment of European communism is the lineal father of the Asian policy.[12]

When debating the Truman Doctrine, Taylor appeared to be fully aware that the colonial powers were going to lose their grip on subject peoples. He believed that Britain and France wanted the United States to help pick up the pieces of their crumbling empires. They wanted the United States to fill the economic and political vacuum resulting from the inability of the two great prewar powers to maintain the status quo. Many American investors apparently were willing to do just that as long as they had governmental support. Taylor saw Truman's foreign policy as directly opposed to the nationalism of subject peoples. At the same time he contended that it was impossible to buy friends with foreign aid.

It was not Taylor's position or purpose to laud everything Russia did and to criticize all his own country's actions. Viewing the causes of the Cold War as a shared responsibility, Taylor asked only that the United States and the Soviet Union get together to discuss their differences and work out solutions. Taylor believed that both of the great powers wanted peace but that unfortunately neither was willing to compromise. His continual agitation for a World Republic and for strengthening the United Nations was prompted by his desire to avoid another war.

Coming to Taylor's defense in 1954, Wallace summarized the goal and the appeal of their third party. "The vast majority who voted the Progressive Party ticket were not Communists but peace-loving people who believed it was possible to arrive at such an understanding with Russia as to make possible the building of a strong United Nations. . . . It was of the utmost importance that

---

[12] Walter LaFeber, *America, Russia, and the Cold War, 1945-1966* (New York: John Wiley, 1967), p. 259. For other works—all written since 1960—which basically agree with Taylor's view of foreign policy, see Gar Alperovitz, *Atomic Diplomacy: Potsdam and Hiroshima* (New York: Simon and Schuster, 1965); Martin F. Herz, *Beginnings of the Cold War* (Bloomington: Indiana University Press, 1966); Fred J. Cook, *The Warfare State* (New York: Macmillan, 1962); David Horowitz, *Free World Colossus* (New York: Hill and Wang, 1965); Ronald Steel, *Pax Americana* (New York: Viking Press, 1967); D. F. Fleming, *The Cold War and Its Origins*, 2 vols. (Garden City, N.Y.: Doubleday, 1961); and Marshall D. Shulman, *Beyond the Cold War* (New Haven, Conn.: Yale University Press, 1966). Whether Taylor was motivated by idealism or whether he was naive is not really the question. The fact is that these recent revisionist scholars, although not referring directly to Taylor, give his position new and added significance.

such an understanding should be arrived at before Russia got the atom bomb. That the effort was not made at that time is the greatest tragedy of history."[13]

By repeatedly pointing out how his own country was in part responsible for the Cold War, Taylor became suspect, but he himself believed that what he was doing was patriotic. He often relied on the Christian teaching, possibly learned from his preacher father, that if a person's brother was making a mistake, that person had an obligation to point out the mistake to his brother. There is no doubt that Taylor feared the world would be destroyed if atomic warfare erupted, and he believed that the Cold War was leading mankind to such a catastrophe.

In 1922 Walter Lippmann wrote regarding public opinion, "There is the world outside and there are the pictures in our heads. Man behaves not according to the world as it really is but to the world as he thinks it is."[14] In the early years of the Cold War it was (as it still is) difficult to separate what was real from what was imagined. Taylor's attempts to separate the real from the imagined were the source of his disagreement with the Truman foreign policy. Time alone will determine the correctness of his position.

American efforts to stabilize and protect Western Europe and the Mediterranean area were construed by Taylor, and by Soviet Russia, to mean capitalist expansionism. In the Soviet view, the Truman Doctrine and the Marshall Plan were potential challenges to Russian hegemony in Eastern Europe, and the historic Soviet concept of security made such hegemony essential.

It is doubtful that Glen Taylor completely understood the prevailing currents of his time. However, bipolarization of the world was what Taylor feared most and what he fought to avoid. His crusade before, during, and after his involvement with the Progressives is reminiscent of the futile efforts of the idealistic Don Quixote. A great many Americans were frustrated by the inability of the two great powers to cooperate in efforts toward world peace and international stability after four years of wartime cooperation. The events of the postwar period led some Americans to believe they had been betrayed by Russia. The fate of Eastern Europe, the very real trauma caused by the existence of awesome atomic bombs, the Hiss and Fuchs espionage cases, and the fall of China

---

[13] *New York Times*, October 21, 1954, p. 17.
[14] Walter Lippmann, *Public Opinion* (New York: Harcourt, Brace, 1922), p. 26.

led directly to the national hysteria of McCarthyism. Taylor's utterances concerning shared responsibility rang hollow and traitorous to many ears tuned in to emotional anti-communism.

One effect of this emotional climate was that rational, clear perception and calculated, measured analysis became increasingly difficult. In addition, there was a reaction against the New Deal and wartime centralization. The bureaucracy had doubled and many people viewed their own government as being too large and distant for their desires. The net result was that extremist anti-communism became for some an ideology. With this kind of political turmoil prevailing, it is clear in retrospect that Taylor was battling "windmills" which would eventually defeat him.

A man of heart and emotion, Taylor's main purpose was to help people be contented and happy. Nearly everything he sponsored or advocated as a senator was designed to give something to the common man and the underdog. His support of price controls, minimum wage increases, civil rights legislation, and CVA, as well as his opposition to Taft-Hartley, were aimed at bringing a greater portion of America's resources and wealth to the "little man."

Taylor also was in large part responsible for several measures which fostered the prosperity and promoted the well-being of Idaho citizens. He worked to secure the atomic energy plant near Arco; the Palisades, Lucky Peak, and Libby dams; and the reactivation of Mountain Home Air Force Base. He also deserves partial credit for the millions of dollars appropriated for flood control, irrigation, schools, roads, and hospitals in Idaho. It is obvious that Idaho's interests were not neglected while Taylor served in the Senate.

Taylor's type of liberalism was indeed strange considering that he was uneducated, came from the West, and had a rural background. The militant liberalism that he advocated is usually associated with urban, eastern, and highly educated individuals. Since Taylor was none of these, why did he vote the way he did? More important, why did he take the foreign policy positions that led to his political demise? There is no doubt that his depression background prompted many of his attitudes on domestic policies, and the influence of his father cannot be discounted. The men and women who advised him in Washington—George Curtis, Foy Blackburn, Al Keefer, Jerome Spingarn, Verda Barnes, and Irene Burton—were all liberals of various shades. Taylor also associated with Progressive policy formulators such as John Abt, Lee Pressman, Clark Foreman, Rexford Tugwell, and many others during 1948, but there is no evidence that he was influenced by them prior to the Progressive crusade or after. Once Taylor had established himself as a spokesman for the common man and an advocate of peace, he received a barrage of mail from many liberals throughout the country. Of course, this influenced him a great deal, especially when people agreed with his past positions and encouraged the Idaho senator to pursue his existing course.[15]

When asked who influenced him and why he advocated certain programs and opposed others, Taylor's response was typically western: "Just plain old horse sense!" He hastened to explain that anyone devoted to democracy, equality, and peace would have seen that the issues confronting the Senate and the nation in the Cold War period cried for solutions. The solutions, from Taylor's point of view, were any legislation designed to bring world peace, civil equality, and economic democracy. He does not blame anyone for leading him astray, nor does he believe that what he did was in error.[16]

Glen Taylor cannot be dismissed as a joker, an opportunist, an embarrassment to Idaho, or a Communist sympathizer; he was a complex man. In an early appraisal of Taylor, which was perceptive and quite accurate, John Gunther wrote: "Glen Taylor, no matter what people in Boise or Pocatello, Idaho, may tell you, is not a clown, not a hillbilly, not a buffoon. On the contrary, he is an extremely serious man. He has a nice dry wit, abundant common sense, fertility of mind, and a . . . sense of showmanship."[17] Taylor's misfortune was that he became involved in politics during an era that demanded swift, adept political maneuvering; and the liberal from Idaho, guided by his heart as often as by his head, instead remained true to those convictions which he had formulated during the depths of the depression. His last words on the Senate floor epitomized Taylor's idealism. Glen Taylor told his colleagues: "At one time I stated on the floor of the Senate that I was going to vote my convictions, as though I never expected to come back. All I can say is that I did vote my convictions, and I did not come back."[18]

[15] Unfortunately Taylor's papers are not available to researchers. There are numerous examples of letters written to Wallace and Taylor during the 1948 Progressive crusade in the Wallace Papers.
[16] Interview with Taylor, June 14, 1967.
[17] John Gunther, *Inside U.S.A.* (New York: Harper, 1947), p. 108.
[18] *Cong. Rec.*, 81st Cong., 2d sess., 1951, 96, pt. 12:17116.

Bibliographical Essay

MANUSCRIPTS

Recent historical research is often difficult because of its closeness. On the one hand potentially valuable manuscript collections are closed, but conversely, many historical participants, with an eye directed toward the researcher, launder their papers to the point that they lose value. Although Glen H. Taylor denies that he has a collection, as such, he does possess sufficient material that would have been helpful. He is presently contemplating an autobiography and was reluctant to release private holdings for research. This fact is a major limitation of this biography, especially in the significant task of attempting to discover who tried to influence Taylor during his Senate career. He willingly allowed me to look at campaign literature, was fun to interview, and answered mailed inquiries promptly and honestly. Because of the lack of a manuscript basis, the biography is only a political biography and under-emphasizes the personal life of Taylor.

However, many other collections were of value. Merle Wells, the Director of the Idaho State Historical Society, was very helpful in steering me through that collection. Governors C. Ben Ross, Champ Clark, Barzilla Clark, Charles C. Gossett, Arnold Williams, and C. A. Robins left their papers at the society. All these collections contained references to Taylor, yet the state politicians seemed to treat the maverick senator as a twentieth-century version of the bubonic plague. August Rosquist, for many years the Idaho AFL leader, placed his papers in the Idaho facility as well. They are very good to illustrate Taylor's obvious pro-labor bias as well as to show how some Idaho labor leaders turned against him. Mr. Wells is in the process of gathering and cataloging the Senate papers of Taylor's contemporaries: John Thomas, Henry Dworshak, Bert Miller, and Charles Gossett. Of course, when Herman Welker's papers are opened, they should tell a lot about the McCarthy period. Another valuable Idaho collection is that of John Corlett of the *Idaho Daily Statesman* (Boise). Mr. Corlett is still very active and has his collection in his possession, but he was very helpful and cooperative.

A number of collections were used at three presidential libraries: the Franklin D. Roosevelt Library at Hyde Park, New York; the Harry S. Truman Library at Independence, Missouri; and the Dwight D. Eisenhower Library at Abilene, Kansas. Roosevelt's Official File and Personal File contained very little about Taylor and his brief association with Roosevelt. Some communications were exchanged, but for the most part they involved routine Senate work. Of course, Roosevelt died shortly after Taylor went to the Senate. The Truman Library proved to be excellent for primary sources on Taylor's Senate career. Truman's Official File and Personal File are filled with information concerning Taylor's personal and political relationships with Truman. These files contain thousands of boxes, but are indexed well and with the assistance of the staff are attainable and useful. Many of Truman's papers relating to foreign-policy decisions are still unavailable and will contain pertinent information regarding the origins of the Cold War. There are numerous smaller collections at the Truman Library which proved useful. The Democratic National Committee Clippings File, the Stephen Mitchell Papers, and the Howard McGrath Papers contain a vast amount of information on the Democratic party. These papers were especially useful in assessing reactions to Taylor's separation from the party and his subsequent reconciliation. Many Truman assistants such as Clark Clifford, David E. Bell, Charles Murphy, and Joel D. Wolfsohn deposited their papers at the Truman Library. They contain a limited amount of information on Taylor, but what they contributed was useful and necessary. These collections contained attitudes of Truman's close advisers which proved helpful. Frank McNaughton, a Washington correspondent and author, has particularly helpful material in his papers. McNaughton recorded hearsay, rumors, and speculations which provided another dimension of research. Papers pertaining to Taylor at the Eisenhower Library are limited. Limited references concerning Taylor's attempted political comeback in 1954 and 1956 are in the Eisenhower general file and the Howard Pyle Papers. All the above cited presidential library's staffs were helpful and cooperative. The main limitations of those facilities is that many controversial issues are still classified, but this is expected.

As yet, there is no central collection for the 1948 Progressive party. The University of Iowa in Iowa City will develop one of significance. The Henry A. Wallace Papers will provide the nucleus for that archival depository. Wallace's papers regarding Taylor were somewhat disappointing. There is actually more recorded interchange during the mid-1950s than during the 1948 campaign. This is probably due to the looseness of the party organization and the increased use of the nonwritten forms of communication. Curtis D. MacDougall, the author of *Gideon's Army*, a three-volume work on the 1948 Progressives, has deposited his research notes and drafts of manuscript at the Iowa Library. MacDougall was a Progressive candidate for the United States Senate from Illinois. The staff at Iowa are quite aggressive in creating a good research center. Further research could be facilitated if the Progressive files could be consolidated. Individual party participants have left their collections at various locations; for example, Naomi Achenbach Benson's Papers are at the University of Washington and Genevieve Fallon Steefel's are at the Library of Congress. The New York Public Library contains some items of particular value. The *Citizen*, a Progressive tabloid published only twice, and *Songs for Wallace*, published by People's Songs, are both there. People's Songs was an organization of liberal protest-song writers who often attended Progressive rallies.

Perhaps the best Taylor collection is held by the AFL-CIO Committee on Political Education in Washington, D.C. The Glen H. Taylor file is a comprehensive newspaper clipping collection from all the major newspapers in the nation. For day-to-day coverage of Taylor as a senator, this material is very helpful. The research staff of the AFL-CIO COPE is totally cooperative. This collection also has Taylor's voting record on all key issues, not just labor.

GOVERNMENT DOCUMENTS

One of the best sources through which to study a senator is the *Congressional Record*. Glen Taylor rarely said anything on the Senate floor that was not directed to his Senate colleagues. He spoke frequently on controversial issues, using the floor as a stage upon which to deliver emotional orations. Much of what Taylor said to the Senate was ignored by the press because Taylor was not too concerned about advance press releases and prior notice. Later in his career, when his aides did hand out prepared copies, the advance speech had little to do with what he said on the floor.

The *Record* contains all his utterances, and since the debates over foreign and domestic policy comprise much of this manuscript, this source was most valuable. The Appendix to the *Record* also has interesting information about Taylor and his activities.

Glen Taylor was less vocal during the hearings conducted by congressional committees. As many scholars have pointed out, hearings and the transcripts are often subject to congressional censorship. Besides, numerous committees proceed in executive or closed session and the transcript may never be published. Senators also have a habit of speaking "off the record" on key issues. Thus their statements cannot be recorded.

Taylor initiated and was most involved with the Theodore Bilbo hearings in 1946. Those hearings (U.S., Congress, Senate, 79th Cong., 2d sess.; 80th Cong., 1st sess., Special Committee to Investigate Senatorial Campaign expenditures, *Report, Mississippi*) were conducted throughout the fall and winter of 1946. Taylor was not a member of the committee, but prepared a brief and testified before them against Senator Bilbo. The published report on the hearings contains Taylor's presentation of a case against Bilbo for violation of the Fifteenth Amendment. When the Committee decided that Bilbo was not guilty, Taylor responded by introducing the resolution which would have denied the Mississippi Senator his seat.

The proposed Columbia Valley Authority also involved Taylor at the committee level. He was a member of the Committee on Interior and Insular Affairs and was active late in his Senate career (U.S., Congress, Senate, 81st Cong., 2d sess.), Committee on Interior and Insular Affairs, *Columbia River Basin*. When his own Committee failed to get a CVA bill on the floor, Taylor turned to the Committee on Public Works (U.S., Congress, Senate, 81st Cong., 2d sess.), Committee on Public Works, Columbia Valley Administrators.

After Taylor left the Senate, he was involved in Senate hearings on his 1948 Progressive activities. Senator Herman Welker called a special subcommittee (U.S., Congress, Senate, 83rd Cong., 2d sess.), Subcommittee to investigate the Administration of Internal Security Act and Other Internal Security Laws of the Committee of the Judiciary, *Communist Propaganda,* and called a group of ex-Communists to appear before him. Taylor wanted to appear before the subcommittee but was never subpoenaed.

The eight-volume *Public Papers of the Presidents of the United*

States, Harry S. Truman (Washington, D.C., 1965) is an excellent primary source on the entire Truman presidency. These collected documents are indexed and very usable. The main question concerning this type of publication is how and why certain documents are selected and others are not. It is valuable even though there is not much on Glen Taylor.

Accurate statistics on Taylor's numerous elections can be found in the *Biennial Report of the Secretary of State,* State of Idaho, Department of State, Boise, 1938–1956. These are the official results of all primary and general elections on the county basis. These reports were particularly useful in determining centers of political power for Taylor.

ORAL INTERVIEWS

Oral history is an ancient technique that is currently enjoying a revival. Many of Taylor's contemporaries in Idaho are still active and have not deposited their official or personal papers in an archive. A tape recorder and a note pad therefore became part of my research arsenal. The most significant interviewee was Taylor himself. Taylor's interview was a delightful experience because he was so open, frank, and willing. If a question was asked which struck a particularly responsive chord, Taylor responded as if he were out on the stump. Taylor is in the process of writing an autobiography and plans to emphasize his pre-political and post-political careers. He is the best source on his life up to political prominence. Mrs. Dora Taylor was also a valuable source for the biography.

Glen Taylor is still either hated or loved in Idaho. There is little objectivity and the mere mention of his name brings an emotional response. The most vocal Taylor detractors are former leaders of the state Democratic party. Robert Coulter and James H. Hawley of Boise, Charles C. Gossett of Nampa, B. A. McDeavitt of Pocatello, and Claude J. Burtenshaw of Logan, Utah, are good examples. There is no way that they can say anything positive about Taylor. They view him as an ego-motivated maverick with no concern for the party and its long-term success. To other Idahoans like Joe R. Williams, John Schoonover, and Merrill D. Tonning, of Boise and the late F. M. Bistline of Pocatello, he was a positive force as a senator, but made a tragic mistake by joining the Wallace third party movement.

The Idahoans who viewed Taylor with some degree of objectivity were reporters like Sam H. Day, editor of the *Intermountain Observer;* Henry Fletcher, manager of radio station KSEI in Pocatello; and John Corlett of the *Idaho Daily Statesman* in Boise. Day was especially helpful on Taylor's last Idaho campaigns. His contribution by reporting Idaho politics for nearly twenty years makes him a tremendous resource.

In order for oral history to be of value, the interviewer needs to be as knowledgeable as possible about the topic and the individual. The researcher must become enough of a journalistic prober to press beyond the surface appearance. There is much more involved than turning on a tape recorder and letting an individual talk off the top of his head. Properly approached, oral history is a delightful and provocative form of research.

PRESS

Glen Taylor always claimed that every Idaho daily newspaper was against him except one and that one, the *Lewiston Morning Tribune,* was neutral. When Taylor first entered politics, the paper that watched him the closest was a Boise weekly, the *Idaho Pioneer.* Not only did it report on Taylor, but the editor, Frank Burroughs, obviously detested the ex-actor's politics. Taylor was always pictured as the buffoon or clown and never as a serious candidate. Burroughs contended that Taylor used campaigning as a means of economic survival.

There are not many Idaho daily newspapers, but those that exist were researched extensively. The *Lewiston Morning Tribune* proved to be most objective and useful. The *Pocatello Tribune,* and its successor, the *Idaho State Journal* (Pocatello), the *Idaho Daily Statesman* (Boise), the *Idaho Free Press* (Nampa), the *Twin Falls Times-News,* the *Caldwell News Tribune,* and the *Idaho Falls Post-Register* were basically anti-Taylor in their editorials and reporting. Out-of-state papers with a significant Idaho circulation were much the same. Heavily Mormon southeastern Idaho subscribes to the Salt Lake City papers, either the *Salt Like Tribune* or the *Deseret News.* Both of these dailies have Idaho sections and report on Idaho politicians. The *Salt Lake Tribune* is excellent because it has been indexed for the modern period. Northern Idaho subscribes to Spokane, Washington, papers. The *Spokesman-Review* and the *Spokane Daily Chronicle* follow Idaho politics for the benefit of their Idaho readers. Even such prominent northwestern papers as the *Seattle Post-Intelligencer,* the *Seattle Times,* and the *Portland Oregonian* had a considerable amount of material on Taylor.

The most beneficial non-western newspapers used in this research were the *New York Times,* the *Daily Worker* (New York), *PM* (New York), the *St. Louis Post-Dispatch,* the *Christian Science Monitor,* and the *Washington Post-Times Herald.* The fact that the *New York Times* is indexed makes it great as a location source which can lead the researcher to other newspapers. So much of Taylor's time as a Progressive was spent in and around New York City, which makes the *Times* of added value. The *Daily Worker* was owned and edited by the Communist party. It proved to be an excellent source on Glen Taylor. Once the party became convinced of Taylor's liberalism, they followed his activities on a daily basis. Naturally, there is ideological basis for the paper and their interpretations reflect the ideology, but as a source it was very useful.

The very fact that Glen Taylor does not have a collection of personal papers made newspaper research even more imperative. It is a tedious type of research, but due to microfilm and microprint, it was not totally unpleasant. Thorough and complete research is necessary because first-time reporting is often unclear and fragmented. Many papers never go beyond the initial fragmented facts, but all in all they reflect attitudes and opinions.

SECONDARY LITERATURE

There is a dearth of information on twentieth-century Idaho history. Merrill D. Beal and Merle Wells, *History of Idaho* (New York, 1959), is the best textbook approach to the period. Some studies are being done which should contribute to Idaho's history. Michael P. Malone, *C. Ben Ross and the New Deal in Idaho* (Seattle, 1970), is a fine presentation of the period prior to Taylor's entry into politics. Two biographies of Senator William E. Borah—Claudius O. Johnson, *Borah of Idaho* (Seattle, 1967), and Marian C. McKenna, *Borah* (Ann Arbor, Mich., 1961), contributed to Idaho political history. An edited collection of essays brought together by Richard Etulain and Ben Marley, *Idaho's Heritage* (Pocatello, Idaho, 1973), should also prompt new research possibilities. Senator Frank Church's career will undoubtedly encourage historical studies. Researchers are doing more on natural resources and economic development. Leonard J. Arrington, a native Idahoan, is encouraging research in the Gem State, and most of the results are forthcoming.

Glen Taylor received considerable coverage by *Time, Newsweek, Colliers*, the *Nation*, and the *Progressive*. Richard Neuberger, later a senator from Oregon, wrote numerous articles on Taylor such as "Cowboy on Our Side," *Nation* (August 24, 1946); "Glen Taylor: Crooner on the Left," *American Mercury* (September 1948); "Glen Taylor Rides Again," *Nation* (May 20, 1950); "Glen Taylor: Left-wing Minstrel," *Progressive* (April 1948); and "Singing Cowboy to United States Senator," *Progressive* (May 1945). These are mostly biographical sketches, but contain insights into Taylor's current plunge into the headlines. Kyle Crichton, "Idaho's Hot Potato," *Colliers* (June 30, 1945), and Frank Gervasi, "Low Man on the Wallace Poll," *Colliers* (May 8, 1948), are similar to Neuberger in their approach. Taylor campaigns in 1950, 1954, and 1956 are covered superficially in the *Western Political Quarterly*—Boyd A. Martin, "The 1950 Election in Idaho," 4 (1951); Merrill D. Beal, "The 1954 Election in Idaho," 7 (1954); and Boyd A. Martin, "The 1956 Election in Idaho," 10 (1957). John Gunther's *Inside U.S.A.* (New York, 1947) contains a delightful section on Taylor, and John Gerassi's *The Boys of Boise* (New York, 1966) has a little on Taylor, but most of his book concerns the sensationalism surrounding the alleged homosexual crisis in Boise during the 1950s. William C. Pratt has also done some research on Taylor's career. His "Glen H. Taylor: Public Image and Reality," *Pacific Northwest Quarterly* (January 1969), and "Senator Glen H. Taylor" in *Cold War Critics*, ed. Thomas G. Paterson (Chicago, 1971), were quite good.

There is a tremendous amount of material coming out on the Truman period. Truman's own two-volume *Memoirs* (New York, 1956) is always a starting point for research. Margaret Truman Daniels's *Harry S. Truman* (New York, 1972) contributes little to her father's autobiography. Richard Kirkendall's edited work *The Truman Period as a Research Field* (Columbia, Mo., 1967) is very valuable. Two other edited collections are of special significance: Barton J. Bernstein and Allen J. Matusow, *The Truman Administration: A Documentary History* (New York, 1966), and Louis W. Koenig, *The Truman Administration: Its Principles and Practice* (New York, 1956). Two general historians of the period are Cabell

Phillips, *The Truman Presidency* (New York, 1966), and Eric F. Goldman, *The Crucial Decade and After* (New York, 1960). Although these works are weak in interpretation, they are readable and give a good overview of the Truman presidency. Truman's *Mr. Citizen* (New York, 1953); Robert S. Allen and William V. Shannon, *The Truman Merry-Go-Round* (New York, 1950); Frank McNaughton and Walter Hehmeyer, *Harry Truman, President* (New York, 1948); and I. F. Stone, *The Truman Era* (New York, 1953), are weak because of their closeness to the period and the climate that existed while they wrote.

Historians are now examining the Truman period piece by piece and their research is quite revealing. Barton Bernstein has authored a number of significant articles. His "Clash of Interests: The Post-war Battle Between the Office of Price Administration and Agriculture," *Agriculture History* (January 1967), is excellent in showing difficulties among special interest groups. That article, added to Harvey Mansfield and others, *A Short History of O.P.A.* (Washington, D.C., 1947), gives a good picture of the OPA continuance conflict. Bernstein has also contributed other articles on economic and labor history of the Truman period. Taylor was actively engaged in the preservation of a liberal Fair Deal, and these articles are sympathetic to his point of view. "The Removal of War Production Controls in Business, 1944–1946," *Business History Review* (Summer 1965), and "Walter Reuther and the General Motors Strike of 1945–1946," *Michigan History* (September 1965), are other works of significance. Bernstein's in-depth research together with R. Alton Lee, *Truman and Taft-Hartley* (Lexington, Ky., 1966), and Robert L. Branyon, "Antimonopoly Activities during the Truman Administration" (Ph.D. diss., University of Oklahoma, 1961), contribute to a better understanding of domestic difficulties. Susan Hartman has written a very fine volume entitled *Harry S. Truman and the Eightieth Congress* (Columbia, Mo., 1971), which details Truman's stormy relationship with the Congress elected in 1946. She carefully illustrates that the foreign policy reactions which elevated Truman in the public eye were passed by that *Reform during the Truman Administration* (Columbia, Mo., 1966), "whipping block" Eightieth Congress. Richard O. Davies, *Housing* is an example of the frustration experienced by Fair Deal advocates on key domestic issues. An interesting parallel article is one written by Davies, "Mr. Republican Turns 'Socialist': Robert A. Taft and Public Housing," *Ohio History* (Summer 1964). Taft who fought

Truman on many labor issues found himself advocating publicly financed housing programs. One of the most enjoyable revisionist volumes is Allen J. Matusow, *Farm Policies in the Truman Years* (New York, 1970). There has not been a great deal written on the Taylor-championed Columbia Valley Authority. John R. Waltrip's "Public Power during the Truman Administration" (Ph.D. diss., University of Missouri, 1965) is a fine study of public power, but the CVA is not central to the study. Robert Tininenko tried to get at the problem of a coordinated CVA effort in his "Middle Snake River Development: The Controversy over Hells Canyon, 1947–55" (Master's thesis, Washington State University, 1967). His description of the method by which private power won over public power in the development of the Snake River makes this study important. W. Darrell Gertsch is currently writing a detailed study of the upper Snake River's economic development which should add to the literature on the topic. An early description of the proposals for increased TVA type authorities is Wesley C. Clark's "Proposed Valley Authority Legislation," *American Political Science Review* (February 1946). Clark's essay is only descriptive and lacks historical perspective or results. Much can be learned about the politics of water resource development from Richard Polenberg, "The Great Conservation Contest," *Forest History* (January 1967), and Arthur Morgan, *Dams and Other Disasters* (New York, 1971). Both Polenberg and Morgan blame competing governmental agencies as much as private power for the failure to pass meaningful legislation. Morgan is especially critical of the Army Corps of Engineers for building dams on a hit-and-miss basis without ecological consideration. David E. Lilienthal's two-volume autobiography, *The Journals of David E. Lilienthal* (New York, 1964), is very useful for any study of reclamation and conservation projects.

Taylor was in the vanguard concerning both civil and human rights. Truman has received some historical credit for moving the nation toward an increased awareness of minority rights. William C. Berman, "The Politics of Civil Rights in the Truman Administration" (Ph.D. diss., Ohio State University, 1963), is a pivotal work in analyzing who was pushing civil rights legislation such as anti-lynching and anti-poll tax bills and why they could not pass. Richard Dalfiume, *Desegregation of the U. S. Armed Forces* (Columbia, Mo., 1969), is another volume of significance. He discusses not only the executive orders that led to desegregation but also the Truman Civil Rights Commission recommendations and the Fair Employment Practices Commission. Both of these commissions' reports need further examination. Barton Bernstein accepts Taylor's judgment that Truman was never committed to civil rights. In his essay "The Ambiguous Legacy: The Truman Administration and Civil Rights," in his *Politics and Policies of the Truman Administration* (Chicago, 1970), Bernstein challenges those who have given Truman credit for advancing civil rights. Instead, Bernstein maintains that Truman never really tried to get FEPC, anti-poll tax, and anti-lynching bills passed.

Taylor's involvement in the 1948 Progressive Party is considered in a number of contemporary as well as historical accounts. Many of those writing in 1948 considered Wallace and Taylor as communist dupes. Some good examples are Charles Angoff, "Wallace's Communist-Front Party," *American Mercury* (October 1948); former Communist Louis F. Budenz, "How the Reds Snatched Henry Wallace," *Colliers* (September 18, 1948); and Norman Thomas, "Wallace Party Launched," *Christian Century* (August 4, 1948). Rodney Gilbert's "Thin Line of Heroes Back Wallace's Party," *Saturday Evening Post* (May 6, 1948); Freda Kirchway, "Wallace: Prophet or Politician," *Nation* (January 10, 1948); and Saul K. Padover, "Party of Hope," *Saturday Review of Literature* (April 17, 1948), are much more objective in their approach to the whole Progressive effort. The best secondary accounts of that specific third-party movement are Karl M. Schmidt's *Henry A. Wallace: Quixotic Crusade* (Syracuse, N.Y., 1960) and Curtis D. MacDougall's three-volume eyewitness account, *Gideon's Army* (New York, 1965). Schmidt is openly sympathetic to the Wallace-Taylor movement, but objectively handles the brief history of that movement. MacDougall, a Progressive candidate for the Senate in Illinois, uses the thesis that America erred by not electing the maverick New Dealer. MacDougall's notes and research make a fine contribution. More analysis of the movement has been written at the thesis and dissertation level. Albert Bilik, "A New Party: Success and Failure" (Master's thesis, Columbia University, 1949); Harvey V. Brandt, "The Ideological Function of the Progressive Party of 1948 (Master's thesis, Columbia University, 1949); John C. Brown, "The 1948 Progressive Campaign: A Scientific Approach" (Ph.D. diss., University of Chicago, 1949); and Merrill R. Moreman, "The Independent Progressive Party in California, 1948" (Master's thesis, Stanford University, 1950), are necessary contemporary accounts. Bilik assesses the reasons for Progressives' failure at the polls, but he postulates that they succeeded in moving Truman to the left. It is Brandt's and Brown's contention that Communist influence on the Progressive campaign and platform was apparent, but that the Communists were never dominant. Moreman's study of California illustrates what a poor national organization existed and how local Progressives were left on their own. On the Progressive-Communist issue, the two most renowned studies of the Communist party in the United States agree. Irving Howe and Lewis Coser, *The American Communist Party: A Critical History, 1919–1957* (Boston, 1967), and David Shannon, *The Decline of American Communism* (New York, 1959), claim that the Progressives would have organized without Communist assistance. The Communists supported Wallace and because of the times contributed to his disastrous showing at the polls. At no time was the Progressive party Communist-led or dominated. The effect of the Progressive party on other liberals is being researched and the results are most interesting. Allen Yarnell's very fine dissertation, "The Impact of the Progressive Party on the Democratic Party in the 1948 Presidential Election" (Ph.D. diss., University of Washington, 1969), demonstrates how Truman chose to move left and recapture Wallace-type liberals rather than go to the right to reclaim the Dixiecrats. Alonzo Hamby, "Truman and the Liberal Movement" (Ph.D. diss., University of Missouri, 1965), believes that Truman became the leader of the liberal movement but that foreign policy and congressional opposition thwarted his domestic leadership. Clifton Brock's well-received study *Americans for Democratic Action* (Washington, D.C., 1960) finds the middle ground between Hamby and Yarnell. Many liberals were convinced that Truman could lead and they decided to stay with him and persuade him to their position. The very fact that Truman was president and Wallace was a third-party challenger dictated which way ADA would go. The two best secondary accounts of the 1948 campaign are Jules Abels, *Out of the Jaws of Victory* (New York, 1959), and Irwin Ross, *The Loneliest Campaign* (New York, 1968). Their focus is naturally much more on Truman than it is on the splinter party. Robert Shogan's article "The 1948 Election," *American Heritage* (June 1968), is well written but adds nothing of significance.

The political extremism of the postwar period as epitomized by Senator Joseph R. McCarthy has been examined by a number of scholars. Walter Goodman, *The Committee* (New York, 1968), is

an excellent account of the House Un-American Activities Committee. A good portion of the book is devoted to the Truman years.
Since Taylor was victimized twice by extremist campaigns, this
book was of great value. Another fine work is Earl Latham, *The
Communist Controversy in Washington* (New York, 1966), which
analyzes the whole question of Communist influence in the nation's
capital. The work done by Athan Theoharis in *Politics and Policies*
of the Truman Administration, ed. Barton J. Bernstein (Chicago,
1970), is noteworthy in many respects. Theoharis examines internal
security and the loyalty oaths and arrives at the conclusion that
Truman's programs must bear some responsibility for the creation
of a Joseph McCarthy. His "The Rhetoric of Politics: Foreign
Policy, Internal Security, and Domestic Politics in the Truman Era,
1945–1950," and "The Escalation of the Loyalty Program" are
excellent in this regard. Richard Rovere's *Senator Joe McCarthy*
(Cleveland, Ohio, 1959) is a perceptive journalistic account of
McCarthy's impact. Rovere was in Washington and observed the
whole phenomena. Two positively brilliant surveys of phases of
the type of extremism which defeated Taylor are Michael Paul
Rogin, *The Intellectuals and McCarthy: The Radical Specter*
(Cambridge, Mass., 1967), and the provocative book by Robert
Griffith, *The Politics of Fear: Joseph R. McCarthy and the Senate*
(Lexington, Ky., 1970). Taylor stands tall in that he did not buckle
under to fear as did many of his colleagues.

My thesis is that Glen Taylor was indeed a prophet without
honor. More than minority human rights and ecological considerations, Taylor's primary concern was world peace. Only once did
he attempt to formalize his opinions in print: "Why a World
Republic," *Free World* (December 1945), is nothing more than an
eloquent plea for international sanity. The same logic was used
against the Truman Doctrine, the Marshall Plan, and NATO. Many
of Taylor's contemporaries left elaborately detailed accounts of
their role in the origins of the Cold War. Truman's *Memoirs* (New
York, 1956) present the Truman view. Secretary of State James F.
Byrnes wrote *Speaking Frankly* (New York, 1947), and one of his
successors, Dean Acheson, added *Present at the Creation* (New
York, 1969). Winston S. Churchill is very cautious and deliberate
in *Triumph and Tragedy* (Boston, 1953). His finger is always
pointed at the other person. George F. Kennan, *Memoirs, 1925–1950*
(Boston, 1967); William D. Leahy, *I Was There* (New York, 1950);
Robert Murphy, *Diplomat among Warriors* (New York, 1964);

Henry A. Wallace, *Toward World Peace* (Boston, 1948); and Walter Bedell Smith, *My Three Years in Moscow* (Philadelphia, 1950), are others in positions who wanted to tell their stories. Three other published sources were of value as well. James Forrestal, secretary of defense and the favorite target of Wallace and Taylor, took his own life during the Truman period. Walter Millis edited *The Forrestal Diaries* (New York, 1951), and they are quite candid concerning Forrestal's beliefs concerning the origins of the Cold War. Arthur Vandenberg, Jr., ed., *The Private Papers of Senator Vandenberg* (Boston, 1952), is an excellent account of Truman's maintenance of bipartisan support for his foreign policy. Henry S. Stimson and McGeorge Bundy, *On Active Service in Peace and War* (New York, 1948), is must reading for the period.

Cold War historiography is in continual flux, bust most scholars fit in either the "revisionist," or the "traditionalist," or the "neutral" categories. Several general revisionist works are available. It is my contention that Taylor's position of 1945–1950 was close to that posture assumed by the revisionists. Walter Lippmann, *The Cold War* (New York, 1947), is a pathbreaker because he questions the basic assumptions behind the evolution of containment. D. F. Fleming's pivotal two-volume history, *The Cold War and Its Origins* (New York, 1961), prompted further research throughout the past decade. Other revisionist works of significance and controversy are Gar Alperovitz, *Atomic Diplomacy: From Potsdam to Hiroshima* (New York, 1965); Walter LaFeber, *America, Russia, and the Cold War* (New York, 1971); Ronald Steel, *Pax Americana* (New York, 1967); David Horowitz, *Free World Colossus* (New York, 1965); David Horowitz, ed., *Containment and Revolution* (Boston, 1967); N. D. Houghton, ed., *Struggle against History* (New York, 1968); Thomas G. Paterson, ed., *Cold War Critics* (Chicago, 1971); Lloyd C. Gardner, *Architects of Illusion* (Chicago, 1970); Richard J. Barnet, *The Economy of Death* (New York, 1970); Richard J. Barnet, *Intervention and Revolution* (New York, 1968); Richard J. Barnet and Marcus G. Raskin, *After Twenty Years: Alternatives to the Cold War in Europe* (New York, 1965); Gabriel Kolko, *The Roots of American Foreign Policy* (Boston, 1968); Gabriel Kolko, *The Politics of War* (New York, 1967); William A. Williams, *The Tragedy of American Diplomacy* (New York, 1962); Fred J. Cook, *The Warfare State* (New York, 1962); and Adam Ulam, *Rivals: America and Russia since World War II* (New York, 1971). These works were used to strengthen the interpretation that Taylor was intellectually justified in questioning American motives following World War II.

Many historians are convinced otherwise. The most recent attack on the revisionists comes from John Gaddis, *The Cold War* (New Haven, Conn., 1972). Other traditional interpretations are John Spanier, *American Foreign Policy since World War II* (New York, 1965); Seyom Brown, *The Faces of Power* (New York, 1968); Wilfrid Knapp, *A History of War and Peace* (London, 1967); Dexter Perkins, *The Diplomacy of a New Age* (Bloomington, Ind., 1967); G. F. Hudson, *The Hard and Bitter Peace* (New York, 1967); Paul Y. Hammond, *The Cold War Years* (New York, 1969); Herbert Druks, *Harry S. Truman and the Russians, 1945-1953* (New York, 1966); and the American diplomacy textbooks of Thomas A. Bailey, *A Diplomatic History of the American People* (New York, 1969); and Robert H. Ferrell, *American Diplomacy* (New York, 1969). Ferrell's diplomatic biography, *George C. Marshall* (New York, 1966), is a firm defense of containment policies as is Joseph Marion Jones's discussion of the origins of the Marshall Plan, *Fifteen Weeks* (New York, 1955). In an essay by Arthur M. Schlesinger, Jr., "Origins of the Cold War," *Foreign Affairs* (October 1967), the revisionist position is attacked by discussing the numerous differences between the Soviet Union and the United States. Although Schlesinger blames the Soviet Union, he concludes with the "shared responsibility" interpretation. Another famous diplomatic historian, Norman A. Graebner, basically agrees with Schlesinger. Graebner's "Global Containment: The Truman Years" *Current History* (August 1969) is an example. John Luckas's popular *A New History of the Cold War* (New York, 1966) also finds the middle ground.

There is no doubt that the Vietnamese tragedy has had an impact on Cold War historiography. Many scholars, upset by the conflict in Indochina, have searched for historical causes. Why would an atomic power reach a position of defending a totalitarian state in a civil war? If the answer is containment, then Taylor was right about the results of Truman's foreign policy.

Index